John Feather

Publishing, Piracy and Politics

An Historical Study of Copyright in Britain

MANSELL

First published 1994 by
Mansell Publishing Limited, *A Cassell Imprint*
Villiers House, 41/47 Strand, London WC2N 5JE, England
387 Park Avenue South, New York, New York 10016–8810, USA

British Library Cataloguing in Publication Data
A catalogue record for this book is available from the British Library.

ISBN 0–7201–2135–3

Library of Congress Cataloging-in-Publication Data

LC–CIP Card No: 94–7320

Typeset by York House Typographic Ltd., London
Printed and bound in Great Britain by Biddles Ltd, Guildford and King's Lynn

Contents

Acknowledgements

My interest in the history of copyright is, in one form or another, more than twenty years old. In such a long period of time, I have inevitably accumulated many intellectual and academic debts, some of them perhaps unrecognized by my creditors. In particular, however, I should like to thank, for various forms of assistance, John Adams, John Barnard, Terry Belanger, Maureen Bell, David Foxon, Peter Jaczi, Paul Marret, David McKitterick, Robin Myers, the late J. C. T. Oates, the late I. G. Philip, Paul Sturges, Michael Turner, Christine Vanden Bossche and Martha Woodmansee. My secretary, Irene Martindale, gave invaluable help in the final stages of preparing the copy, and Veronica Higgs was a tolerant and friendly editor. Carolyn Pritchett was an eagle-eyed proofreader.

Earlier versions of parts of this book have appeared elsewhere. Part of Chapter 1 was originally prepared as a paper for a conference of the Society for Critical Exchange, held in Cleveland, Ohio, in April 1991. It was subsequently published as 'From rights in copies to copyright: the recognition of authors' rights in English law and practice in the sixteenth and seventeenth centuries', *Cardozo Arts & Entertainment Law Journal*, 10 (1992), pp. 455–73. The sections of Chapter 2 dealing with the 1710 Act began life as a paper given to the Oxford Bibliographical Society in 1980, and subsequently published as 'The book trade in politics: the making of the Copyright Act of 1710', *Publishing History*, 8 (1980), pp. 19–44. Three further papers in the same journal have been drawn upon for some parts of Chapters 3, 4 and 5; these are 'The publishers and the pirates: British copyright law in theory and practice, 1710–1775', *Publishing History*, 22 (1987), pp. 5–32; 'Publishers and politicians: the remaking of the law of copyright in Britain 1775–1842. Part I: legal deposit and the battle of the library tax', *Publishing History*, 24 (1988), pp. 49–76; and 'Publishers and politicians: the remaking of the law of copyright in Britain 1775–1842. Part II: the rights of authors', *Publishing History*, 25 (1989), pp. 45–72. I am grateful to the various organizations, publishers and editors for their hospitality, but should perhaps emphasize that all of these papers have been very substantially revised and augmented for their partial re-appearance here.

John Feather
Loughborough University
July 1994

Introduction

Copyright is a legal device which is used to protect certain forms of property. These forms include books, drawings, plays and music, but extend also to other forms of writing, published and unpublished, and media other than print, including photographs, films and videos, recorded sound, computer software and electronic databases. Copyright is as wide-ranging and as complex as the forms of property which it seeks to protect. Moreover, it does not stand alone, for it is only part of the wider field of the law of intellectual property, which is concerned with all the recordable and reproducible products of the human mind, including inventions, designs and artistic creations.

This book is a history of some aspects of copyright in the United Kingdom, and is particularly concerned with it as a factor in the relationship between the authors and publishers of books and other written matter (such as magazines and newspaper articles), and as an element in the economics of the book trade in general and the publishing industry in particular. The main focus, therefore, is on copyright in written language, or in what the law now calls a 'literary work', that is, anything (provided that it is the coherent result of conscious effort) which uses language as a medium of communication, whether it is a novel or an advertising slogan.

Copyright in written works (a more neutral term which will be used except in the strictest legal contexts) cannot, however, be seen in isolation. Although this book is intended primarily as a contribution to the history of the British book trade, it must range more widely. Rights exist in graphic, dramatic and musical works, and more recently in works recorded in media which are not dependent upon paper, print, writing or drawing. The law has sometimes treated these separately, and sometimes together, and there have often been influences flowing in both directions; these we must attempt to trace.

More generally, because copyright is primarily a legal concept, we cannot ignore its legal as well as its economic history. Copyright is defined by statute and enforced by litigation. Since the statute law first concerned itself with copyright at the beginning of the eighteenth century, legislation has been at the centre of all matters relating to it. The law has been interpreted, discussed and enforced; sometimes it has been ignored, it has frequently been criticized, and it has occasionally been changed. All of this is relevant to this history. We need to trace the development of the law and of the interpretation of the law, both as it was seen by the lawyers and as it was understood by those most directly affected by it, the authors and the publishers.

Our concern, however, is not only with the technicalities of legal history. The development of the law was influenced by social, economic and technological factors. Copyright law not only regulates the relationship between authors and publishers, but also intervenes in the relationship between authors and readers, and between both authors and the book trade, on the one hand, and, on the other, society at large. It is concerned with products which have never been, and can never be, wholly neutral. For most of the period covered by this book, the printed word was the only medium of mass communication which could transcend time and distance. By using it, writers could seek to influence both the thoughts and the actions of their readers. Others who sought to exercise such an influence could employ writers to exploit this potential. The printed word was a social and political instrument of great power, which no one who sought to exercise power could ignore.

The power of the printed word was of particular importance in Britain, for, during more than half of the period covered by this book, parliamentary politicians, and more particularly members of the House of Commons, were at the heart of the power structure. They were dependent, however remotely, on the opinions and votes of electors, and therefore inevitably sensitive to any issue which concerned the circulation of printed matter and of the ideas which it could transmit. British copyright, therefore, also has a political history, not only because it touches upon the property rights of individuals, public bodies, private corporations and the state itself, but also because it is concerned with a form of communication of vital interest to politicians.

An appreciation of the legal and political issues in the history of copyright is an essential foundation for any analysis of the more introspective concerns of publishers and authors. For the former, an effective law of copyright is a necessary condition for the conduct of business. Publishers, and all those who cluster around them to form the group of activities loosely called the 'book trade' (such as booksellers, printers and bookbinders), need some guarantee that their investment in a book will be protected. Their problem can be stated quite simply: the publisher pays the author, the printer and all others involved in the production of a book, before any copies can be sold. Once the book is published, however, others can (in a purely technological sense) copy it without incurring more than a fraction of the expense incurred by the original publisher. The law of copyright, therefore, seeks to prevent such copying (and to punish it if it takes place) in order to protect the commercial interests – the property rights – of the first publisher. Copyright is a property which has, historically, more often belonged to a publisher than to anyone else.

When we turn to the place of the author in this set of relationships, we are moving onto less certain ground. We need to consider such issues as plagiarism, creativity and originality, complex enough in themselves, but apparently made more so by modern literary critics who question the very idea of the 'author'.[1] But we can see the deconstructionists themselves as being a part of the history of authorship. Our concern is not with the philosophical concept of the 'author' (legitimate as that may be as a subject of study and speculation), but with changing attitudes of, and towards, those who write. Our concern is not with the history of authorship *per se*, but with how authors have seen themselves, and how others have seen them, as a part of a social and economic system.[2]

It is often argued that in English law, and in jurisdictions influenced by English law (especially the United States), it is the social dimension of copyright which has tended to predominate in legal thinking and legislative provision. It is argued that, by contrast, French law, and the law in those countries influenced by the Napoleonic Code, emphasizes the position of the author, deriving the theory of legal protection for copyright from the idea that the creator has a moral right to be regarded as the proprietor of the creation. To some extent this contrast is valid, but it ignores both the social dimension of French law, and (more importantly for our purposes) the role of the writer as one of those involved in the relationships created by the English law. What is true, however, is that the author was a comparative latecomer into the development of copyright in England, rather than being its starting-point as was the case in France.[3]

The main narrative of this book is concerned with the development of the relationship between authors and publishers in so far as it was, and is, regulated or influenced by the law of copyright. The story is long and complicated; because of that complexity, and because of the detail which is necessary to support the narrative, it is useful to summarize the underlying argument before it is stated and demonstrated at length.

The origin of copyright in England is clear enough: it began as a device developed within the London book trade in the sixteenth century to protect the investments of those involved in printing and publishing. There was no statutory framework for this device, although it was to some extent supported by the official status of the book trade's guild, the Stationers' Company, which was able to enforce its collective will on its members and had a wide range of monopolistic powers over the printing and selling of books.

Authors had no significant part in these early developments, partly because the book trade excluded them from its own arrangements, but also because of their social and economic position. The idea of the book being written for printed publication was a recent development; printing itself was not yet fifty years old in the year 1500, and those who were then writing were the first generation of authors who had grown up with the printed book. Their predecessors had expected their works to be circulated only in manuscript, and to a very limited audience. The idea of the named personal author was also new. Although the names of some medieval and classical authors were known, books were more usually referred to by their titles than by the names of their authors (*Canterbury Tales* rather than 'Chaucer'), and there was little interest in authors as individuals. During the fifteenth and sixteenth centuries, there was a fundamental intellectual shift which profoundly changed this attitude. Although individuals were still seen as a part of a divinely ordained and regulated society, they were also seen as identifiable people with existences which could be associated with names or locations. These names began to appear on their books, and some authors became widely known. The first generation included Erasmus and Luther, whose names (and, in some form, ideas) were known to thousands who had never read their works.[4]

The gradual development of the idea of the writer as an individual was combined with less elevated matters to bring authors into a new kind of relationship with publishers. The driving force was economic. In the last third of the sixteenth century, the English book trade was, for the first time, on an economically sound base, and was becoming highly competitive.[5] The publishers needed books to publish, and only writers could provide them. A few authors began to exploit this, and by the end of the century there are some rudimentary suggestions of the recognition, at least *de facto*, of their right to financial reward for the works which they wrote.

There was still a long way to go. Copyright remained primarily a concern of the book trade for over a century after 1600. Through all the political and constitutional upheavals of the seventeenth century, the London book trade devised ever more ingenious mechanisms to protect the growing body of copyrights which its members owned between them. After the Restoration of Charles II, the Printing Act of 1662 brought statutory control to the trade for the first time, and there was an implicit recognition of the system of copyright protection which the trade had developed. When the provisions of that Act lapsed in 1693, the trade successfully agitated for new legislation which finally came in 1710 with the so-called Copyright Act of that year.

The passage of the 1710 Copyright Act is a defining moment in this history, but it needs careful analysis. Entitled an 'Act for the Encouragement of Learning', it says nothing and implies little about the rights of authors. It is essentially concerned with the protection of the rights of certain members of the book trade, and to a far lesser extent those of the buyers and readers of books, with a token gesture towards the good of society at large by creating favourable circumstances for the writing and (more especially) the publishing and selling of works of culture and learning. Nevertheless, despite its origins in the inner circles of the book trade, the 1710 Act did eventually provide the statutory basis on which authors could assert their own rights. Alexander Pope and his literary associates were particularly active in exploiting (and extending) their rights under the Act, and it was indeed in that circle that the very word 'copyright' was first used.[6]

During the middle years of the eighteenth century, the 1710 Act was the subject of a succession of complex legal cases in both England and Scotland, in which authors and publishers alike sought to use it for their own purposes. The legal arguments turned essentially upon whether or not the Act had created new rights, or had merely confirmed rights which already existed in common law.

This was an issue of great importance in the book trade, for if the Act meant what it apparently said, then copyrights ceased to exist after 28 years (with some exceptions) and a book could then be printed and published by anyone. In 1774, the House of Lords effectively decided that this was exactly the case, and publishers had to seek more diverse sources of revenue than the reprints of popular works which had become one of the mainstays of the London book trade.

This gave the authors another opportunity to strengthen their own position. By the middle of the eighteenth century, many authors were reasonably well-paid for their work, but it was not until the end of the century that they began to seek more equitable rewards.[7] At the same time, as in the sixteenth century, the very idea of authorship was changing. New ideas about originality and creativity, and the creative process itself, gave the author and his or her personality a prominence which they had never previously enjoyed. No longer merely seen as a social being, serving the welfare of society as a whole, the author was now an individualist as well as an individual, expressing his or her own thoughts through writing. The very concept of originality had to be redefined.

This generation included two writers whose role in the history of copyright was to be crucial, Sir Walter Scott and William Wordsworth. The former was perhaps the first to exploit to the full the economic potential of authorship; the latter was a key figure in the reform of the law in the first half of the nineteenth century. In essence, it was argued by Wordsworth and his supporters that the 1710 Act was unfair to authors; indeed it ignored them. They sought a new law which would allow authors themselves throughout their lifetimes, and their heirs after their deaths, to reap the financial rewards of authorship. In a series of new laws, in 1814, 1836 and 1842, the justice of their cause (and the effectiveness of their lobbying) was recognized. The 1842 Copyright Act, which was to remain essentially unchanged for the rest of the century, gave a period of *post mortem* copyright, as well as apparently unambiguous lifetime rights. It was, however, almost as unsatisfactory as a piece of legislation as the 1710 Act had been. It was an authors' act (and more particularly a *literary* authors' act), just as the 1710 Act had been a book trade act, and it concentrated on books to the exclusion of almost everything else. It was ambiguous about abridgements, anthologies, magazine and newspaper articles, translations, dramatizations and many other matters which were of great importance, to authors and publishers alike. The complexities of the issues defeated even the most ardent of reformers, however, and it was not until 1911 that a new Act, much simpler than its predecessors, took account of new forms of publication, and forms which had been ignored by the framers of the legislation of 1842.

In its turn, the 1911 Act became inadequate. It was overtaken by social and technological change, and was partly replaced in 1956. The thirty years after that, however, saw the pace of change increase, with the development of new reproduction techniques for printed matter (most obviously photocopying) and whole new technologies of which copying was the very essence; video was one example, but by far the most important by the 1980s was computing. A new law in 1988 grappled with some of these complexities, and provided a reasonable basis for protecting both publishers and authors at the end of the twentieth century.

The main narrative of this book is concerned with the details of these events, and with the analysis of their significance for authors and publishers. There are, however, some other issues which arise and which cannot be entirely ignored. One is an historical accident: the legal rights of certain libraries to claim for themselves a copy of each new book published in the United Kingdom. This began as a private arrangement between Oxford University and the book trade in 1610, was extended to Cambridge and the Royal Library by statute in 1662, and was confirmed and again extended in 1710 and in 1801. At the beginning of the nineteenth century no fewer than eleven libraries in England, Scotland and Ireland were entitled to free books. There is no necessary link between copyright and legal deposit. In some countries, entitlement to the former depends upon completion of the latter, but that has never been the case in the United Kingdom. In British law, the link between the two is entirely fortuitous. The 1662 Printing Act was, as its title suggests, concerned with a wide range of book trade issues (principally relating to the censorship of printed matter) of which legal deposit happened to be one. It was under pressure from the universities that the 1710 legislation, which was in part derived from that of 1662, revived the deposit clauses of the Act as well as protecting copyrights. Consequently, in all subsequent copyright legislation, legal deposit was also a potential issue.

In the early nineteenth century, this essentially irrelevant matter came to dominate the debate about the reform of the law of copyright. The 1814 Act (the most badly drafted of all British copyright legislation) remained unchanged for nearly thirty years because the earliest attempts to improve it (in 1818) became inextricably entangled in a quarrel between the publishers and the legal deposit libraries. The question was not resolved until 1836, and only then could the problems of the law of copyright itself be addressed. Until that time, however, the history of copyright has to take account of the consequences of the association between copyright and the legal deposit system.

One other matter also has to be considered. This book is primarily concerned with the British book trade, and hence with British copyright law. For a very long time, the British book trade was insular in a metaphorical as well as the literal sense. From the beginning, it was primarily concerned with books in English; books in Latin and modern foreign languages were imported to satisfy the small market for them. The English language was virtually unknown outside Britain, to the extent that as late as the seventeenth century British authors like Bacon, Milton and Newton who sought a wider audience wrote in Latin. With the development of British colonies overseas, however, and the phenomenal growth of British influence in continental affairs after 1688, this changed. There was a demand for English books outside Britain, which was only partly met by exports. Publishers on the continent, and in the colonies, began to reprint British books, a practice which the English law could not prevent.

After American independence, the practice grew apace in the United States, and when the rest of Europe was reopened to British travellers after 1815, the problem became acute there also. For most of the rest of the century, the development of means of copyright protection across international boundaries was a matter of concern to both authors and publishers. Among the authors, Charles Dickens was particularly active in attempting to protect his rights in the vastly profitable American market for his works. Gradually, order was brought to trans-border copyright issues, and some of this development influenced the subsequent development of domestic law, especially in forcing a limited reconciliation of the legal traditions of Britain and France.

The development of an international law of copyright had brought the two traditions into inevitable conflict. In France, copyright was understood as a 'moral right', the *droit d'auteur* to be recognized as the creator of the work and to have control over its use. English law was more pragmatic, and essentially concerned with the property rights of whoever could prove ownership, regardless of the owner's role in the creative process. The first multinational copyright agreement, the Berne Convention of 1886, recognized both authors' and proprietors' rights. Over the following century, English practice and thinking were gradually influenced by the French concepts, until in the 1988 Act the principle of the 'moral right' of writers to be recognized as the authors of their works was, at last, acknowledged.

This long history begins in the early days of printing, with the wooden presses and hand-cast type of a new craft. It ends in a world of universal electrostatic copying and instantaneous world-wide digital communications systems. But the fundamental issues, and the dilemmas which they pose, have perhaps changed less dramatically than the economic, social and technological environments which have produced them. Communications technologies depend upon the existence of that which is to be communicated. Ideas, information and works of art are the product of the human brain, not of the media in which they are stored and through which they are transmitted and retrieved. These intellectual products are created so that others can receive and benefit from them. That presents the central dilemma: authors wish to communicate, and to be rewarded for doing so, but only by imposing restrictions on the mechanisms of communication can the rewards of creative endeavour be assured. The law and practice of copyright have evolved over four centuries as an attempt to resolve this problem. How successfully this has been done will emerge in the remainder of this book.

1 The Origins of Copyright 1475–1640

When Caxton introduced the art of printing into England in 1477, he brought it to a country in which there was already a flourishing commercial manuscript-book trade. Some printed books were already in the country,[1] and a few were probably on sale. The bulk of the trade, however, was in books copied in commercial scriptoria, either bespoke by customers or made speculatively for the booksellers.[2] The concept of copyright was meaningless in this trade, and there was no reason why it should have developed. The stationer or scrivener recovered his investment in copying a manuscript as soon as it was sold. In what was essentially a bespoke trade, this was an almost immediate return. In other words, there was little or no stock of books (other than 'second-hand' books, which were to be found in the shops), and therefore no economic imperative to protect a long-term investment.

The introduction of printing into the trade led to fundamental changes in the economics of book production. The producer (later to be called the 'publisher', but at this time normally the owner of the printing shop) had to invest in a press and in type; he was an employer of skilled labour, and he needed a stock of consumables such as ink and paper. All of this represented a substantial capital investment, on which the return was necessarily slow. When printing became the principal means of production, as it had done in southern Europe by 1480 at the latest, the trade became highly competitive, and the printers began to look for a means of protecting their investments.

It was from this need for economic protection that the concept of the 'privileged book' began to develop. The 'privilege' was a form of special protection given to an individual printer by secular or ecclesiastical authorities. The first was that granted by the Republic of Venice to Johann Speyer in 1469. Speyer was the first printer in the city, and it was in everyone's interests to protect his position.

His privilege gave him an exclusive right to print books in all Venetian territories for the next five years.[3] As the Italian book trade developed rapidly during the 1470s, the need for protection became more acute. In 1481, the Duke of Milan granted to Andrea de Bosiis the right to print or publish Jean Semoneta's *Sforziade* for the next five years. Other such privileges followed in Milan and elsewhere, and the practice was soon imitated in France.[4]

The early Italian and French examples of book privileges show a distinction which was to be carried over into English practice in due course: there were privileges which protected individual texts and those which protected individual members of the trade. To these was subsequently added a third category: the privilege which protected particular types of books, such as school books, or books in Greek.

The legal basis for granting book privileges in England was the exercise of the Royal Prerogative. The extreme assumption was that all written works (like all other property) could be disposed of by the Crown, although in practice this was always modified, and the full claim was never authoritatively sustained. Even so, in the early seventeenth century, when the claims for prerogative powers were reaching their height, the Solicitor-General, Sir Thomas Coventry, took a strong stand in an opinion which he wrote in 1618: 'Wee do not conceive that either the ordinans or the decree can restrein yor power and prrogative to grant privilege, where it shalbe needfull or convenient . . .'[5] This position was not without support, although it contradicted many practices which had developed over the previous century.

Royal grants of privileges to members of the English book trade apparently began in 1504. In that year, Henry VII appointed William Facques as King's Printer, and to give some substance to this grand-sounding title Facques was also granted the unique right to print royal proclamations, statutes and other documents issued by the Crown.[6] In one sense, this grant was similar to that made by the Venetian Senate to Speyer, for it gave Facques a privileged position in the trade. On the other hand, it also restricted him, for his privilege extended only to the specified groups of publications. What distinguished those publications, apart from their official origin, was that they were of unknown or collective authorship, a principle which was soon to be applied to the granting of other privileges in very different materials. The privileges of the King's (or Queen's) Printer were both extended and limited during the rest of the sixteenth century. Gradually, the Printer's privilege came to include Bibles and service books, as well as the statutes and proclamations, giving him a major commercial advantage over his rivals in the trade. Not surprisingly, this was to arouse resentment, for in the process of extension, the nature of the privileges subtly changed.

In 1553, Mary I took away from the Queen's Printer the right to print books of common law. Instead, she gave it to Richard Tottel, a well-established printer who was already a leading member of the trade and well-known as a publisher of law books. Tottel's privilege was, however, unusual in two ways: first, it not only granted him the sole right to print books of common law, it also explicitly forbade others to do so; and secondly, and in a significant extension of previous practice, it granted him rights not only in those common law books already in existence, but also in all of those which were written in the future. This was indeed a comprehensive provision.[7]

It was not to remain unique for long. By the mid-1570s, there were similar privileges in primers, prayer books, school-books, service books, almanacs and prognostications, Bibles, New Testaments, the Book of Common Prayer, catechisms, the ABC (the elementary reading book prescribed for general use), the Psalms in metre, Latin grammars, other Latin books and music (and ruled music paper). The list is formidable, and the more so when it is understood that much of it was in the hands of two or three printers.[8] These privileges were essentially different from that granted to Facques in 1504, for the class privileges granted the absolute rights in books written by others to individual members of the book trade, whether or not the author wished to grant those rights. No longer did the privileges only apply to anonymous works, or those of collective authorship.

All of the grants made in England before the middle of the sixteenth century protected texts or categories of texts, usually in the name of a particular printer who was given the sole right to print the books in question. A third category of grants of privilege begins to emerge in the 1560s. These used the same mechanism as the earlier privileges, Letters Patent granted by the Crown, usually following a petition from the would-be grantee. The first indisputable example is in 1563, when Thomas Cooper, at that time Master of Magdalen College School in Oxford, was granted a patent to protect his revised edition of the Latin dictionary by Sir Thomas Eliot, and his own *Thesaurus Linguae Latinae*. The privilege was to last for a period of twelve years, during which time the books could only be printed by him or with his explicit permission.[9]

There were a few subsequent examples of similar practices with other books and authors. In 1573, for example, Ludovick Lloyd was granted sole rights for 8 years in his English translation of Plutarch, with the important rider that no other translation was to be published in that period.[10] This was more comprehensive than Cooper's patent, and suggests that there was little consistency in the way in which such grants were made. Each was a response to a particular case, although cumulatively they began to establish a set of precedents. The variety of grants, however, is further emphasized by one made to the printer Henry Bynneman in 1580; he was granted a 21-year privilege for the latest revised version of the Eliot dictionary, and for Cooper's continuation of Languet's *Chronicle*, with the very significant addition of all dictionaries and chronicles. What had been a patent for particular titles had been transformed into another class patent, analogous to Tottel's rights in common law books.[11] A third example, which was also slightly different from its predecessors, was that granted to the bookseller Richard Field in 1592, which gave him the sole and unlimited right to print Sir John Harington's translation of Aristo's *Orlando Furioso*.[12]

It has been argued that these books, with their individual grants of privilege through Letters Patent, represent the only form of author's copyright which was recognized in England before 1640.[13] In fact, when we look at them more closely, a rather different picture emerges. Almost without exception, they are learned works which had involved their authors in long periods of compilation, and sometimes in great expense. Protection was necessary not only to reward the author, but also to protect the investment of the publisher in such large and slow-selling works. This was clearly the case with Lloyd's Plutarch, which was effectively protected from competition (which was possible) and not merely from reprinting (which was, in practice, unlikely). The renewal of Cooper's expiring privilege in favour of Bynneman when it expired is another example of the same phenomenon, for no publisher could be expected to keep such important works in print without some guarantee for his investment. Indeed, most of the privileges granted by patent to particular texts were not granted to authors at all, but to publishers. In 1574, for example, the bookseller Thomas Vautrollier was granted a 10-year privilege for a whole series of books, including Beza's edition of the New Testament, Lambinus's editions of Ovid and Cicero, and the *Thesaurus* of Marloratus;[14] these works of learning, written in Latin and all to be printed as large and expensive folios, needed some form of protection if they were to be published in England at all. That was clearly the purpose of the grants of privilege to individual titles; if a living author were the beneficiary of such grants, that was a purely coincidental consequence.

The privileges granted by Letters Patent were based upon the claim made for the Royal Prerogative, a claim which was unchallenged during the sixteenth century, even if some of the consequences were to be the subject of disputes inside the book trade. Their effect (and probably their intention, although we have no direct evidence) was to ensure that certain categories of 'essential' books were readily available, but that the trade in them was orderly and organized. Some of these texts, such as successive versions of the prayer book, or the proclamations and statutes, were politically sensitive; others, such as the school books, were socially necessary; some, like the learned works and the translations, were culturally desirable; yet others, like the almanacs, were very profitable. Individual members of the book trade, and a handful of authors and translators, benefited from these arrangements, but they certainly did not constitute a general system for protecting rights in books. Even so, when Elizabeth I came to the throne in 1558, Letters Patent were the only public mechanism recognized by law or custom by which a printer, publisher or author might protect his work and his investment. The whole system of protection, such as it was, depended upon the goodwill of the Crown towards individuals, and the willingness of the courts (which had not apparently been tested at this stage) to uphold the claims made for the prerogative. The books that were protected, important as they were in their different ways, were only a minority; for the majority, at a time when the output of books was consistently increasing from year to year, there was no legal mechanism at hand to protect their creators and producers.

For that purpose, a separate, and ultimately more successful and long-lasting, system was developed within the book trade itself. By the middle of Elizabeth I's reign it was already recognized that the privileges granted by patent covered only a minority of books. An investigation into the operations of the patent system, in 1583, concluded that the:

> . . . Stationers hath diuers copies seueral to themselues, wch they enioye as fully as if they have the Quenes preuilege for euerie of them . . .

> . . . euerie of them [the stationers] hath of order seuerall to him selfe any boke that he can procure any learned man to make or translate for him, or that can come to his hand to be the first printer of it.[15]

In this obscure prose lies the key to an understanding of the origins of copyright in England.

Several questions arise out of it. Who were the 'Stationers'? What was this special position which they obviously occupied? What was the 'copie' which they claimed or owned? What were the benefits of such ownership? In answering these questions, the book historian can perhaps help the literary scholar and the legal historian to understand the origins and early development of both the idea and the practice of copyright.

The 'stationers' were the freeman of the Company of Stationers of London, the trade guild, or livery company, to which members of the book trade belonged. Although it can trace its history back to the beginning of the fifteenth century, the Company's most glorious era begins with its reorganization in 1557, the last year of the reign of Mary I.[16] The Queen granted the Company a virtual monopoly over printing and bookselling both in London and throughout the kingdom. This was confirmed and amplified by Elizabeth I when she succeeded her half-sister in the following year. Such powers were not unusual, for most trades were controlled by and through livery companies and those companies were granted powers to ensure that their authority could be upheld. This was not benevolence on the part of the crown, but an attempt to maintain good economic order. In the case of the Stationers' Company, this also entailed helping the crown to ensure that unacceptable printed matter was not put into circulation.[17]

In 1559, Elizabeth I issued a set of Injunctions which dealt with the crucial issue of the government and organization of the Church, and it was in this context that rules were made governing the control of the press. No book was to be published unless it was properly licensed by censors appointed by the Crown.[18] The Company was required to police the trade and thus to assist the Crown in the enforcement of the Injunctions against unlicensed printing. This was a great responsibility, which the Company exercised only imperfectly, partly because the Crown had other means of enforcement, and did not give it sufficient powers to carry out the work which might have been thought to have been given to it.[19] Nevertheless, the Company did try to take its obligations very seriously, and established procedures which were intended to ensure that the Injunctions were enforced, in so far as that was its responsibility.

The Company established a system of recording licences to print; these were listed in a volume known to scholars as the 'Stationers' Register', although known at various times in its history as the 'Hall Book', the 'Register Book' and the 'Entry Book', and possibly other names as well. In 1557–58, the first year of operation under Mary's Charter, a list of titles was recorded in the Register with the annotation: 'lycensed to be printed by the master and wardens'.[20] There is a similar series of entries for 1558–59,[21] and although the record may be incomplete, it is clear that the practice of entering licences to print first became usual, and then, quite soon, compulsory. As early as 1557, a stationer was fined twenty shillings by the Company for printing a book before it had been entered,[22] and in the December of the same year another stationer was fined four shillings for printing a book 'contrary to our ordenaunces that ys not havynge lycense from the master and wardyns'.[23]

All of this requires a little further interpretation. What are the 'ordenaunces'? The use of the word 'our' suggests that we are here considering some internal regulations, rather than a document emanating from official sources. And what exactly is the licence apparently being issued by the Master and Wardens?

The first of these questions can be easily, although not very satisfactorily, answered. When the Company began its new chartered life in 1558–59, it had to create for itself the internal institutions through which it would function. It followed the well-established patterns of the City livery companies,[24] by having various annually elected officers, including a Master and two Wardens who acted with him, and by making rules which provided the framework within which the members of the Company could exercise their rights and meet their obligations. In the Stationers' Company, these rules were devised by the officers, and by a small circle of advisers, which was later to be formalized as the Court of Assistants. The Court was to be of some importance; it was the self-electing electoral body for the wardenships and the mastership, and also regulated disputes between members of the Company. For the moment, however, in its embryonic form, it concentrated on drafting regulations. Only a draft version of this first effort survives, but the Ordinances were finally agreed in 1562, and revised from time to time thereafter.[25]

The Ordinances help us to understand the licences, although they do not fully explain their force. In the 1558–59 draft, one clause reads as follows: 'Euery boke or thinge to be allowed by the stationers before yt be prynted.'[26] This apparently unambiguous statement certainly reflected current practice, as is illustrated by the fines in December 1557, which were for precisely this offence. But it does not explain by what authority the 'stationers' issued this licence, or what force it had, if any, outside the Company itself.

It is clear that the licence was, in practice, granted by the Master and Wardens. The form of words in the Register varies, but the gist is always the same. Yet it is unambiguously clear that under the 1559 Injunctions, the power of censorship rested with the Privy Council and other designated officials of church and state. Had this crucial authority been delegated to the Stationers' Company? Almost certainly not. The Master and Wardens were signifying that in their view there was nothing to prevent the publication of the book, a statement for which the only completely acceptable evidence would be the permission of the official licensers. In practice, it seems that many books were not formally licensed at all, and that the Master and Wardens took upon themselves the awesome responsibility of agreeing to allow the book to be published.[27]

The original purpose of entries in the Stationers' Register is clear: it was a record of the fact that, in the opinion of the Master and Wardens, the book had been properly licensed, or that it could be printed without giving offence. It was soon, however, to take on a very different and more extensive meaning.

An example will illustrate this extension. At some time in the year 1563–64, John Sampson was fined twenty pence by the Company for printing what are called 'other mens copyes',[28] a phrase that becomes familiar in the Company's records in the next eighty years. It was indeed used in each of the following two years to justify fines on other stationers.[29] Even in 1563, it was not entirely without an apparent precedent. Before the Ordinances were formally adopted in 1562, William Copland had been fined twenty pence (in 1558-59) for printing a book 'of master Bradfordes'.[30] These entries and others seem to establish that possibly in the late 1550s, and certainly before 1565 at the latest, it was understood within the Company that the 'licence' issued by the Master and Wardens and recorded in the Register, was not merely testimony to the right to print a particular book, but to the unique right to do so. Here we have, in all but name, the concept of copyright.

Within a very short time, these 'copies' were, logically enough, being treated as pieces of property. Such a view was, of course, the only real justification for the fines. In printing another man's copy, the offender was infringing his property rights, and was to be duly punished by fine, and in some cases by also paying compensation to the sufferer. It followed, however, that if copies could be the subject of illegal or irregular transactions, they could also be the objects of legitimate trade. In the late summer of 1564, we have the first record of a transaction involving rights in a copy. Two copies were registered in the name of Thomas Marsh, 'which he boughte of' Luke Harrison.[31] In 1566–67, we have the first example of a joint registration by two stationers of the same copy, in which they apparently owned equal shares.[32] Gaps in the record from the later 1560s to 1576 leave some questions outstanding, but by 1576 when the surviving Register resumes, and became much more detailed, there can be no doubt that there was a well-established and generally accepted pattern of copy ownership, including transfers by purchase, inheritance and gift, subdivision into shares, and similar commercial activities. Other evidence that copies were treated as property is scattered throughout the early records of the Stationers' Company. As early as 1579, a copy was used as collateral against a debt;[33] similar practices at a later date included using copies to secure mortgages.[34]

How did the system operate? No set of regulations survives which describes the day-to-day practice, which in any case clearly evolved over a period of time through trial and error and precedent, but the basic rules are fairly clear. The most basic was that every book had to be entered in the Register. This is clear from fines on stationers who did not enter their copies,[35] although it was not made explicit until as late as 1637. In that year, a decree of the Court of Star Chamber required that in addition to being licensed, every book 'shall be also first entred in the Registers Booke of the Company of Stationers'.[36] The distinction between licence and entry is also quite explicit here, and the distinction is clearly between the official licence, and the internal arrangements of the Stationers' Company.

When the copy had been duly entered, it was the sole and perpetual property of the person or persons who had registered it, provided that he or they had the right to make the entry in the first place. The latter point is important, for a number of entries are indeed conditional, and the reservations expressed in some of the conditional entries reveal both practices (sharp and otherwise) and uncertainties.

These conditional entries are not uniform, for each deals with a specific and unique case. In 1580, for example, the Wardens were unhappy about the contents of a book, and ordered it to be entered with the proviso that those in whose favour the entry was made 'promese to bringe the whole impression therefore into the Hall in case it be disliked when it is printed'.[37] In this case, the Wardens were clearly concerned that the book might be politically or religiously unacceptable. Two general points arise out of this: first, the book cannot have had a licence from the censors, or the doubts could not have arisen, and secondly, the Wardens clearly were not themselves empowered to act as censors on behalf of the Crown.

Fear probably lay at the root of many of the conditional entries in the Register. Even an author, if he were sufficiently influential, might be a cause of concern to the Master and Wardens. In 1581, a book on the education of children was entered with the reservation that if it had any contents 'preiudiciall or hurtefull' to Roger Ascham's *Schoolmaster* 'then thys Lycence shalbe voyd'.[38] Ascham had been Elizabeth I's tutor, and was still highly favoured by her; he was not a man to be annoyed or even, it would seem, refuted in print.

Even more interesting, however, for our present purposes are those conditional entries where the doubts concern the legalities of the ownership of the copy rather than its contents. A number of entries in the 1580s have such comments as 'vpon condicon that no other man be interested in yt',[39] and 'soe much . . . as Doth not belong to anie other of this Companie'.[40] These cases, which are a few among many, clearly show that the principal concern of the Stationers' Company was to regulate the trade for the benefit of its members. This was their interpretation of their obligation under the Charter to maintain order in the book trade. They had, in effect, created for their own purposes a new kind of property, and developed a system for exploiting it.

The legal basis for what the Company was doing lay in the Charter, which incorporated the state's perception of the need to organize and regulate all forms of economic activity. The economic benefit which this conferred on some members of the book trade was coincidental to the fundamental principles involved. Riding on the coat-tails of censorship, and always treading very carefully in cases of doubt, the first generation of officers of the Stationers' Company laid the foundations for the domination of the English book trade by themselves and their successors for the following century, and for an influence over its affairs which was to survive even longer than that. For the historian of the book trade, the real significance of the early history of copy ownership lies in the fact that it was the motive force behind a critical change in the balance of power within the trade itself. For more than a century after the invention of printing, it was the printers, with their command of the limited technical facilities for book production, who controlled the trade.

It was certainly the printers who dominated the Stationers' Company during the first ten or fifteen years after the Charter was granted. During that time, they were able to protect themselves to some extent by limiting the number of presses and printing houses (another point at which the interests of the more economically powerful members of the Stationers' Company coincided with those of the state), but gradually their power slipped away from them.[41] It was the copy-owning booksellers who succeeded them as the leaders of the trade, for they gradually came to control the very product on which it depended for its continued existence: the right to publish books. The printers became, as they have remained ever since, the paid agents of the copy owners. The copy owners reinforced their dominance of the Company throughout the late 1570s and early 1580s, and gradually took control of the Court of Assistants, and hence of the senior offices. By the end of the 1580s, they were ready to use that dominance to form the policies of the Company in their own interests, and to exert political and legal influence outside the narrow circles of the book trade itself.[42]

The power of the Stationers' Company as a whole, and of the copy-owning booksellers within it, was further enhanced by the Company's gradual absorption of the rights protected by Letters Patent, thus uniting the older system of copy protection based on the direct use of the Royal Prerogative with the newer, and less official, mechanisms developed within the book trade. By the early 1570s, the patent rights were a cause of serious concern within the trade, to the extent that they were threatening to disrupt the cosy arrangements with which the senior members of the Company were very satisfied.

To understand this complex, but important, series of events, we need to consider the history of the rights in copies granted by Letters Patent. During the first decade of the reign of Elizabeth I, a number of existing patents were renewed, and others were created. The effect was that nearly all of the most profitable books were controlled by a handful of printers and booksellers, and there was no legal means by which anyone else in the trade could become actively involved in their publication. Four men were particularly prominent in this respect: Christopher Barker, the Queen's Printer (who controlled the Bible, the New Testament, the Book of Common Prayer, statutes, proclamations and other official documents), William Seres (primers and other private prayer books, and school books, among others), Richard Tottel (common law books) and John Day (the *ABC*, the Catechism, and the Psalms in metre). All four men were prominent in the Stationers' Company, and were part of the group of Master Printers who at that time still dominated the Court of Assistants. A protest against the Company and a protest against the patents could easily merge into one.[43]

It was the Day patent which was to bring matters to a head, and to lead to the first detailed official investigation of the trade since the incorporation of the Stationers' Company. Apart from the Queen's Printer himself, Day was the most important of the patentees. The *ABC* alone was one of the most valuable of copies, and it was merely one of those which he controlled.[44] In 1577, a group of Freemen of the Stationers' Company petitioned the Privy Council against the Day patent, and the Court of Assistants also found itself dealing with a number of cases involving the patent books. Neither body was particularly sympathetic to the claims against the patentees, but the seeds of trouble were being sown. All sorts of complications were beginning to arise, as the Company's customs came into conflict with external social, economic and political forces. In 1578, for example, Richard Jones entered a Welsh translation of the *ABC* in the Register, and Day, as patentee, objected. The Court of Assistants considered the matter, and reached the Solomonic judgment that, while the copy of the Welsh version did indeed belong to Jones, he was to print it in Day's name as the latter's assignee.[45]

Day was not the only victim. Even Christopher Barker was not exempt, and in 1578 he complained to the Privy Council that his patents as Queen's Printer were being infringed by 'diverse printers of the Cittie of London'. In fact, the printer in question was apparently Richard Tottel, who was printing abridgements of the statutes (which belonged to Barker) under the cover of his common law patent![46] The situation was becoming ridiculous, and could not be allowed to continue.

It was exacerbated by real piracy, that is the reprinting of patent books without the permission of the patentees. When Day appealed to the Privy Council about the infringement of his rights, it was found that Roger Ward had printed at least 10,000 copies of the *ABC* without permission.[47] This is, in itself, a testimony to the economic importance of the patent books: at that time, a normal print run rarely exceeded 500. Moreover, Ward was neither the only pirate nor the worst. In the same year, John Wolfe, the most depredatory of the pirates, illegally printed both the *ABC* and the *ABC with the Little Catechism*. This was not his first brush with the law. He had already infringed Barker's rights, and Barker had turned to the Privy Council for redress. He had also infringed patents in Latin grammars in 1581, when yet again the Privy Council had ordered him to desist.[48]

Throughout the late 1570s and the early 1580s, piracies of the patent copies and grievances against the patentees were a disturbing undercurrent which brought the trade to the attention of crown officials. The Privy Council occasionally reminded the Stationers' Company of its duty to protect the patentees, and of its right to search for, and confiscate, pirated books,[49] but the truth was that there was little that it could do in most cases except to accept the *status quo*. The causes of the difficulties were not far to seek. Barker himself, in a report to the Privy Council in 1582, put his finger on one of them, which was the growing power of the booksellers and the relative decline of the printers: '. . . the Bookesellers being growen the greater and wealthier [,a] nomber haue nowe many of the best Copies . . .'[50] These 'copies' were, probably, those which were entered on the Register, rather than the patent copies, of which the great majority still belonged to printers. What Barker had identified was that the possession of the non-patent copies was also becoming profitable, and that this was widening the gulf between the patentees and the rest of the trade. The increasingly confident copy-holding booksellers wanted to share in the good fortune of the patentees by finding some means of publishing the most profitable books of all. At the same time, however, the number of men qualified to work in the trade, especially as printers, was also growing, and there was not enough work to go around. Gaps were developing between privileged and unprivileged, between patentees and the rest of the trade, between the rich and the poor.

The pirates proved intractable. In the early 1580s, Wolfe's printing shop was raided and his presses and other property confiscated by the officers of the Bishop of London (who was one of the official book licensers in his diocese). The City of London tried a more ingenious and more subtle mechanism, presumably under pressure from the Privy Council, or the Bishop, or the patentees or perhaps even the Stationers' Company, or some combination of them: it transferred Wolfe from the Fishmongers' Company, of which he was a Freeman, to the Stationers', and ordered the latter to give him enough work to satisfy him. This ploy was partially successful, but not really a solution.

There was official concern at the highest levels about these disturbances. Any disruptions in the book trade opened up the possibility of unlicensed printing. Eventually, the Privy Council appointed two commissioners to investigate the situation, and they uncovered what had happened in the trade in the previous fifteen or twenty years, bringing to the Privy Council's attention the internal system of regulation which the Stationers' Company had developed. The outcome was a decree issued by the Court of Star Chamber in 1586 which reinforced the existing licensing system, and to a large extent confirmed the position of the patentees. There were, however, some concessions. The number of Master Printers, apprentices and journeymen was to be limited, thus easing the problem of too many men competing for too little work. Print runs were limited to 1,500 copies of each edition, another provision which had the same effect. Other clauses reiterated the duties and rights of the Stationers' Company, including the restriction of printing to its Freemen (except in Oxford and Cambridge under licence from the respective Vice-Chancellors), the Wardens' rights of search and seizure, and the requirement to observe the rulings of the licensers. The licensing system was strengthened by increasing the number of officials involved in it, and there was some limited recognition given to the force of an entry in the Register. It is, perhaps, an exaggeration to argue that 'The ecclesiastics guarded against "dangerous" works, and the wardens against piracy',[51] but those were certainly the respective priorities of the parties involved. The concern of the Crown, however, was first and foremost to prevent the printing of seditious and heretical books, and secondly to ensure that its authority was respected. The protection of the alleged rights, and commercial interests, of a small group of comparatively insignificant London tradesmen was, if it were considered at all, a very minor part of the whole arrangement.[52]

Nevertheless, the 1583 Commission and the 1586 Decree did have a significant long-term effect on the development of copyright law and practice. John Day died between the time when the

Commission reported and the official response to its findings and recommendations. His son, Richard, inheriting both the patents and the long struggle to protect them, reached an agreement with Wolfe, in which the latter became one of five assignees of the Day patents.[53] This took the sting out of the attack on the patents, and the other patentees cut their losses and followed suit. The patent rights had now become a very different kind of property. Although they clearly derived from the exercise of the prerogative, they were, equally clearly, an integral part of the book trade, being owned by consortia of printers and booksellers who profited from them. Increasingly the patent copies were being treated like copies to which the claim rested on an entry in the Register, and the Company began to take a rather different interest in them.

Under the stricter regime imposed in 1586, the Court of Assistants could not afford to be seen to be lax. Within a matter of weeks it used its reconfirmed powers to search Roger Ward's premises (again), seized books he had printed in breach of the patents in Latin grammars, catechisms and primers, and ordered his presses to be destroyed.[54] At the same time, and perhaps even on the same day, the Wardens confiscated presses belonging to a group of five men on the grounds that they were intended to be used for printing Latin grammars in breach of the patent.[55] This was draconian indeed! Such actions had their effect, and we hear little more of such overt breaches of the rights of the patentees.

The Court, however, also concerned itself with the arrangements which the patentees and the developing groups of owners of patent rights were making for themselves. It began to regulate the operation of these groups, and, in particular, made rules which required the owners to ensure that some of the poorer members of the Company benefited from their good fortune. They required, for example, that the printing should be undertaken by some of the less prosperous men, and they made arrangements for the equitable distribution of the profits according to ownership of rights and printing undertaken for the owners. By the middle of the 1590s, this operation had its own Treasurer, and was beginning to take on the appearance of a business on its own account. When James I came to the throne in 1603, the arrangements were formalized. Letters Patent were issued which formally vested the patent rights in the Company.[56]

The Court divided the rights into shares of a notional capital of £9,000, held according to rank in the Company in units of £50, £100 or £200, of which there were 60, 30 and 15 respectively. The business was known as the English Stock, and became one of the most important activities of the Stationers' Company in the publishing trade. The Stock eventually came to include not only the Day and Seres patents, but also those for almanacs and prognostications, which were to prove profitable until well into the eighteenth century. The shares themselves were highly sought prizes, for in the early seventeenth century the annual dividend was running at between 12 and 13 per cent per annum.[57]

The transformation of the patent books into the English Stock was a response to the need for the Stationers' Company to be seen as an effective and willing agent in the regulation of the press for the benefit of the Crown. But it also had clear benefits for the Company itself, and especially for its most powerful members on the Court of Assistants. The evolution of the English Stock is also, however, a significant event in the history of copyright, for it established on a clear legal basis the rights in some of the most valuable copies in the trade. At the same time, although probably coincidentally, it confirmed the role of the Stationers' Company in the establishment and enforcement of such rights. The English Stock copies unequivocally had their origin in the exercise of the Royal Prerogative; the Stationers' Company had transformed them into commercial properties.

This was clearly in line with the rapid contemporaneous developments in practice with regard to rights in other copies, those entered in the Register. The 1586 Star Chamber decree strengthened the hand of the Company in enforcing registration (and all its other internal regulations), and thus facilitated the emergence of a new and clearer understanding of the nature and implications of copy ownership.

It is clear that the idea of rights in copies, that is, the unique right to print a particular text, was well-established before the end of the 1580s, and probably earlier. At the same time, it was also claimed, and probably established *de facto*, that such rights could normally only belong to a Freeman of the Stationers' Company although, in exceptional cases, this could be overridden. In 1598, members of the Company were required by the Court of Assistants to desist from the practice of entering copies on behalf of non-members.[58] An order of 1607 was even more explicit: copies were to be entered only by Freemen of the Company, resident in London; no Freeman was to help anyone else to enter a copy; and no copy was to be printed without entry.[59] The Company went to great lengths to prevent the ownership of copies outside its own membership. In

1605, it was alleged that Edmund Weaver had entered ten copies on behalf of Thomas Wight, who was not a member of the Company; this was allowed only on the condition that Wight was to 'dispose of them to any freeman of this Companye'.[60] The Stationers' Company thus achieved two objectives at once: it maintained order within the trade, and it ensured that its members had a collective monopoly over it.

The Stationers' Register had become the only means of proving ownership of rights in the vast majority of copies which were not the subject of Letters Patent or part of the English Stock. A number of incidents at the turn of the sixteenth and seventeenth centuries demonstrate this. The case of Thomas Wight is one interesting example of what could happen. Wight could never exploit these copies for himself, other than by selling them to a member of the Company; but entry, even in the name of another, established his rights in them, and hence the legitimacy of any subsequent transactions. There are many episodes from about 1600 onwards which leave no doubt about the Company's internal interpretation of a Register entry. In 1603, for example, when, following the usual practice, the copies of the late Robert Dexter became the common property of the Company when he died intestate, there was a rider that the order included 'all other copies and bookes wherin Robert Dexter Deceased had Right by entranc [*sic*] in the hall book'.[61] There are several points of interest here: first, an entry in the Register is proof of ownership; secondly, rights are obtained and established by the act of entry; and thirdly, the rights of deceased Freemen revert to the Company as a whole, presumably to avoid them going into the hands of those not in the trade.[62] Indeed, there is even some evidence that the value of shares in the Stock attracted men from other companies.[63]

The absence of an entry in the Register could be fatal to any claim about the ownership of a copy. An interesting, if negative, example is that of the rights in 'the book of Dcor ffaustus', not Christopher Marlowe's play, but the English translation of the German 'Faust Book' which was his main source. On 18 December 1592, the Court of Assistants ruled that the copy was owned by Abel Jeffes, if no entry could be found for it in the name of Richard Oliffe who also claimed it.[64] No such entry was found (and indeed none exists), and the copy was duly considered to belong to Jeffes; in 1596, he was able to transfer his share to Edward White. In fact, the whole story is more complicated than this very brief summary suggests, for no one involved was an exemplary member of the

Company, and there was almost certainly a good deal of sharp practice hidden beneath the curt entries in the Register and the Court Book.[65] Even so, the principles involved are clear enough: Oliffe's claim had to stand or fall on the existence of a valid entry in the Register.

Although entry was the only *proof* of ownership, it is important to recognize that the Register was merely a record of established rights; an entry could not, by itself, confer those rights. The conditional entries exemplify this, for they, in effect, refer to external and higher authorities for adjudication. The registration customs could also, however, be used in different ways. This is exemplified by entries for copies in which rights are clearly deemed to exist, and to be legitimately owned by a member of the Company, but for which there had been no previous entry. Examples are found at intervals from 1600 onwards. On 2 July 1602, for example, thirteen copies which had belonged to a deceased member of the Company were entered to William Leake; of these, earlier entries can be found for only nine. Despite this, however, the ownership of the four unentered copies, and of the right to transfer them, was never successfully challenged.[66] In 1607, a similar transfer took place of a group of sixteen copies, now entered to John Smethwicke, 'whiche dyd belong to Nicholas Lynge'; several had not previously been entered, but no question was raised about the legitimacy of the transfer.[67] One final example will suffice to establish this point, and it is perhaps the clearest of the three. Dekker's play *The Shoemaker's Holiday* was written in 1599, staged in 1600 and published in the same year by Valentine Simmes.[68] There is no entry in the Register, but in 1610 it was transferred by Simmes to James Wright without any difficulty or challenge.[69] From these and other examples, it is clear that while entry was the only proof of ownership of a copy, and was indeed required under the Company's Ordinances, its absence was not necessarily an obstacle to exercising the rights of ownership provided that there was no substantiated challenge. Perhaps it was for this reason that almost half of those books published before 1640 which were not part of one of the patents were apparently never entered in the Register.[70]

A challenge to the right of publication might come from one of three principal sources, although such cases are unusual. The first was from within the Company itself. This was the business of the Court of Assistants, and was indeed their principal formal involvement in disputes about copy ownership. Their first concern was, of course, to ensure that they did nothing to annoy powerful outside interests, but they were also committed, for commercial reasons, to maintaining strict control over the conduct of the members of the book trade. The Court Books and the Hall Books are full of minutes and entries, many of them impenetrably obscure in their details, which reflect both the disputes which arose and the Court's efforts to mollify everyone involved in them, while ensuring that its own authority was not blatantly flouted, and that it did its public duty in relation to the 1559 Injunctions, the 1586 Decree and other crown orders.

The second source of objections, far fewer in number, but taken very seriously when they did arise, was the various official bodies which might object to the contents of a book rather than to the commercial arrangements for its publication. In other words, these are not really copyright issues at all, but rather issues relating to the enforcement of the licensing regulations concerning the censorship of books.

The third group of complaints came from outside both the book trade and the official circles concerned with censorship of the press, although the use of the word 'group' implies a degree of cohesion which did not exist. Nevertheless, this third category of complaints is of particular interest, for it consisted of those who argued that they had some sort of prior claim on the ownership of whatever it was that was claimed as a piece of property by a Stationer. In other words, they forced the earliest consideration of the nature of the 'rights' in copies.

There are a few sixteenth-century incidents which, at least to the modern interpreter, suggest some rudimentary concept of the rights of the author as well as those of the publisher. In 1582, for example, Henry Denham was ordered by the Court of Assistants to pay the not inconsiderable sum of £4. 6*s*. 8*d*. to Edward White because he had published a book called *The Diamond of Devotion*: 'pte whereof was taken out of a copie of ye said Ed. whites Called the footepath of faithe'.[71] Two years later, another case also (but presumably coincidentally) involved White; *A Book of Cookery* was entered to him on the usual condition that it did not belong to anyone else with the rider that it was 'not collected out of anie book already extante in printe in English'.[72] Are these cases concerned with piracy or with plagiarism? The line is a fine one, and it never became much clearer in the early seventeenth century. In 1618, for example, Thomas Jones was forbidden to print in *The Father's Blessing*, in which he owned the rights, anything which had appeared in Lewis Bayly's *The Practice of Piety*, in which he did not.[73] *The Father's Blessing* is an anonymous (but legitimate) adaptation of *Basilikon Doron* by James I, but despite this special circumstance a general question arises. Was Jones being forbidden to pirate another man's copy or was he being prevented from plagiarizing Bayly's book?

In the reign of James I, the question became more acute because of the King's renewed exercise of the prerogative in relation to rights in copies, as defined by Coventry in 1618.[74] Unlike the Tudor patents, now largely absorbed into the English Stock, the patents granted by James I were generally given to individuals for particular titles, usually books which they had written or were writing. Some of these were connected with particular political initiatives, such as that granted to William Stalling for his *Instructions for Planting and Increase of Mulberry Trees* in 1607.[75] Some were probably simply exercises of patronage in favour of petitioners for royal favours; these may have included George Humble's patent for John Speed's great atlas, the *Theatre of Great Britain*, granted in 1608.[76] Others were rewards or incentives to the authors of great works of learning, such as John Marriott's *Pharmocopoeia Londiniensis* (granted 1616),[77] or, most famously, John Minsheu's pioneering multi-lingual dictionary, *Glosson Etymologicon* (granted in 1611).[78] Whatever the motive for issuing these Letters Patent (which were probably a mixture of political, financial and scholarly), some of them contain the implied recognition of the rights of the author of a work to be its legal 'owner'.

We can see here some glimmerings of an issue which was to become central to the law of copyright in the eighteenth and nineteenth centuries: the relationship between the rights of the author and the rights of the publisher. The concept of plagiarism, however rudimentary it may have been, is a movement towards a recognition of the essential uniqueness of every book, and in those entries in the records of the Stationers' Company we can perhaps see the first stumbling attempts to deal with the key issues of the difference between ideas and the works in which those ideas are expressed. The recognition of the author as a participant in the process of publishing a book was perhaps further reinforced by the granting of protection to particular titles rather than to whole groups of books or to such essentially anonymous works as statutes or prayer books. A fundamental question, although it was not yet raised, was clearly implicit: if a copy was a piece of property, what was its origin? Who created it? At what point in its development did it take on those characteristics which allowed it to be defined and treated as property? It was from such questions that the concept of copyright was finally to emerge.

In so far as these questions were addressed in England before the Civil War, they seem to have arisen in one particularly complicated context: printed drama. An understanding of this is essential, but it requires a little preliminary explanation.

The serious study of many of the issues that have been under consideration in this chapter had its origins in the study of the textual and theatrical history of the Elizabethan and Jacobean drama, and particularly in the complex relationship which existed, or was presumed to exist, between playwrights, theatrical companies and printers and publishers. As a generalization, it is not a serious misrepresentation to say that plays were written by authors working on commission for theatrical companies. Some of these companies were effectively owned by an individual. One such was the Admiral's Men in the later part of Elizabeth I's reign, whose owner, Philip Henslowe, kept a detailed, if somewhat confused, account of his dealings with playwrights and others.[79] It is clear that after Henslowe had paid his dramatists, their plays then went into the Admiral's Men's repertory for as long as they could hold the stage. Other companies, of which the only significant example was the Chamberlain's Men (which became the King's Men in 1603), were, in effect, joint stock companies. We have no similar business records for such a company. The whole issue is confused by the fact that Shakespeare was a principal shareholder in the Chamberlain's/King's company, and that his plays, after 1598, were written for, and hence belonged to, that Company. There was nothing unusual about this arrangement: it was the standard pattern of the dramatist writing for the Company (whether he was employed by it, or was a part owner of it) and the play then becoming part of the stock which the Company owned and performed.[80]

None of this would have been of any significance to the book trade, had it not been for the fact that some plays were published. Even that statement needs to be put in context. In a typical year, between June 1594 and June 1595, the Admiral's Men introduced eighteen new plays into their repertory.[81] If we assume that a major professional Company like the Admiral's always worked at that rate, then we would expect it to have introduced between 150 and 200 new plays a decade. This can be compared with the rate of publication. In the fifteen years from 1590 to 1605, eighteen plays were published that can be definitely associated with the Admiral's

Men;[82] in the period from 1597 to 1612,[83] thirty-two plays belonging to the Chamberlain's/King's Men were printed.[84] From this it seems reasonable to conclude that publication was of minimal significance to playwrights and theatrical companies, and that it was the exception, not the rule.

There is a further complicating factor in using any evidence relating to the publication of plays to cast light on the book trade in general. So far as the Stationers' Company was concerned, plays were copies like any other. Some of them were printed in texts which were later recognized by scholars to be deeply corrupt, and yet their publication was not irregular in any way. Shakespeare's *2* and *3 Henry VI* illustrate this point. The first edition of *2 Henry VI* (with the title *The First Part of the Contention of York and Lancaster*) was published in 1594, in a badly mangled text not entirely by Shakespeare.[85] This was entered in the Stationers' Register on 12 March 1594, in a perfectly normal way, by Thomas Millington.[86] Millington duly published editions in 1594 and 1600, and then transferred his rights to Thomas Pavier in 1602, again by a normal transaction in the Register.[87] Pavier published an edition in 1619, and the play was then printed, in a revised and more accurate version, in the folio edition of Shakespeare's works published in 1623, the so-called First Folio, an enterprise to which Pavier was almost certainly a consenting party.[88] *3 Henry VI* has a very similar legal and textual history. Throughout this series of transactions, a corrupt text, which cannot have derived from the author, was treated as if it were a perfectly normal copy. From the trade's point of view that was indeed precisely the situation.

Are these textually corrupt editions, and similar 'bad' quartos of other Shakespeare plays, piracies? In the answer to that question lies the relevance of all of this in the history of copyright. It is crucial to maintain a clear distinction between 'piracy' as it was understood in the book trade and 'piracy' as it might have been understood by the theatrical companies. So far as the book trade was concerned, piracy could only take place if the rights of a member of the Stationers' Company were infringed, or if a text protected under Letters Patent were printed by someone other than the patentee and without the patentee's permission. The theatrical companies took a different view, and on a few occasions they intervened, or attempted to intervene, to prevent the publication of plays from the repertory. The most notorious case was in 1619, when the Court of Assistants ordered as follows: '. . . vppon a ler from the right hoble the Lo. Chamberleyne It is thought fitt & so ordered That no playes that his Matyes do play shalbe printed wthout consent of some of them.'[89] The Court could not ignore an order from such a source, but it must be seen in the context of its equally compliant reaction to other orders from civil and ecclesiastical authorities when they sought to prevent the publication of particular books. Some such cases involve an attempt to protect the author or his work for some reason, and that is in fact the case here. The King's Men had their own reasons for seeking to protect their plays from publication at that time, and they merely followed the normal contemporary practice of turning to their most powerful patron (in their case the King operating through one of the Great Officers of State) to help them, as indeed he did.[90] Despite alleged instances of earlier interventions by theatrical companies to prevent the publication of their plays (especially in corrupt texts), there is no real evidence for the practice.[91]

The whole episode in 1619 is full of lessons about the normal rather than the exceptional. A powerful patron could put pressure on the Court of Assistants to order the members of the Company not to print particular books, even if there were no legal reason why they should not do so. On the other hand, the Court was recognized as the governing body of the trade, and it was also recognized that it controlled the rights in copies and the way in which these were exercised. We can also see quite clearly that the copies were regarded as property, to be protected in this case just as they might be traded in others. Most revealingly, however, there is an underlying assumption that they 'belonged' to the King's Men, even though some of them had been printed and were the subject of legitimate entries in the Register. Once again we have glimmerings of the concept that the rights originate with the author.

The conclusions to be drawn from the exceptionally complex rights in plays accord with those suggested by the granting of patent rights in individual titles and the attempts to prevent the kind of piracy which verges on plagiarism: there was some limited recognition of authors' rights in the first half of the seventeenth century. We can find other fragments of evidence of individual incidents and of general practices which support this view. We know, for example, that authors were paid for their copy. In itself, this proves nothing, except that the booksellers did recognize that in acquiring a copy for entry and publication they were acquiring something which had already taken on the status of property. Can they have believed that they were only buying a piece of paper rather than what was written on it? It would be perverse to argue, and probably wrong to assume, that any such distinction would have suggested itself. As early as the late 1580s, the playwright Robert Greene was accused of selling a play twice, once to the Queen's Men and then again to the Admiral's. The accusation itself is more interesting to us than whether or not it was true: it was clearly thought to be credible that a man should write a play and then sell it. He can only have been selling what would later be called his intellectual property, his copyrights.[92]

These are straws in the wind, and again a case from the theatrical world, but there are others. Before 1600, we can see the beginnings of a distinction between manuscript and printed works. In the 1590s, Thomas Nashe indicated that printed publication was one way to prevent illicit copying of works by scriveners, at a time when the circulation of literary works in manuscript was still common.[93] In effect, an astute author like Nashe could take advantage of the system of copy protection developed within the Stationers' Company. Once a book was in print, it was protected by the Company's regulations, and there is evidence for the exploitation of this system by authors seeking to protect themselves against the unauthorized printing of their works, or the printing of inaccurate or incomplete texts.[94] Again the examples are few, and, perhaps inevitably, concern literary texts rather than the mass of ordinary books; but the signposts are there if we will read them. Before the death of Elizabeth I it was recognized that authors had rights in the books which they wrote, and that those rights could be translated into money by the sale of the copy to a member of the Stationer's Company. That Stationer could then use the Company's own mechanisms to protect both his investment and, if it were a matter of concern, the reputation of the author.

By the second decade of the seventeenth century, there was a reasonably effective system of copy protection operating in England. The Royal Prerogative was the source of it; it had no statutory basis. Through Letters Patent, through the Charter of the Stationers' Company, and through the prerogative courts such as Star Chamber, the Crown controlled the printing and book trades. Although the primary motive was to control the content and distribution of books, a coincidental consequence had been to develop a system which protected the commercial interests of individual members of the trade. The patent rights in privileged books, some subsumed into the English Stock of the Stationers' Company, were the oldest and perhaps the most extensive group of protected copies. But the number of copies protected by the

Stationers' Company's own regulations was growing every year, and the Court of Assistants was assiduous in trying to ensure that rights were protected and that disputes were fairly adjudicated. Copies were treated as property, and their owners regarded with the respect accorded to the holders of property, whether they were printers, booksellers, theatrical entrepreneurs or even authors.

Although the system thus established under the Crown and its various agents and agencies, including the Stationers' Company, was reasonably effective and reasonably stable, there were changes during the reigns of James I and Charles I. One of these was the use of Letters Patent by James I to protect or reward or profit from the work of particular authors. These, however, were not the only extension of the patent system in his reign. Class patents, like those which had caused so much trouble in the 1570s and 1580s, were still being issued, and included new patents for songs and hymns, granted by James I, and for ballads and other material printed on one side only, and newsbooks, granted by Charles I.[95] Some of these led to serious difficulties, especially when the interests of the patentees conflicted with those of the trade in general, or indeed of the Stationers' Company itself. George Wither's patent for hymns was particularly troublesome, and caused many years of dissension in the trade, and a good deal of damage to the authority of the Court of Assistants.[96]

The whole system, including the Wither patent, became entangled in the general opposition to the use of patents to establish economic monopolies which was manifested in the House of Commons throughout the early seventeenth century. Even Elizabeth I had some difficulty on the issue in her last Parliament, and matters became far worse under the less experienced, less well-respected and less politically astute James I.[97] In the parliaments of 1614 and 1621, there was a ground swell of opinion against monopolies and monopolists, including the Stationer's Company, and this reached its climax in the Parliament of 1623–24. The outcome was the Monopolies Act of 1624,[98] which severely limited the Crown's powers to grant monopolies under Letters Patent, and brought those which existed under the control of the common law courts rather than the prerogative courts. The one exception to this legislation was for 'grants of privilege heretofore made or hereafter to be made for, or concerning printing'.[99] Why should this have been so? We do not know, but we may guess that the wish to restrain the press was widespread.

The campaign against monopolies in the book trade continued, but it was largely carried on from within, by dissatisfied members of the trade, who, like Wolfe fifty years earlier, felt commercially disadvantaged by being excluded from the system. George Wither was the leader of the opposition on this occasion, and he was silenced, as Wolfe had been, by being given a patent of his own, in this case in hymns, granted in 1623. But the Stationers' Company refused to cooperate with him, and he continued his attacks, most notably in a pamphlet entitled *Schollars Purgatory, Discouered in the Stationers' Commonwealth*, published in 1624. Eventually the dispute with Wither was resolved, but the underlying problem re-emerged in 1641 when so many long-standing grievances were given their most eloquent airing.[100]

Despite these troubles, the Stationers' Company continued to exercise its authority as best it could over the printing trade. This authority was reinforced from time to time. A Proclamation issued in 1623 confirmed the Star Chamber decree of 1586, and again recognized the importance of the Company's own regulations. In imposing a penalty of six months' imprisonment for illegal printing, it defined this as including any printing 'contrary to any allowed Ordinance, set downe for the good Governaunce of the Company of Stationers . . .' and even overrode the rights of copy owners, by applying the penalty to such books 'though lawfull or allowed to bee Printed by such to whom the Printing thereof doth belong . . .'[101] In 1636–37, the trade petitioned William Laud, as Bishop of London and hence the licenser in his diocese,[102] for a new Star Chamber decree to confirm its position and its authority. This was duly granted, and issued in 1637. It is important in the history of copyright only in being the first document issued in the name of the Crown to require entry in the Register, but otherwise it merely confirmed existing practices, increased penalties for those who infringed against the regulations, and generally tried to ensure good order in the trade.[103]

The Star Chamber decree of 1637 was to prove to be the high-water mark of royal regulation of the English book trade. In fact, it was to last, like the political and constitutional system on which it depended, for only three years, before a wholly new set of circumstances provided the context in which the book trade had to work. Even that upheaval, however, was not great enough to undermine some aspects of book trade practice which had evolved in the previous century. By 1640, the concept of rights in copies was one of the cornerstones of the trade, regulated both by the

Stationers' Company and by the Crown. Three generations had passed since the Stationers had begun to evolve their copy registration and transfer conventions in the early years of the reign of Elizabeth I. Copies which were not part of the English Stock or of the patent monopolies were exploited to the profit of their owners. Even authors had learned how to play the system. The ownership of copies had come to represent an important element in how the London book trade worked, and how it saw itself in relation to customers, competitors and the state. The copies were investments, less tangible perhaps than presses and printing houses, but nevertheless representing the key to economic success in the book trade. The next two decades were to prove that it would take more than civil war, regicide and republicanism to change the practices of the copy-holding booksellers.

2 From Custom to Statute 1640–1710

By the year 1640, there was an effective, if somewhat eclectic, system of copy protection in place in the London book trade. It consisted essentially of two elements: the copies protected by privileges, deriving from Letters Patent, and those protected by the mechanisms of the Stationers' Company as part of its own internal arrangements. Ultimately, both of these were dependent upon the authority of the Crown and the exercise of the royal prerogative, either directly or indirectly. If the prerogative powers of the Crown were diminished, or its authority undermined, there would be immediate consequences for the organization and stability of the book trade.

The trade could not be isolated from the general effects of political and social change. Although the 1624 Monopolies Act had apparently recognized its special position, the continued debate about the role of the state in the legal infrastructure of trade in general had inevitable consequences for all economic activity. Within the Stationers' Company, as in many livery companies at the beginning of the 1640s, there was a party which opposed the monopolies exercised by the ruling oligarchy, and which gradually came to identify itself with the anti-prerogative party which emerged both in the Short Parliament of April 1640 and, more effectively, in the Long Parliament which first met in November in the same year.

The struggles within the book trade mirrored the wider struggles in the state, but they were also important because of the growing recognition of their possible effect on the use of the printed word as an instrument of propaganda. This was critical at a time when two opposing factions had almost equal access to printing facilities, and both recognized their significance. When Charles I left London to lead his army against the rebellious Scots, he took a printer with him, and a number of proclamations were printed as a result. This practice was followed throughout the Civil War.[1] Parliament also took a hand in the matter, and exercised an increasingly tight control over the regulation of the press in London from 1641 onwards.[2]

The increasing exercise of authority by Parliament, and particularly by the House of Commons, had some significant implications for the copy-owning booksellers. The system of protection for the unprivileged copies depended on the use of the Stationers' Register, and the general acceptance of its meaning within the Company. Anything which affected the rules of entry had implications, usually unintended, for the ownership of rights in copies. It is important to recognize, however, that it was the privileged copies, and especially those which constituted the English Stock, which were of greatest importance to the leading members of the trade. It was these copies which provided the most profitable work, and it was with the protection of these rights that the Court of Assistants was principally concerned. The copies protected only by custom, whether or not they were entered in the Register, were, of course, a serious matter for their owners, but of far less general consequence for the trade as a whole.

The finer points of book trade practice were of no concern to those directing or resisting a revolution. What was of critical importance was the control and effective use of the press as an instrument of propaganda. From the earliest days of the Long Parliament, its members concerned themselves with this issue, for the licensing system effectively collapsed as the prerogative courts lost their moral, and subsequently legal, authority. The House of Commons was particularly sensitive on these issues, and began to address them early in 1641, with the intention of ensuring that its views were fully and accurately represented in print.[3] Any effect on the system of copy protection was entirely coincidental and unintended, but it was, from the trade's point of view, inevitable.

Their first battle was fought to protect the privileged copies, and particularly the English Stock. The attack on them was renewed early in 1641 with a pamphlet published by Michael Sparke, entitled *Scintilla, or a light broken into dark warehouses*. Sparke was deeply involved in the trade in the import of English Bibles, in breach of the privileges of the King's Printer and the universities,[4] but his attack on monopolies was politically astute and brought him much support. It caused a real crisis in the Stationers' Company,[5] because it found clear echoes in the Commons, which had already concerned itself with the implications of the Bible patent.[6] Two years later, John Milton referred back to this affair in *Areopagitica*:

> . . . there was in it the fraud of some old *patentees* and *monopolizers* in the trade of book-selling; who under pretence of the poor in their Company not to be defrauded, and the just retaining of each man his severall copy, which God forbid should be gainsaid, brought divers glosing colours to the House, which were indeed but colours, and serving to no end except it be to exercise a superiority over their neighbours . . .[7]

The view that the shareholders in the English Stock were interested in exploiting it only for their own advantage, and not in order to provide work for the poorer members of the Company, was widespread both inside and outside the trade, and, whether or not the accusation was a fair one, it provided a potent weapon to the opponents of the trade establishment.

Even before the publication of *Scintilla*, however, the Commons had begun to take an active interest in the affairs of the trade, by establishing a committee to investigate it in February 1641.[8] The trade was now seriously concerned, and, when the Lords also began to show an interest in its affairs, it pre-emptively complained in March 1641 to that House that the breakdown in the control of the press was wrecking its economic stability.[9] This was, however, of little concern to either House as events moved at an ever-increasing pace. In October, the Court of Assistants agreed to consider the Company's affairs, and to report on them to the House of Commons, presumably in response to the committee established in February; its report would specially concentrate on the 'Ordinances and Rights concerning the Entry of Copies'.[10]

There was, however, a growing conflict of interest, and not only in the matter of monopolies. There were two separate, although related, issues at stake: the control of the press in order to use it for propaganda (while suppressing the propaganda of others), which was the interest of Parliament; and the retention of long-established rights which had a multiplicity of economic implications for their beneficiaries, which was the interest of at least some members of the trade. The problem for the latter was that they were neither united nor unanimous. The very public opposition of some members of the Company to the continuation of its historic role (whatever their own motives may have been) proved both an excuse and an opportunity for intervention by authority. In practice, it was the view of Parliament (and particularly that of the

House of Commons) which ultimately prevailed, and, as a result, it was the control of the press, rather than the rights in privileged and other copies, which dominated the debate and the legislation in the late 1640s and early 1650s. This had implications for the copy-protection practices which had developed within the trade, but only rarely directly impinged upon them.

One interesting example of the almost casual way in which this happened is in a House of Commons order in January 1642, which was principally concerned with licensing arrangements, but added coincidentally that 'the Master and Wardens of the Company of stationers shall be required to take special Orders, that the Printers do neither print or reprint anything without the Name and consent of the Author . . .'[11] The requirement to print the name of the *licenser* had theoretically existed since 1632, and had been reiterated in 1637,[12] but this apparent concern for the author was new. The real purpose was, of course, to enable easy identification of the authors of unacceptable books and pamphlets, and we should certainly not ascribe any motive beyond that to the framers of this Order. Even so, they show a clear recognition that it is the author who is ultimately responsible for the book.

After the outbreak of war in 1642, the House of Commons had weightier matters on its mind, and its interest in printing was thereafter wholly confined to propaganda. It was not until the spring and early summer of 1643 that it returned to the general principles involved in the control of the book trade. By that time, the Court of Assistants had, to some extent, reasserted its own authority, at least to the extent of pacifying Sparke. The *Ordinance for the Regulating of Printing*, issued by the Commons on 14 June 1643,[13] recognized the 'diligence of the company of Stationers', and gave some support to their historic claims. All books were to be licensed, and the licence printed in the book,[14] but they were also to be 'entred in the Register Book of the Company of Stationers, according to ancient custom'. Once a book was duly entered it was not to be reprinted 'without the license and consent of the Owner or Owners thereof'. The Register itself reflects little of this, except in the growing caution of the officers and members of the Company. An entry in August 1643 records that Richard Harpur registered '. . . two things wch were printed before the Ordinance came forth . . .',[15] but no other Stationer seems to have taken the same precaution. What is significant, however, is that from late 1644 until the mid-1650s, the form of the entries changes from its traditional wording, omitting the Wardens, and including instead the names of the licensers, or referring to Commons committees, the Clerk of the Commons, or powerful individuals including both Fairfax and Cromwell.[16]

Throughout the interregnum, the power and status of the Stationers' Company was undermined. The 1647 *Ordinance against Unlicensed or Scandalous Pamphlets and for the Better Regulating of Printing* makes no mention of the Company at all,[17] and in its 1649 successor it clearly plays a subsidiary role. That legislation, *An Act against Unlicensed and Scandalous Books and Pamphlets, and for the Better Regulating of Printing*,[18] prescribed detailed mechanisms for licensing, and particularly for the licensing of newsbooks, which were to be recorded in a special register by the Clerk of the Parliament, and, almost as an afterthought '. . . in the Register-book of the Company of Stationers, according to ancient custom'.

The newsbooks were, however, an area of particular political sensitivity, and during the 1650s the control of them became almost absolute.[19] For less inflammatory publications, the Company did find some official support for its position. There was a specific statement that English Stock titles were not to be pirated:

> . . . nor any Book or Books, or part of any Book or Books, now entered in the Register Book of the said Company, or which hereafter shall be duly entred in the said Register Book, for any particular member of the said Company, without the like consent of the owner or owners thereof.[20]

This at least allowed the Court of Assistants to protect, however tenuously, the continuing existence of rights in copies as recorded in the Register. There was, however, not even the pretence of leaving the Company in control of the book trade in the final piece of Commonwealth legislation, in January 1653. The control of the trade passed to the Council of State, and the Master and Wardens were merely left with a series of duties and obligations, supported by the reassertion of their rights to search for and seize illegal books, and rewarded by granting to the Company half of the value of the fines levied on those associated with the writing, printing, publishing and selling of such books.[21]

The 1653 Act was in force until the Restoration of Charles II in May 1660. Licensing was strictly enforced, but, within the system, the Court of Assistants continued to operate as best it could. There was, perhaps, a more cautious approach to potentially contentious issues. When Richard Hodgkinson complained in 1653 that William Leybourne had pirated a copy which belonged to him, he produced his licence as evidence of ownership. Confronted with such authority, the Court referred the matter for a later decision.[22] In another case, in 1656, concerning a dispute between Thomas Warren and Francis Leach, the Clerk eventually suggested that the Court of Assistants should take legal advice before determining a course of action; nothing more seems to have happened.[23] These are mere straws in the wind, although the latter is not wholly without significance in suggesting a reference to the law as well as to custom. Also of some interest are a few entries in the Register which suggest that copy ownership practices were still evolving and changing even under the difficulties of the times. In particular, there is a noticeable growth in the transfer of shares in copies, as opposed to copies as a whole. In May 1656, for example, William Lee, Daniel Pakemen, Gabriel Bedell and Thomas Collins jointly entered *Reports in the Exchequer*, the official record of the Court of Exchequer for 1606 to 1614; the first two each owned one-third shares and the others one-sixth each.[24] Such complex joint ownership was becoming more common, if not yet usual; it was also in 1656 that John Harrison's widow transferred his one-sixteenth share in Lancelot Andrews's sermons to Octavian Pulleyn,[25] and Giles Calvert transferred to Mary Simmons a one-fourth share of volumes two, three and four of the works of Joseph Caryl. In the latter transaction the phrase 'parte or share' is used, apparently for the first time, as a description of the nature of the property.[26]

In May 1660, however, the trade found itself in a legal vacuum. Interregnum legislation was deemed to have no force, but the book trade had operated under decrees from the prerogative courts, which were also not to be restored. A few minor actions were taken by administrative decree. An Order-in-Council in June ordered the Master and Wardens to seize all republican books; Milton's *Pro populo anglicano defensio* and his refutation of *Eikon Basilike* were both banned by proclamation in August;[27] and, in a strange echo from the distant past,[28] it was ordered on 1 October that the Master of the Revels was to authorize all plays before they were printed.[29]

Obviously, however, more than this was needed, a fact recognized by the Court of Assistants on the same day: 'The Table taking notice of the great want of a Law for restraining the Exorbitances of Printing & securing propriety [*sic*] in Copies . . .'[30] The Court noted that a Bill was already in front of the House of Commons, and took steps to ensure that the Company's interests were represented. The minute of the Court's discussion makes it clear that the protection of copies was at least as important to the trade as was the regulation of the press. It is, however, significant that, from the very beginning of post-Restoration attempts to legislate for the press, the Court of Assistants linked the two issues of censorship and copyright, thus enabling it to present an argument in favour of its own commercial control as one for the protection of the state.

No legislation was passed in 1660, and by the summer of 1661, it was regarded as a matter of urgency. In early July, the House of Commons, 'taking Notice that several traiterous, schismatical, and scandalous Pamphlets have been printed since his Majesty's happy Restauration', ordered that a Bill should be prepared 'for the Regulation of Printing'.[31] The essence of the proposal was to establish the new office of Surveyor of the Press, whose occupant would oversee book-trade matters and would have wide-ranging powers. The Stationers' Company was to be a part of the system, and indeed was to be firmly enmeshed in it by forcing all members to take an oath not to print unlicensed books, and, in another proposal, giving a committee of twelve members of the Company the power to prosecute offenders.[32] In the meanwhile, however, the Solicitor-General was ordered to prepare a Bill to give the King statutory power to regulate the press 'till it be otherwise provided for'.[33]

The Bill to regulate the press passed quickly through the Commons, getting its Second Reading on 26 July and its Third Reading the following day.[34] It then ran into trouble in the Lords, where it was amended to protect the houses of peers from search by officers looking for illegal books. The Commons rejected this amendment, and the Bill was lost at the end of the Session.[35]

The loss of the Bill merely exacerbated the problem. On the one hand, Charles II and his ministers wanted to control the press, and on the other, the Court of Assistants wanted protection for copies and, especially, for the English Stock. Piecemeal legislation, such as the Royal Proclamation against Milton's works, or to prevent the unlicensed printing of almanacs, only made the situation more confused,[36] and, inevitably, a new Bill was introduced into Parliament in 1662. The Commons was left in no doubt as to the importance attached to the proposed legislation:

> Mr Secretary Morice acquainted the House, from his Majesty, That, next to the Bill for settling the Forces of the Kingdom, his Majesty held, that the Bill, now depending, for regulating the Press, and to prevent the Printing of libellous and seditious Books, did most conduce to the securing of the Peace of the Kingdom.[37]

After this message, it was not surprising that the Bill passed fairly quickly through both houses, and received the Royal Assent on 19 May.[38] In various guises, the 1662 Printing Act was to provide the legislative framework for the trade until 1679, and again from 1685 to 1694.

Despite Cyprian Blagden's view that in 1662 'the clock was firmly put back to 1637',[39] the Act actually included a number of important innovations, including the appointment of a Licenser (Sir Roger L'Estrange) and a statutory requirement for entry in the Register. The latter brought the whole business of entry and copy protection firmly within the orbit of the common-law courts for the first time, despite the parallel survival of the privileged copies, and the patents of the King's Printer which had been created and protected by the exercise of the prerogative. In practice, the power and prestige of the Stationers' Company was damaged, although not yet fatally so, by the Printing Act of 1662 and its successors. There is no evidence in the Court Book that the Company was ever consulted about the Bill as it passed through Parliament; it seems to have offered its support to the proposals.[40] The printers even tried to break away to form their own livery company, an idea which had been floated as early as November 1660,[41] and was rejected in 1663 largely because L'Estrange was unhappy about it rather than because of the views of the Court of Assistants.[42]

The book trade now had to operate within the provisions of a law which was specifically and avowedly designed to control the output of the press. The law required that all books should be licensed before publication, and that the fact of licensing should then be recorded in the Stationers' Register. It was this requirement to enter the licences in the Register which ensured the survival of the system of copy protection which the trade had evolved before the Civil War. This now consisted of three elements: the patents of the King's Printer and the universities, together with a few patents for individual titles; the English Stock (which was a specialized variant of the patent system); and the copies secured to their owners by custom supported by entry in the Register and the practices of the Stationers' Company.

Increasingly, the Court of Assistants was more concerned with the English Stock than with any other aspect of copyright regulation, and was vigorous in its defence. In 1666, for example, Neville Simmons was allowed to enter Tobias Ellis's *The English Schole* only on the condition that 'this booke be not prejudiciall to the Companie of Staconers, or anie other mans rights, &c'.[43] Despite the apparent inclusiveness of the last clause and the '&c', this was clearly a move to protect the school-book monopoly of the English Stock.

It was, however, the almanac monopoly which came to dominate the Stock in the late seventeenth century, and for the next hundred years. Almanacs were vastly popular throughout the period, and represented a regular source of income for the shareholders. There were two complications in their enjoyment of this profitable monopoly: legal claims, and piracy. The university presses both claimed that their own Letters Patent gave them the right to print privileged books, including almanacs. Various agreements were reached between the Company and the universities during the seventeenth century, including long periods when almanacs were printed at Cambridge for the English Stock,[44] but there was always a sense of unease about the potential damage to the Stock's profits from university intervention in this trade. Piracy was more insidious, but sometimes easier to control. It was always a factor in the London almanac trade, and the Court adopted various ploys to deal with it, including, on one occasion, fining a pirate and depriving him of his shares in the Stock, and then reaching an accommodation which resulted in his election as Master a year later![45]

The Company, however, also used more formal mechanisms for protecting the English Stock, including the law itself. It was the 1662 Act which made this possible, for it provided the basis on which a body of case law could be developed. As early as the autumn of 1667, the Company and the patentees of Roll's Abridgement (which was part of the Law Patent) sought the views of the Court of Common Pleas on the legality of the monopoly. The Court unequivocally upheld the patents, as having been granted under the prerogative, because 'The King hath a general prerogative [in relation to printing] at common law . . . time out of mind'.[46] This general judgment was of particular relevance to the English Stock. In 1677, King's Bench held that the almanac patent derived from the prerogative, and therefore was not an illegal monopoly, because the King 'may grant the printing to whom he will'.[47] Moreover, the justices added that their view was supported by the 1662 Act in which 'it is impliedly granted that the printing of all books is restrainable, or grantable by the King's patent'.[48]

This broad view of the prerogative powers of the Crown, and their particular application in the book trade, was generally advantageous to the Stationers' Company, and we find an increasing recourse to the courts in disputes between the Company and pirates, and between individual stationers, from the 1660s onwards.[49] On at least one occasion, the Company sought the views of the Solicitor-General on a copyright issue; the issue was a comparatively trivial one (whether or not marginal annotation created a new copy), but the action itself was significant.[50] In a by-law approved in January 1678, the growing relevance of the law to the trade's affairs was recognized, implicitly, when the Court of Assistants made an attempt, perhaps somewhat anachronistically, to try to control it by ordering that:

> . . . when any difference or differences shall hereafter arise between any Member and Members of this Company for Copy Right[51] or any thing relating to Printing bookselling or Bookbinding That then before any Accion or Suite be Commenced They shall first make their application to the Master Wardens & Assistants in a Court . . .

There was a £10 fine for going directly to law.[52] There is evidence that this by-law was enforced. In April 1678, Thomas Fabian was given permission to sue Henry Harris for infringing his rights in 'his Coppy Entitled Flavells Navigacon Spiritualized'.[53] In 1682, Robert Pawlett was given an even more inclusive permission to sue, in the name of the Company, any member who had printed or imported any of his copies without his permission, although the Company carefully indemnified itself from any costs arising out of the case.[54] Ironically, no such permission is recorded in what seems to be the only fully reported seventeenth-century case of an individual stationer suing another individual stationer for breach of copyright, *Ponder v. Braddill* in May 1678.[55]

In general, the law supported the Stationers' Company and the shareholders in the English Stock, although it did so for political rather than economic reasons. The report of the final hearing of *Company of Stationers v. Seymour* in King's Bench in 1677 is perhaps the most explicit statement of the position. The Court referred to an earlier case regarding the Law Patent determined by the House of Lords, and argued that the case for the almanac monopoly was 'stronger':

> The Lords, in the resolution of that case, relied upon this, that printing was a new invention, and therefore every man could not by the common law have a liberty of printing *law-books*. And since printing has been invented, and is become a common trade, so much of it as had been kept inclosed never was made common; but matters of State, and this

> that concern the Government, were never left to any man's liberty to print that would . . . Queen Elizabeth, King James, and King Charles the First, granted such patents as these, and the law has great respect to common usage . . .[56]

This was apparently a resounding reaffirmation of the position of the Crown and of the English Stock as a beneficiary of the Crown's exercise of its powers. But there was a sting in the tail. Having quoted precedents, and looked deep into the history of patents, the Court added that 'There is no particular author of an almanack; and then, by the rule of our law, the King has the property in the copy'.[57] This was a modification of the extreme position held by Coventry in James I's reign,[58] for it seemed to acknowledge that books which did have an identifiable author were not subject to the exercise of the prerogative in the same way.

This did not, however, mean that there was no royal intervention in securing rights in copies to individuals. There are a few post-Restoration examples of the earlier practice of granting patents to individuals for their books. An example in July 1661, when Miles Dodson was a given a 31-year licence for his *God and the King*, should probably be regarded as atypical because of both the timing (when there was no legislation) and the delicate subject matter.[59] The few remaining examples include Ogilby's patents for his illustrated editions of Virgil, Homer and Aesop, granted for 15 years in 1666, and duly noted by the Court of Assistants, and John Fuller's 10-year patent for his father's *Worthies of England* in 1663.[60] In general, however, patents for individual titles had vanished before the end of Charles II's reign, although a few class monopolies were still granted outside the English Stock, including one for Welsh almanacs in 1680,[61] and perhaps a *de facto* monopoly on music.[62] For the protection of particular titles outside the patent books, entry in the Register remained the only mechanism.

The use of the Register as a record of licences was compulsory under the 1662 Act. The Court of Assistants thus had a sanction which it never had before 1640, despite the various regulations about entry which had been made both by the Company itself and by the state in various guises. The Court was now in a very different position. Although its hand was indeed stronger, it was itself, as was the whole trade, under the constant surveillance of the Surveyor of the Press, and was obliged from time to time to take measures to convince officials of its seriousness. In 1674, for example, it ordered Robert Clavell, the publisher of the *Term*

Catalogues, quarterly lists of newly published books,[63] to print in his catalogue 'only such [titles] as are entred in the Register booke belonging to the Company . . .' The reason was simple: he had been putting 'unlicensed bookes into his Catalogue'.[64] Two years later, this ruling was generalized to the effect that no catalogue was to be published until the Clerk of the Stationers' Company could attest that every book listed in it was duly licensed.[65]

Although the requirement to license and enter new books was specified in the 1662 Act and its successors, the interpretation of the entry within the trade was an internal matter. Here the Court of Assistants followed its own precedents. There was never any question that rights derived from entries before 1662 (and indeed before 1640) were still regarded as valid. When Humphrey Moseley, who had been active in the trade since the 1630s, died in 1661, his widow sold his copies to Henry Herringman, who, on the strength of them, became the leading literary publisher of the late seventeenth century, for his purchases included Milton, Donne and many of the Cavalier poets. He added contemporary literature, especially Dryden, to this list, much of which was eventually bought by Jacob Tonson, and laid the foundations of his family's successful three generations in the trade.[66] Other examples abound of pre-Civil War copyrights clearly recognized after 1662; perhaps the most famous are the rights in Shakespeare, which descended intact, and with surprisingly little challenge, until the late eighteenth century.[67]

For so long as the 1662 Act was in force, the Court of Assistants could ensure that copies were entered in the Register, and that the Company's own rules were then obeyed. The lapse of the Act in 1678–79 therefore provoked something of a crisis. The key political issue was the control of the press, but this now passed outside the orbit of the Stationers' Company.[68] For the Company, the key issue was that of copy protection. The 1678 by-laws, and the likelihood of litigation which they assumed, were an attempt to address this issue as it became apparent that the legislative underpinning of the system might vanish. Indeed, the Court of Assistants was sufficiently concerned to appoint a committee in March 1679 to 'attend the drawing and passing of an Act of Parliament',[69] presumably to replace the lapsed Act in whole or in part. The Company was already aware of the significance of the statute law for the conduct of its affairs. The English Stock cases which referred back to the 1662 Act affirmed its importance, and in 1674, the Court of Assistants had directed that entries in the Register 'shall be with a

Saluo Iure cuilibet', explicitly recognizing the superior force of law over custom.[70]

It is in this context that *Ponder v. Braddill* is of some interest.[71] The case was a complicated one concerning Bunyan's *Pilgrim's Progress*. The work had been duly licensed, and then properly entered on the Register by Ponder on 22 December 1677; it was published early in 1678.[72] It was an immediate success, and was reprinted twice in the same year; according to Ponder, there were also piratical reprints at the same time, one or more of them by Thomas Braddill (or Braddyl). It was the beginning of a long series of disputes between the two men over this valuable copy; its importance is that Ponder's case was based on legal ownership attested by entry in the Register. In fact, the case was withdrawn before it was determined, and the legal force of an entry in the Register as a record of ownership remained in some doubt.

There was, however, no doubt in the minds of the Assistants. From 1678 onwards the number of entries in the Register declined dramatically in the absence of legal sanctions. The efforts of the Court of Assistants to enforce entry and to prevent piracy seem to have been in vain,[73] and it was doubtless a matter of great relief when, on 5 June 1685, the Commons in James II's first Parliament appointed a committee to look at expiring laws, and also ordered 'That the same Committee have Power to present a Bill to this House, for regulating the Printing Press'.[74] It duly did so, and a Bill reviving the 1662 Act received the Royal assent on 2 July.[75] This restored the position to that which had existed in 1678 before the expiry of the earlier legislation, and offered a little more stability, for the new Act was to be in force for seven years, and until the end of the next session of Parliament thereafter.[76]

Long before the 1685 Act expired, the political system of which it was a product had vanished for ever. The Glorious Revolution, however, had no immediate effect on the law. The Act was in fact renewed in March 1693, and the licensing system was enforced with some rigour; in turn this meant that copies had to be entered in the Register and the Court of Assistants had its traditional powers restored to it.[77] Nevertheless, the Court was in trouble. There was general agreement in the early 1690s that there was a need for licensing to control the opposition, and more particularly Jacobite, press. This did not, however, mean that there was a consensus about the role of the Stationers' Company. The legislative process of 1693 brought both old and new grievances to the surface. There were objections to the monopolies on the patent books, both those of the King's Printer and of the English Stock. There were also claims made that entries in the Register were being falsified to establish 'rights' which did not actually exist. The truth of the latter accusation cannot be established; what is certain is that there was still a widespread and growing resentment, both inside and outside the trade, about the role of the Stationers' Company, and of those who controlled the Court and the English Stock.[78]

There was also a different kind of opposition to the renewal of the 1685 Act in 1693. Not all of its opponents were concerned with issues of trade; at least one, John Locke, also addressed issues of principle. He argued that the Stationers' monopoly made books too expensive, and that they merely made profits from the fruits of other people's work. This view did not prevail in 1693, but in the winter of 1694–95, when the Act came up for renewal once more, Locke mobilized a group of his friends in the Commons in the hope of engineering the defeat of the Bill. The Court of Assistants was not idle, but it was somewhat complacent. It was taken by surprise when the Commons rejected the Bill on 11 February 1695, and immediately began to agitate for its revival.[79]

The final lapse of the law which began as the Printing Act of 1662 marks a turning-point in the history of the English book trade, and in the history of the freedom of the press in England. So far as the latter was concerned, the lapse of the Act led to the abolition of pre-publication censorship, although this by no means created a 'free' press overnight. For the trade, the immediate consequences were potentially catastrophic. Much of the superstructure of protection which the Stationers' Company had so carefully erected and so assiduously defended was swept away. Although the patents, and hence the English Stock, were unaffected, little else remained the same. There were no more restrictions on the number (or location) of printers, or on the numbers of journeymen or apprentices. There were no restrictions of the import of books. Above all, there was no longer any legal obligation to enter new books on the Stationers' Register, and, given the absence of any unambiguous precedents, certainly no guarantee that the courts would uphold the claims of the copy-owning booksellers.

The book trade was, of course, not alone in its concern about the absence of any legislation relating to publishing, but the politicians were far more interested in the other and more important implication for licensing. Indeed, the trade was now to pay the price for its own history. Ever since the middle of the sixteenth century, its practices in relation to copy ownership and the

Table 2.1
Book trade bills 1695–1710

Date	House	Outcome
1695	C	Commons rejected Lords' amendments
1695–96	C	In committee at end of session
1696	C	Ordered but never brought in
1697	C	In committee at end of session
1698	C	Defeated on Second Reading
1698	L	Ordered but never brought in
1699	L	Passed; defeated on Second Reading in Commons
1701	L	Defeated on Second Reading
1704	C	In committee at end of session
1707	L	In committee at end of session
1710	C	Royal Assent 6 April 1710

Sources: CJ; LJ.

protection of rights in copies had been derived from, and indissolubly linked to, the system for the control of the press by the state. This had been as true in the Interregnum as at any other time. For the leading members of the trade in 1695, the regime imposed by the 1662 Act and its successors was the normal environment in which they were accustomed to work, despite (or perhaps because of) the unhappy experience of the period from 1679 to 1685. But unless the politicians could find some way to restore licensing, there was, or so it seemed then, no obvious way to restore some sort of order to the book trade.

On the very day, 11 February 1695, on which the Bill to renew the 1693 Act was lost, the House of Commons established a committee to draft a new Bill.[80] This was merely the first of what was to prove to be a long line of such bills, fifteen in all between 1695 and 1714, which, in one form or another, sought to regulate the affairs of the book trade[81] (see Table 2.1). The first of these fifteen bills was very different from the 1693 Act and its predecessors. It proposed that printing presses should be registered, and that printed sheets should be sent to the licensers before publication. There was, however, no attempt to restore the privileged position of the Stationers' Company. There was to be no geographical restriction on printing, no requirement to enter licences in the Stationers' Register, and no ban on imports. This Bill passed the Commons, but the provisions about licensing were amended in the Lords, and it was lost when the Commons refused to accept the Lords' amendments.[82]

All the successors of the 1695 Bill (except the 1710 Copyright Act) were similarly lost when they became entangled in the machinery of Parliament. Only five reached a Second Reading in either House: one passed (in 1710), three were rejected on a division, and one was lost when Parliament was dissolved on the death of Queen Anne. All the others died in various stages of procedure. It was not lack of parliamentary time which led to these failures. When both houses wanted to enact a law they could do so very quickly.[83] Indeed, the 1710 Copyright Act went through all its stages to the Royal Assent in just over three months. The explanation for failure was quite different: there were too many opposing interests in conflict with each other.

For most of the politicians, the only reason to be interested in any of these bills was in the hope of reviving the licensing laws. Robert Harley, later first earl of Oxford, dominated the politics of the period, first from the Speaker's chair, then from the office of the Secretary of State, and finally from the Treasury. Harley was obsessed with the press. This was not entirely surprising, for he was the first major politician to be exposed to the perils of an unlicensed press at a time of great political discord.[84] The first decade of the eighteenth century saw both the publication of the first successful daily newspaper, and the emergence of Daniel Defoe as the first great journalist. Yet within living memory, news had been regarded as a state secret, and its printing and distribution a state monopoly. Until the Glorious Revolution, news and its dissemination had been effectively controlled by the Secretary of State's office, and the official *London Gazette* had for long periods been the only licensed newspaper.[85] After the Revolution, the situation inevitably changed, but the final lapse of the licensing law created a wholly new and uncontrolled situation. The government could now only protect itself through the courts by looking for very broad interpretations of such common-law offences as seditious libel,[86] or by using parliamentary procedures such as prosecutions for breach of privilege or contempt of the House.[87] All this happened at a time of unprecedentedly fierce party conflicts, especially after all Queen Anne's children predeceased her and the High Tories began to look towards a Stuart restoration as their only salvation. It is hardly surprising that successive governments, even when led by moderate Tories like Harley, should have sought some means of controlling the press. Even if licensing did not always work, as had been argued in 1694 and 1695, it did provide some vestigial legal protection.

Certainly, the Bill presented in April 1695 was intended to restrain the press, as was that presented in the new session later in the same year by Harley himself. Both bills, however, provoked opposition from many quarters including the book trade. Four days after a House of Commons committee had begun to draft a new Bill in February 1695, John Sims, the Master of the Stationers' Company, called an extraordinary meeting of the Court of Assistants to decide what action should be taken. It was agreed to petition the House, and to authorize the Treasurer to pay the Master and Wardens whatever they needed for this purpose.[88] This petition, whose objective was to ask for protection for rights in copies, was presented to the House on 30 March.[89] On the following day, the journeymen added their voices, asking for the restoration of the geographical restrictions on printing (to London, York and the universities), and for limits on the numbers of both master printers and apprentices.[90]

There was a similar pattern of petitions on subsequent bills. On 5 December 1695, the House received petitions from the printers and booksellers of London and Westminster (the employers) and from the journeymen (the employees), the latter once again concerned to limit the numbers of masters and apprentices.[91] In October 1696, a petition was printed, but never reached the House, because the Bill to which it referred was dropped.[92] This petition began with a nod in the direction of the promoters of the Bill by arguing that both church and state were in need of the protection afforded by licensing. It then, however, came to its real point: piracy was commonplace, imports should be banned, the geographical restrictions on printing restored, and the number of masters and apprentices limited by law. The implication was that the provisions of the 1662 Act, including registration, should be revived. In 1696, the masters petitioned the House on the then-current Bill.[93] In 1704, it was once again the turn of the journeymen, who pointed out that the number of men engaged in the trade had greatly increased since 1695, and asked for restrictions on the number of apprentices, and sanctions against 'interlopers', that is, those who had not served a proper apprenticeship.[94]

There is a common theme which runs through all of these petitions, whatever their specific requests: the desire to restore to the book trade the laws under which it operated before 1695. There are, however, differing motives for wishing to do so, although both masters and men were seeking to protect their investments in the trade. For the journeymen, this meant their skills. For the masters it meant the less tangible, but no less valuable, asset of their rights in copies. We do not know whether the two sides acted in concert, but it is clear that both felt that they would be best served by the revival of the historic powers and assumed privileges of the Court of Assistants.

The book trade, however, was not alone in its interest in these matters. Quite apart from any political or philosophical opposition to the revival of licensing, there were those who used economic and commercial arguments against it. In 1694 or 1695, an anonymous petition, *To the Honourable Members, assembled in Parliament*,[95] had argued that any monopoly was contrary to the national interest, and that one such as that which had formerly been exercised by the Stationers' Company should not be restored once it had lapsed. The petitioner probably touched a raw nerve in the trade when he argued that it was only self-interest which made the Stationers support licensing at all: 'Were it not for their Mammon-Monopoly, the Master, Wardens, &c of the Stationers' Company, would cry out against the slavery and charge of Licensing as much as any of their Brethren.'

The interests of the politicians were, however, completely different, as was clear as early as 1697. In that year, as the end of the Session approached, another licensing bill was still in committee, and seemed likely to be lost when Parliament was prorogued. The House of Commons then gave leave for another Bill to be brought in which would have prevented the unlicensed writing, printing and publication of news.[96] That was aimed both at the newspapers and at the writers of the privately circulated manuscript newsletters which were an important means of communication of political information.[97] This Bill also vanished at the end of the Session, but it showed starkly where the real argument was being pursued, among those who wished to control the dissemination of news and opinion.

Faced with their inability to push licensing legislation through the House, successive governments used different means to pursue their enemies in the press. Between 1695 and 1714, more than thirty printers, booksellers and news-writers were brought to one or other House to answer charges relating to privilege or contempt.[98] It was, however, both a clumsy and an ultimately unsatisfactory way of dealing with the problem. By the spring of 1704, at least three such prosecutions were in hand, and at the same time the Tory majority in the House was slipping away. The ministry dissolved, and Harley became Secretary of State in a new administration which combined Whigs and moderate Tories.

This change in the ministry signalled the end of the attempt to revive the old licensing system. Harley had come round to the view that subtlety was more potent than legislation, and that what he really needed was a knowledge of the state of opinion outside the House so that he could direct his policies accordingly. He used both public and private money to this end, employing agents to keep himself well-informed.[99] His chief agent, and to some extent the controller of the whole propaganda exercise, was Daniel Defoe, in whose release from prison in 1703 Harley had been instrumental.[100] Soon after he began to work for Harley, Defoe went into print on licensing, and also on the associated matter of copyright. Defoe, in his pamphlet *An Essay on the Regulation of the Press*,[101] set out what was, by then, the moderate Tory position on press controls. He argued that the restoration of licensing would make the press a 'slave to party', and the 'first step to restore Arbitrary Power in this Nation'.[102] The latter phrase was an allusion to the Jacobite tendencies of the High Tories, but Defoe was not making the case for a wholly free press. He proposed to specify particular matters of both church and state which should not be allowable, while leaving room for open publication of party political quarrels. He also proposed compulsory imprints, showing the names of author, printer and publisher, and very heavy penalties for infringements of the law.[103]

This inevitably raised the question of the registration, and hence of the protection, of copies. A law which required explicit statements of the authorial and trade origins of a book, would also, he wrote, 'put a Stop to a certain sort of Thieving which is now in full practice in England, and which no law extends to punish, viz. some Printers and Booksellers printing copies none of their own'.[104] Defoe considered that this not only robs authors of their property, and thus discourages the publication of useful and learned works, but also gives rise to the production of unauthorized abridgements, and cheap reprints on poor paper in bad type. In Defoe's view, if authors were granted the right to prosecute pirates, the whole trade in piracies would rapidly come to an end.

It is not clear whether Defoe was exaggerating the difficulties faced by the trade. There was some piracy in the early eighteenth century, especially of popular literary texts, and, of course, the continuing problems with the almanacs and the import of books protected by the patents of King's Printer such as Bibles.[105] What is certain is that he was suggesting a different approach to the whole problem of copy protection. He saw it as being a matter for the author. This was an unusual perception at a time when the whole public debate had revolved around censorship on the one hand, and the property rights of publishers on the other. Even Defoe, however, subordinates the protection of copies to the need for the clear identification of the origins of books so that authors and publishers can, if necessary, be traced by the authorities.

No such Bill as Defoe envisaged was promoted during Harley's secretaryship, but it seems reasonable to assume that in *An Essay* Defoe gave a reasonably accurate representation of Harley's position. He was, after all, working for the Secretary of State, and had recently been released from prison through his influence. Harley, however, had other matters on his mind. A steady stream of prosecutions of books in Parliament and the courts continued,[106] but no attempt was made to reintroduce a licensing bill. Quite apart from Harley's own views, it is unlikely that such a Bill would have commended itself to the Whiggish House elected in 1705.[107] Nevertheless, Defoe's ideas were implanted in the minds of some moderate Tories, as was their presumed authority from Harley. When the House considered copyright legislation in 1707, the ministry was, at worst, sympathetic. In a sense, Defoe's arguments opened the way for a reconsideration of the whole issue of copy protection, by suggesting a slightly different case which might be made for it. Despite Defoe's emphasis on the need for some control of the press, he had also added a further argument in favour of the protection of property. It was, of course, precisely this with which the booksellers had been concerned, and it was central to their various petitions on the bills which had been discussed since 1695. Defoe, however, added a new element: the idea that protection was beneficial to authors as well as to the trade. It was this element, the 'encouragement of learning', as Defoe called it, which the trade now began to emphasize.

The first formal expression of this view was put by thirteen leading members of the trade in a petition presented to the Commons in February 1707.[108] They pointed out that time and money had been spent in writing books, and in printing and selling them, but that the pirates, both English and foreign, were making serious inroads in this property. They therefore asked that what they called 'literary property' (another new phrase) should be secured to the writer or his assignees, or to the purchaser of the copy. The last would, of course, normally be a publisher, but the

Table 2.2
The signatories of the book trade petition 1707

Name	Offices (1)	Trade sales (2)	Conger (3)	Trade subs (3)
Edward Brewster	M, W		x	x
Daniel Browne	M, W	x	x	x
Richard Chiswell		x	x	x
Robert Clavell	M, W		x	x
Freeman Collins	W		x	x
Timothy Goodwin			x (p)	
Charles Harper	M, W			
Henry Mortlock	M, W		x	x
William Rogers			x	x
Samuel Roycroft	W			
Jacob Tonson			x (p+)	x
Benjamin Tooke	W		x (p+)	x
John Walthoe	M, W	x	x (p)	x

Key: M = Master
W = Warden
p = printing conger
p+ = in printing conger

Sources:
(1) D. F. McKenzie, *Stationers' Company Apprentices 1701–1800*. Oxford: Oxford Bibliographical Society (new ser. 19), 1978, pp. 402–4.
(2) Terry Belanger, Booksellers' trade sales, 1718–1768. *The Library*, 5th ser., 30 (1975), pp. 297–302.
(3) Hodgson and Blagden; see note 109.
See also Feather, The book trade in politics (note 98), pp. 30–2.

petition was worded so that the petitioners gave prominence to the protection of authors without in any way compromising their own interests.

These interests were indeed considerable. The thirteen included six former or future Masters of the Stationers' Company, and ten former or future Wardens (see Table 2.2). The most recent entrant to the trade was John Walthoe, and he had been in business for twenty years. All the others were far senior to him. More importantly, all were deeply embedded in the trade's commercial networks. All but two of them belonged to one of the congers, the groups of printers and booksellers who controlled much of the wholesale trade, and were also joint owners of some copyrights. Nine of them were subscribers to the so-called 'trade books' published jointly by the copyright owners and distributed through the congers. At least three of them had either books or copies sold at trade sales. In short, they were all deeply committed to the trade through heavy financial commitments.[109] We can identify here the 'proprietors' who had agitated for over ten years for the restoration of some kind of legislative framework for the book trade, and it is clear that they saw themselves as the mouthpiece of the trade as a whole. Certainly, the partners in the English Stock wished them well. On 1 March 1707, they agreed to pay £30 to the Doorkeepers of the House of Commons for their help with the copyright bill, and authorized Goodwin and Walthoe, both signatories of the petition, to act for them in this matter.[110]

It is quite clear that the initiative for legislation in 1707 came from the inner circles of the London book trade, under the leadership of some of the most influential and deeply involved copy-owning booksellers, supported by representatives of the wholesaling conger and of the English Stock, and with the active support of the Stationers' Company. A Bill was duly presented to the House, and was given a Second Reading on 4 March.[111] This was followed by a short flurry of activity from various quarters. These quarters included the Royal Library, the Archbishop of Canterbury, and both English universities, all seeking to benefit from the possibility of legal deposit,[112] and also, especially in Oxford, a growing concern about how the Bill might affect the already strained relations between the University Press and the London trade about Oxford's claims to print privileged books.[113] In the end, all of this activity came to nothing, for the Bill never emerged from committee.

This was not, however, to be the end of the story, for early in 1710 the matter was raised once more. A new Bill was given its First Reading on 11 January,[114] and once again the book trade went into action through the Stationers' Company. The Court of Assistants held a special meeting on 13 January, and what is described in the Court Book as 'a saving clause for the Company' was read and approved.[115] The Master and Wardens were at Westminster on 7 January, and again on 6 March (and perhaps on other occasions) to attend to the Company's interests.[116]

The proposals in the Bill dealt with three central issues:[117]

1. From a date to be determined, all existing copies shall be confirmed to their present owners for 21 years; new books will be protected for 14 years, with the possibility of a second 14-year term. There are fines for breaches of these rights.
2. From a date to be determined, books shall not be sold at 'High or Unreasonable Price', with the duty of judging complaints on this score being settled on a committee headed by the Archbishop of Canterbury.
3. From a date to be determined, copies of new books and revised editions shall be delivered for deposit to certain libraries.

In addition, two other matters were dealt with:

1. The Act was to have no effect on the rights of the English universities in copies which they owned.
2. Books in Greek, Latin and other foreign languages could be imported, despite any prohibition on the import of books in English.

The preamble to the Bill explains its purpose:

Whereas the liberty which Printers Booksellers and other Persons have of late frequently taken in Printing Reprinting, and Publishing or causing to be Printed, Reprinted and Published Books, and other Writings, without the consent of the Authors thereof, in whom ye undoubted Property of such Books and Writing as the product of their learning and labour remains or of such persons to whom such Authors for good Consideracons have lawfully transferred their Right and title therein is not only a real discouragement to learning in generll [*sic*] which in all Civilized Nations ought to receive ye greatest Countenance and Encouragement but it is also a notorious invasion of ye property of ye rightfull Proprietors of such Books and Writings, to their own very great Detriment, and too often to the Ruin of them and their Families . . .

The whole tone of this was, of course, quite different from that of the licensing bills presented and rejected between 1695 and 1704. The objective was clear: to protect the rights of authors and to encourage the publication of good books.

However noble such an aspiration might have been, it was not easily to be achieved. Four petitions on the 1710 Bill are known, three from surviving printed copies, and one from the *Journals* of the House of Commons. All four were generally favourable to the Bill, although for different reasons. The journeymen, like their masters, had by now abandoned hope of any return to older practices, and prayed generally for the protection of Parliament, supported the Bill on the grounds that piracies were printed by men who had not served apprenticeships, a statement for which they apparently offered no evidence.[118] *The Case of the Booksellers' Rights to their Copies, or sole power of printing their respective books, represented to the Parliament*,[119] supports the Bill because 'The liberty now set on foot of breaking thro' this antient and reasonable Usage is no way effectually to be retained but by an Act of Parliament'. There is no reference to, or even tacit support of, the encouragement of learning or the rights of authors, but a tone of reluctant acceptance of the need for legislation.

The other two representations to the House, which seem to be the 'official' book trade petitions, were rather more generous. The first of them, *The Booksellers' Humble Address to the Honourable House of Commons, in behalf of the Bill for Encouraging Learning*,[120] offers seven reasons for passing the Bill:

1. It confirms common-law rights.
2. It offers redress for which common law does not provide.
3. It provides a mechanism for the publication of books at reasonable prices, as had happened when common law was confirmed by statute in 1662.
4. If the Bill is rejected the trade will be ruined.
5. The trade has tried not to offend in the years since the lapse of licensing.
6. If the trade is ruined, there will be no public benefit.
7. The Bill will not restrain the freedom of the press.

This strange mixture was politically astute. First, the petitioners clearly assert that they are seeking nothing new, merely the protection of their existing rights. Secondly, they need such protection if their trade is to survive. Finally, the Bill does not inhibit the freedom of the press, and in any case the trade is so well-behaved that such inhibitions would be superfluous. In political terms, this was close to the Defoe–Harley position of three years before, and there was nothing in it which would seriously offend the Whigs or the moderate Tories whose votes were needed to carry the Bill into law.

The petition does, however, raise the issue of common-law rights which was to be of great significance during the next 65 years,[121] and also seems to argue that there is no requirement to take advantage of the benefits which statute law offers:

> For no man will be obliged thereby to Register his Copy unless he pleases; and without the Author's leave it cannot be done at all. The Press therefore under this Law will be as Free as ever, and Un-registered Books and Pamphlets always unappropriated.

To the petitioners, the two important points here were, first, that registration was voluntary, and secondly that unregistered copies had no owners. Both of these provisos assume the superior force of common law over any new statute, and imply that the proposed Act is merely supplementary to existing law and practice. They cleverly disguised this point with nods to both authors and Whigs.

The second trade petition, *More Reasons Humbly Offered to the Honourable House of Commons for the Bill for Encouraging Learning, and for securing property of copies of books to the rightful owners thereof*,[122] is concerned entirely with these alleged common-law rights. This time, Parliament is explicitly asked to confirm existing rights, on the grounds that the current situation merely encourages piracy, and ruins honest members of the trade who buy their copies lawfully. It is suggested that there is no need for time limits on such ownership, and there is a mere nod towards the title of the Bill in the suggestion that the prevalence of piracy discourages the publication of learned works.

In the event, much of what the trade wanted was granted by the House of Commons. The Bill was given its Second Reading without difficulty,[123] but at the Report Stage on 25 February various amendments made in committee were accepted.[124] Most of the changes were minor, adding dates, sizes of fines, additional deposit libraries, and the like. Two amendments, however, were both long and significant, and clearly reflect the success of the trade's lobbying and petitioning. The first deleted all references to authors in the preamble, which now read simply:

> Whereas Printers, Booksellers, and other Persons have of late frequently taken the Liberty of Printing, Reprinting, and Publishing, or causing to be Printed, Reprinted and Published Books, and other Writings, without the Consent of the Authors or Proprietors of such Books and Writings, to their very great Detriment, and too often to the Ruin of them and their Families . . .

Nothing is left about the 'undoubted Property' of the authors, the 'good Consideracons' for which they sell their rights to booksellers, or about the obligations of 'Civilized Nations' to protect and encourage learning. The preamble was now concerned only with protecting a piece of property which was not actually described in the Act itself.

Some of this was perhaps verbiage, but the second major amendment suggests that the concern was not merely stylistic. The original third paragraph of the Bill ran as follows:

That where any Author shall hereafter compose or write any book or books and shall reserve to himself ye Copy or Copies of Such book or Books share or shares thereof Or any Bookseller printer or other person who hath already purchased or acquired or shall hereafter purchase or acquire ye Copy or Copies of any book or Books Share or Shares therefore in Order to print or reprint ye same That in any or either of these Cases from and after the Tenth Day of April, One thousand seven hundred and ten . . . [there shall be protection and penalties].

Every word of this from 'where any Author' to 'any or either of these Cases' was deleted, for those words were anathema to the trade. The Bill clearly envisaged that authors might retain some or all of their rights, and thus continue to enjoy them after publication. That might still be possible, but so explicit a statement struck at the root of the prosperity of the whole legitimate London book trade.

The trade had one final victory; its 'saving clause', which had exercised the minds of the Assistants on 13 January, was there. There was to be none of Defoe's scheme for compulsory imprints. The Register was to be the official record of copy ownership, and entry was, apparently, to be required as a precondition of claiming and defending rights. It was in this form that the Act for the Encouragement of Learning received the Royal Assent on 4 April 1710, and came into force on 10 April. It was the first English statute concerned solely with the ownership of copies, and has come to be regarded as the first copyright act.[125]

The trade had not won on every point. The price controls, if they could be enforced, were potentially irksome, and, more importantly, there were time limits prescribed in the Act, exactly as there had been in the original Bill. All new copies were protected for 14 years, with a second 14-year term if the copy were re-registered; existing copies were protected for 21 years. But in 1710, this seemed too far in the future to be a matter of concern.

Nevertheless, in general, this was a very satisfactory outcome for the book trade in several respects. Most importantly, it had gained recognition of rights in copies, and a means of legal redress against pirates. At the same time, it had succeeded in watering down the original proposals to the point at which authors had their existence acknowledged but their rights undefined or ignored. It was even more significant for the future that it had also managed to avoid any precise statements about the nature of rights in copies. This is, indeed, one of the oddest features of the whole debate. At no stage does anyone involved seem to have asked exactly what it was that the trade and law sought to protect. Nowhere does the 1710 Act define 'copies' or 'books' or 'rights'; it merely assumes an understanding of them.

That assumption was, of course, wholly accurate so far as the principal supporters of the final version of the Act were concerned. The leading members of the book trade who had led the support both for a law and for a particular form of law had no real interest in precise definitions. They knew exactly what traditional rights and practices were being protected. Indeed, they considered that the only form of protection which their historic common-law rights needed was some easier means of recourse to the courts in order to act against pirates. For the trade, the 1710 Act represented a simple continuation of legal and commercial practices which had developed since the middle of the sixteenth century, but which had been under challenge in the absence of any statutory authority since 1695. Certainly the Stationers' Company was satisfied. On 18 April, the Court of Assistants appointed a committee (which included six of the 1707 petitioners) to make arrangements for keeping the Register properly, and on 1 May agreed that the Company and the Sharers in the English Stock should bear equally the costs incurred during the Bill's progress.[126]

In all important matters, the trade thought it had what it wanted, yet this apparent victory was to prove chimerical. The 1710 Act was fraught with problems because of its very imprecision. Not everyone shared the trade's complacent and conservative interpretation of what it said, what it meant and what it implied. Above all, perhaps, the world outside and around the book trade was changing. Authors were expecting to be paid more, and to some extent their expectations were being met. The book trade was booming, and there were plenty of people in it who had little interest in, or respect for, its customs, conventions and historic forms. To a large extent, the concern for copyright was a concern of a small group of copy owners in London. It is true that they had a dominant position in the trade, but they were, perhaps, just a little too confident about the strength and permanence of that position in 1710. During the next half-century, their confidence was to be undermined by attacks from many quarters: authors, pirates, printers in Ireland, Scotland and Holland, lawyers and even readers. The 1710 Act, far from being the end of a story, as the trade must have hoped, was in fact the beginning of another equally complex sequence of challenging events.

3 Defining the Law 1710–1800

The 1710 Copyright Act has been seen as a landmark in the history of copyright law, and in the history of the book trade, in Britain. This is indeed the case, but it was an unintended consequence of the actions taken by those who had promoted the legislation. The Act had been evolved from two overlapping and sometimes conflicting groups of interests. On the one hand, there was a sense among some politicians that the lapse of licensing in 1695 had been a mistake which ought to be rectified. On the other, there were copy-owning booksellers who sought to protect their existing properties against the alleged depredations of pirates. The latter hung on to the coat-tails of the former for as long as they could. Only when it became clear that pre-publication censorship was no longer achievable did they begin to fight for themselves and openly admit their objectives. Even then, they surrounded themselves with the cloak of respectability embodied in the phrase 'the encouragement of learning'.

As a result, the 1710 Act was to prove to be a thoroughly unsatisfactory piece of legislation. Although it was treated as a Public Bill,[1] it was, in effect, a law designed by its promoters to defend a group of property rights vested in a small number of owners and shareholders. It lacked in definition, especially of the key concepts of copies and rights, and, despite the amendments introduced as the Bill passed through the Commons, still left many loopholes for the ingenious. It was an essentially conservative measure, promoted by men whose interests were in preserving the *status quo*. Indeed, it was so conservative that it took little account of developments within the book trade itself, in some of which its promoters were active participants. Above all, it wholly ignored the authors of books, and certainly was not intended to confer any additional rights upon them. All of this was to prove costly for the trade throughout the rest of the eighteenth century.

At the beginning of the eighteenth century, the book trade was changing rapidly. This was, in part, a result of the lapse of licensing. After 1695, there were no restrictions on printing in either London or the provinces. The London printing trade became rather more competitive, and at the same time a few printers began to go to work in the larger provincial towns. They, however, presented an opportunity rather than a threat to the London trade. The provincial printers produced weekly regional newspapers, and their distribution networks formed the basis for a larger, more active and better financed network of provincial bookshops than had ever existed before. The London publishers thus had easier access to provincial markets, which they were able to develop and exploit as the provincial towns themselves became more prosperous throughout the century.[2]

An associated change was the development of new methods of wholesaling. The conger system, which had begun to develop in the 1680s, may have been, in origin, a part of the copy-owning booksellers' response to the lapse of the Printing Act in 1679.[3] A group of 'tradeing booksellers',[4] between six and eight in number, worked together to market their books. All of them were copy owners, and some copies were owned jointly by two or more in the group. This group, which came to be known as the 'conger',[5] was trying to protect its common interests. The books in which they owned copies were marketed through the conger and thence into the retail trade. All the members of the conger thus had a strong interest in preventing the piracy of any of the copies belonging to any of them, since this represented a potential loss of trade. The wholesaling conger continued to operate, in various forms, until the middle of the eighteenth century; at the height of its operation, in the first decade of the eighteenth century, it was handling some 20,000 books a year, worth about £5,000, a figure comparable with the turnover of the English Stock at that time.[6] Almost all of the 1707 petitioners were active in the wholesaling conger,[7] which, by that time, was a major player in the London book trade.

The wholesaling conger represented a means by which the copy-owning booksellers could protect their property regardless of the law. It was a simple but effective commercial device, but it assumed that leading members of the trade, however much they might be in competition with each other in some ways, could work together for their mutual defence. The same protectiveness can be seen in another practice which developed at about the same time, and which was to play a critical role in the development of copyright during the eighteenth century. Shares in copies had been known since the beginning of the seventeenth century, and were common after the Restoration.[8] They were an inevitable development as the ownership of copies descended through the generations, and became the subject of commercial transactions. Under the Stationers' Company's own regulations, such shares could be owned only by members of the Company and transactions relating to them had to be entered in the Register,[9] but it is unlikely that this practice was sustainable after 1660, and after 1695 it was impossible. This opened up the possibility of ownership of copies outside the book trade, and the apparently inevitable intrusion into the trade's capital base by 'outsiders'.

The mechanism which evolved to prevent this was the understanding among the principal copy owners that they would only sell shares to each other. These transactions took place at private auctions, known as 'trade sales', of which catalogues survive from 1718 onwards.[10] Once a bookseller had been admitted to the sales, he was required to sell any copies which he bought there at a similar sale, a rule which also bound widows and other heirs if they wished to dispose of copies which they inherited. Since most of the really valuable copies were divided into shares, almost all of them passed through the trade sales during the eighteenth century, and contributed to the general pattern of a small group of booksellers who dominated publishing through their ownership of copies and the system of book distribution through the wholesaling conger.

Although all three of these developments – the growth of the provincial trade, the development of the wholesaling conger, and the evolution of the trade sales of copies – can trace their origins to the lapse of the Printing Act and the reaction to that of some members of the trade, all of them took place independently of formal changes in the law. The copy owners and conger members who were involved in 1707 and again in 1710 seem to have regarded the new law as little more than confirmation of existing rights, and may even have seen it as merely one part of a multi-faceted campaign to maintain their own profitably dominant position in the London (and increasingly national) book trade. None of these commercial developments is even hinted at in the 1710 Act, and yet every member of the trade who was involved in promoting that Act knew of them, and many were active, indeed leading, participants. The omission can only be deliberate, and strongly suggests the essentially supplementary nature of the Act as it was seen from within the inner circles of the trade.

Another group who were to be vitally concerned with the 1710 Copyright Act were excluded even from any part in framing it: the authors. Defoe had raised the notion of their rights in his *Essay on the Regulation of the Press* in 1704, but only as a peripheral issue to the 'encouragement of the learning'. Since even that was marginalized in the content (as opposed to the title) of the 1710 Act, it is hardly surprising that authors had little more than a nod to acknowledge their existence, and that what might have been a stronger law to protect their interests was actually watered down in Committee under pressure from the trade.[11] The legal position and status of authors was as vague after 10 April 1710 as it had been before.

In this sphere also, however, there had been evolutionary change which was not reflected in the Act. The rights of authors had been implicitly recognized before the Civil War,[12] and after the Restoration the payment of authors for their copy was an established fact and a normal practice. This led to the formalization of the relationship between author and publisher, and the evolution of the practice of defining that relationship in a contract. The earliest contract of this kind which is still extant is apparently that between John Milton and Samuel Simmons for the publication of *Paradise Lost*, dated 27 April 1667, which, despite the strictures of earlier critics, gave Milton the generous sum of £20 for a long and obscure poem by a regicide who had escaped the scaffold only because of his blindness.[13]

The arrangements between authors and publishers gradually took on a fairly standard form. Broadly speaking, the author sold the rights in the copy to the publisher, although there are variations on this theme even in the late seventeenth and early eighteenth centuries. Whatever the details, the mere existence of such contractual arrangements clearly acknowledged the origin of the rights with the author; yet those rights were still seen as being transferred to a bookseller and then of no further concern of the author. The sums of money involved were typically small. When Dryden sold a work to Tonson for the first time in 1679 (his version of *Troilus and Cressida)*, he, like Milton, received £20.[14]

By 1710, the payment of authors was an established fact, and the normal assumption among all of those involved. Like the book trade's commercial arrangements, this was not recognized in the law, which merely assumed that a copy was in existence when it came into the hands of a bookseller. The law was for the benefit of the 'proprietors', not the creators, of books.

From the beginning, members of the book trade behaved as if the law meant what they wanted it to mean, and ignored those parts of it which they found inconvenient. The attempt to regulate book prices was probably always a vain one, and was abandoned without enforcement ever having been attempted in 1739.[15] Similarly, the clauses requiring the deposit of copies of books in certain libraries were widely and successfully evaded.[16] Copy owners continued to trade in shares, and to buy new copies from authors, apparently without any sense that the law had made their property impermanent.[17] The pre-1710 copyrights were due to expire in 1731–32, but shares in such authors as Shakespeare, Milton, Bunyan, Stanhope and Dryden continued to change hands at high and increasing prices. Eventually, this was to exacerbate the problem, for with the total value of copyrights spiralling into many thousands of pounds, the book trade was in danger of becoming fatally dependent on the permanent popularity of these books and the absence of competition in reprinting them.

The copy owners were concerned with commercial investments, not with legal niceties, but they were always prepared to go to law, even if reluctantly, in their own defence. The late seventeenth-century cases had been largely concerned with English Stock copies, and provided few precedents for judgments on ordinary trade copies, although there were a few exceptions.[18] In practice, however, the courts were moving into new pastures with cases relating to trade copies, and sought their precedents in the common law relating to sale and property. The 1710 Act, if anything, obfuscated rather than clarified the situation.

As a general rule, actions were initiated by the copy owner against an alleged pirate, seeking an injunction to prevent the printing or distribution of the piracy. A typical example is that of Thomas Corbett's *Account of the Expedition of the British Fleet to Sicily*, published by Jacob and Richard Tonson in 1739. The book was popular enough to be reprinted in the same year,[19] and to be pirated.[20] The pirated edition was not difficult to identify; it had the imprint:

> London: Printed and sold by the Booksellers
> in Town and Country.

Such modest anonymity is an almost infallible indicator of an irregular edition.

The pirate was a printer named Mechell, and on 20 April 1739 the publisher filed a suit against him in the Court of Chancery.[21]

From the surviving papers in the case, the complex story behind these editions can be reconstructed. The copy was based on the papers of the late Admiral George Byng,[22] and dealt with his command of the Mediterranean Fleet in the early part of George I's reign. Corbett had sold the copy to the Tonsons on 27 August 1738, and they had entered it in the Stationers' Register on 24 September. It was argued that there was no doubt of Corbett's right to sell the copy, nor of the Tonsons' right to buy it. Mechell and his unnamed associates had, on the other hand, printed their edition with no such rights. The plaintiffs therefore asked the Court to prevent Mechell from selling his edition. The case is unreported, but it is fairly clear that the law was on the Tonsons' side. There was, however, apparently no need to refer to the 1710 Copyright Act in order to establish that fact.

The Tonsons, through three generations, were never averse to going to law, for they owned some of the most valuable copyrights in the trade. Two other occasions included an injunction obtained in 1722–23 to prevent Francis Clifton from pirating Steele's *Conscious Lovers*,[23] and the defence of the rights in Gay's *Fables* by Jacob Tonson III in 1745.[24] The courts invariably found for the plaintiffs in copyright cases, provided that they could prove ownership. The documents adduced in proof might include contracts, letters and other papers, but the 1710 Act was rarely introduced as part of the legal argument. Certainly, there was never any suggestion that any of the properties under consideration had their existence in any way truncated or restricted by the Act. For the Chancery lawyers and judges, a copy was simply a piece of property, inviolable and permanent.

Even so, the statute law had its uses, and was not entirely ignored. Its broader implications did not escape all of those whom it concerned. Alexander Pope, for example, when he granted rights in his works to Bernard Lintot in 1717, did so in a contract which specifically grants those rights for as long as Pope could do so by Act of Parliament, that is, for the 14-year term specified in 1710.[25] This is, however, a rare, perhaps unique, example, of an overt reference to the Act in such a document, and was made by an author already very conscious of his rights, and of the potential offered by the Act for exploiting them.[26] Nevertheless, the law did exist, and it contained a potentially devastating time-bomb in the apparent limitations which it imposed on the existence of copyrights.

There were two such limitations: copies already printed before 1710 were protected for 21 years, and those first printed after 10 April 1710 were protected for 14 years, with the possibility of a further 14-year term thereafter. In theory, therefore, statutory copyrights began to expire in 1724, but the critical date, from the trade's point of view, was 1731 when the pre-1710 copyrights were apparently due to expire. This would have put Shakespeare, Milton, Bunyan, Dryden, and substantial parts of the works of Addison and Steele (including the perennially popular *Spectator*), along with hundreds of other copyrights, out of reach of the statute law.

Even so, the fatal date passed without notice, and nothing might have happened had it not been for another piece of legislation which attracted considerable interest and drew attention to the whole issue of copyright. Early in 1735, the artist William Hogarth, along with George Vertue and other named and unnamed artists and engravers, petitioned the House of Commons for protection against the unauthorized copying of their engraved prints.[27] The artists' petition made specific reference to the fact that they sought similar protection to that already afforded to others 'as the Laws now in being have preserved the Properties of the Authors of Books'.[28]

That perception is of interest in itself, but, in fact, the artists were asking for something rather different. Above all, it was the artists who were asking for legislation, not the printers or printsellers. In effect, they were seeking to protect their artistic designs, as well as the commercial property which those designs embodied. This established a distinction between literary and artistic works which persisted in English law until almost the present day.[29] In other respects, however, the artists did indeed follow the patterns established in the 1710 Act, not least by proposing a 14-year period of copyright protection. It was perhaps the latter which attracted the attention of the book trade.

The engravers' petition was presented to the House on 7 February 1735, and its substance accepted by a Committee appointed to investigate it a week later.[30] A Bill based upon it had its First Reading on 4 March, and passed through both Houses with little difficulty, receiving the Royal Assent on 15 May.[31] The booksellers had a less easy passage. A petition from them was tabled in the Commons on 3 March; in it they argued that because of the prevalence of piracy the value of their property had diminished. Specifically, they asked for legislation to ban the import of books, and also for other appropriate, but unnamed, measures.[32] A Committee was appointed to report on this petition, and it reported back to the House on 12 March.[33] It was agreed that a Bill should be prepared, but this did not appear until 1 May.[34]

The preamble to the Bill followed the booksellers' petition in one important respect.[35] This was in drawing attention to the import of books and stating that this was detrimental to the British book trade. There was certainly a serious problem. It was almost impossible to prevent the import of English books from Holland and Ireland, where they could be legally reprinted without the permission of the copy owners, or even from Scotland, where it was illegal to reprint them. The trade may have exaggerated the problem, but it was a real one.[36] One petition on the Bill made the point that the foreign pirates not only did not have to pay for rights in the copy, but also even added insult to injury by keeping their costs down yet further by using the cheapest paper.[37]

The question of imports was considered at some length by the Committee on the original petition in February and March 1735.[38] The witnesses were selected by the petitioners, that is the copy-owning booksellers, but they also brought along some authors to support their case. The trade witnesses produced some specific examples of imported reprints. Charles Rivington, for example, testified that he and the author were the joint owners of the copy in Philip Miller's *Gardeners' Dictionary*, but that he had bought an Irish reprint in a bookshop in York for only 22*s*. 0*d*., whereas his own, legal, edition cost 25*s*. 0*d*. One witness actually produced copies of books which he claimed were Dutch piracies. The type was identified as Dutch by James Bettenham, a printer. Thomas Ward gave evidence that he had the rights in Burnett's *History of His Own Time*, which was one of the books, and testified that no one else had printed it in England. Further evidence followed to show that paper was more expensive in England (because of import duties), and that both the Dutch and the Irish could therefore undercut the English on the costs of book production. Finally, James Crockatt, another London bookseller, said that he had been in a bookshop in Preston in Lancashire when a parcel of books had arrived from Ireland which had included reprints of English copies.

All of this was telling enough, but the case became even stronger when the authors began to give their evidence. The Committee was told of 29 authors who had had their works pirated, and then some living examples were paraded in front of them. Philip Miller was produced to support the statements of his publisher, Rivington.

John Clarke, Dean of Salisbury, reported that he had recently edited and published the collected sermons of his late brother, Samuel, a philosopher, which he had sold to James Knapton for £1,000. Knapton's plan had been to print the book in ten volumes, and to sell it at £2 per volume in sheets. The whole work had been reprinted in Ireland in two volumes, selling at £1. 6*s*. 0*d*. To add to the respectability of a Dean came one of the most distinguished scholars of the age, Robert Ainsworth. He told the Committee that he had spent twenty years in compiling an English–Latin dictionary, which was now almost ready for the press. He had sold the copy to his publisher for £500, and would receive a further £300 if and when there was a second edition. The 6,000 copies which were planned would cost £3,000 to produce, and were to be sold at 10*s*. 0*d*.; therefore there would be no profit until the second edition, which could not be expected for some time, and protection for this investment was clearly necessary. Finally, the Committee heard from Thomas Mangey, a canon of Durham, who said that he had spent £400 in preparing an edition of the works of Philo Judaeus, but feared that after publication it would be reprinted abroad for about one-third of the English price, because paper was so much cheaper in Holland.

These were carefully selected examples of divines and scholars. Clarke and Ainsworth were both being well-paid for their labours, and all three were clear examples of the encouragement of learning by the protection of property. The witnesses and evidence produced by the booksellers may, however, have had an unexpected, and, from their point of view, undesirable effect, in drawing attention to the authors as a party to the trade's affairs. When the Bill finally reached the House in May, the second point in the preamble was that authors were obliged to sell their books to members of the trade in order to have them published. The statement is ambiguous; it could be interpreted to mean that the Bill was intended to protect authors, while the booksellers could take it as a recognition of the financial value of their investments in copies. In either case, this second strand in the argument for the Bill introduced the authors as a factor by raising the question of the value of the property of which they were the originators.

By the middle of April, before the Bill had been published, the affair was already attracting some public attention, and led to the publication of a number of broadsides and pamphlets. Some of these appear to have emanated from the trade, or to have been heavily influenced by trade views. One of these is almost certainly

A Short State of the Publick Encouragement Given to Printing and Bookselling in France, Holland and Great Britain,[39] in which it was argued that a new and stronger law is needed to replace the 1710 Act, especially in giving protection against imported reprints of English books. According to this anonymous author, it was 'well known' that similar laws were vigorously enforced in France to prevent the import of books into that country, and that in both France and Holland privileges in individual copies were regularly granted and renewed.[40]

The booksellers did not, however, have the field to themselves. The anonymous author of *A Letter to a Member of Parliament concerning the Bill now Depending in the House of Commons* argued that the booksellers' case for the patriotic encouragement of learning and commerce was merely a cover for their own self-interest.[41] He based his argument on his understanding of history, claiming that before 1710 there was no law of copyright and that the 1710 Act was designed to remedy the grievances of authors about this. This was unsustainable as an interpretation of history,[42] but no doubt it had some polemical force. On somewhat safer ground, the author suggested that the booksellers, in asking for a further 21 years' protection on top of what the law already afforded to them, were seeking unprecedented generosity, which was to be compared with the much more limited terms given to inventors.[43] This is the first mention of a proposed 21-year extension of the term of copyright; presumably it was one of several ideas which were in the air to give substance to the booksellers' generalized request for further protection.

Even the spurious history in this pamphlet found some support. One writer who agreed that there had been no such thing as copyright before 1710 suggested that legislation had been necessary then to protect authors and publishers because it was in the late seventeenth century 'when Pyrating of Books first began to be practised'.[44] What was needed was an even stronger law, since piracy was on the increase, especially in prescribing penalties and mechanisms for enforcement. Some of these points were reiterated in a second pamphlet, apparently by the same author, published a few days later.[45]

The Bill which finally reached the Commons on 1 May took account of some of these points. It gave an additional seven years' protection to all existing copies, and seven years to all books published in the future, presumably with the intention that the law would be renewed in seven years' time.[46] Various provisions were also made in relation to penalties for breach of copyright, and for the deposit of books in libraries and the control of book prices. After some debate and various procedural manoeuvres, the Bill seems to have passed through all its stages in the Commons,[47] and was duly sent to the Lords. There it was given its formal First Reading on 6 May, but the Second Reading was twice postponed, and the Bill was lost at the end of the Session.[48]

This Bill is of less interest for itself than for the issues which were raised in its wake. It was no longer possible to pretend that the rights of authors were not at stake. Indeed, one author deliberately drew attention to the deficiencies of the law in a way which was designed to influence Parliament. This author was Alexander Pope who colluded with Edmund Curll to publish a 'pirated' edition of his own letters; Pope then sued Curll. It is a complicated episode, which does little credit to any of the parties involved; its relevance here is that it was an attempt to force Parliament to recognize the claims of authors and the need to give them real protection against the depredations of unscrupulous booksellers.[49] After 1735, it was never again entirely possible to exclude some consideration of the rights of authors when copyright law was under discussion.

A second and even more complex issue was, at least implicitly, raised in the same debates. In comparing books with inventions, the author of *A Letter to a Member of Parliament* was inviting consideration of the nature of the property which was being discussed, and in particular its origin. As authors' rights were asserted, it became ever clearer that the only logical answer to this question lay in the assumption that the property – the copy – was created by the author at the time of writing. Indeed, at least one other pamphlet published in April 1735 starts from this assumption,[50] although the theory was later to be the subject of much ingenious legal argument in the courts of both England and Scotland.[51]

Some of this was indeed considered during the debate in the House of Commons. We know something of what happened there from the brief notes of Thomas Carte, a non-juring antiquary who had himself been the victim of Irish pirates.[52] Carte regarded a single term of 21 years as being the appropriate period of copyright, not least because he was persuaded by the logic of Robert Ainsworth's evidence to the Committee that some books needed to go into a second edition before they could begin to show a profit. Carte also considered, however, that authors needed to have their rights explicitly protected, since only the unspecified 'proprietors' seemed to have rights under the 1710 Act. Carte, however, like many of his contemporaries, did not have a completely clear view of these matters. In particular, he toyed with the idea that, since they were a form of property, copies subsisted in perpetuity, and could not be limited in their existence. This was yet another issue which was in the air in 1735 and which was to reappear several times in a more acute form during the next forty years. All the difficulties really arose from the fact that copyright was still a relatively unfamiliar concept, ill-defined and ill-understood, but nevertheless now quite clearly beyond the private sphere of the book trade. The authors had become major players in the game, and neither they nor the questions which their participation had raised were going to vanish.

In the parliamentary session of 1735–36, another Bill was prepared and printed, and this was unambiguous about its purpose.[53] The preamble stated bluntly that the 1710 Act 'has proved ineffectual to prevent the Publication and Sale of surreptitious Editions, and impressions of Books . . .' The solution proposed was indeed a radical one, and it took considerable account of the rising tide of opinion in favour of authors. The term of protection was to be the author's lifetime and a further eleven years thereafter. If the author died within ten years of publication, protection was to be for 21 years from the date of death, and for posthumously published works there would be protection for 21 years. It was, apparently, this Bill which was brought into the House of Commons on 11 February 1737.[54]

Complications began almost at once. There was a technical issue about the payment of the stamp duties on paper by the university presses which threatened to obscure the more central points.[55] Even so, the issue was not entirely irrelevant, for it was an attempt to 'encourage learning' by reducing the cost of scholarly works, which was, after all, one of the alleged intentions of the 1710 Act. The point is taken up in one of the broadsides published in support of the Bill,[56] in which it was argued that in France and Holland the state encourages the book trade, but in England it taxes paper.

In general, however, it was the trade which leapt upon this Bill, which was, it seems, not to its liking. A broadside which clearly comes from the copy owners was quite explicit about their wishes.[57] Stating that the trade has invested more than £150,000 in copies, it declares that it is necessary to give more 'durable' protection to this property, like that given to other property owners. The emphasis on the rights of the booksellers, as opposed to the authors, is reinforced by a further reference to the need to prevent the import of Dutch piracies. The *Farther Reasons*[58] reinforce these points, reiterating some of the arguments from two years earlier about the need for long-term investment, and hence long-term protection, if learned works were to be published in England.

One other point also begins to emerge again in both *Reasons* and, particularly, *Farther Reasons*: the history and nature of rights in copies. Before 1710, it is argued, rights were both absolute and permanent. In that year, the trade conceded some abbreviation of their rights in order to achieve better legal protection for them in the form in which they continued to exist. What they are now asking for is an extension of that provision. What they did not add, however, was the logical conclusion that this involved recognizing the inherent perpetuity of property rights in copies. Again this was to be a key issue during the next forty years.

The 1737 Bill was lost; it progressed as far as its Second Reading in the Lords, but then never emerged from Committee.[59] The events of 1735 and 1737 proved to be a transient intrusion by the authors into the legislative process in the eighteenth century. The trade, however, still had pressing concerns. In April 1738, a further Bill was promoted, which had but a single objective: to deal with the ever-growing number of imports of foreign reprints of English books. This Bill was rejected on its Third Reading in the Lords, but a similar Bill was reintroduced in the next Session and received the Royal Assent on 14 June 1739.[60] This Act forbade the import into Great Britain of any book written, printed or reprinted there within the previous twenty years, with the exception of books in Latin, Greek or the 'northern languages' (i.e. Anglo-Saxon, Old Norse and so on). The effect of this should have been straightforward: it prevented the import of reprints of books which still had some commercial value. It provided the trade with sanctions against importers of such reprints, and they worked actively to ensure that these sanctions were enforced. By 11 September 1739 the Clerk of the Stationers' Company had reported that he had been in touch with the Commissioners of the Customs, and that they were working on the enforcement of the new law.[61]

The Import of Books Act was the last piece of eighteenth-century legislation which even indirectly affected the law of copyright, but it is merely the prologue to the story of the transformation of the law in practice. In 1710, and to a lesser extent in the 1730s, the trade had succeeded in suppressing any discussion of the rights of authors, but this was a position which could not be sustained in the long term. The bills of 1735 and 1737 had both provoked debates, which partly arose out of contemporary events elsewhere in the book world, which could no longer be stifled. In particular, there were authors who were prepared to assert their rights, and even a few who saw ways of using the 1710 Act to their advantage. The most important of these was Alexander Pope.

Pope was not the first author to take an intense interest in the publication and printing of his work,[62] but he was the first to do so with some semblance of statutory authority to support his claims. He was deeply interested even in the typography of his works,[63] but, in general, he sought to protect both his financial and literary interests by retaining as much control as possible over the printing, publication and dissemination of his books. He made extremely careful contracts with his publishers and printers, often giving them only the right to print a single edition of a specified size and format. As early as 1713/14, Pope negotiated a very profitable and favourable contract with the bookseller Bernard Lintot for the publication of his *Iliad*.[64] Even the great Tonson had to submit to the wishes of Pope. In 1723, the two signed a contract for Pope's *Works* under which the author retained the right to reprint anything he wished, and were he to do so, Tonson's only compensation would be a copy of the reprint.[65] Even this was not enough. In the late 1720s, Pope became deeply involved in the book trade himself, although at one remove through the printer John Wright and the bookseller Lawton Gilliver.

It is impossible to resist the inference that Pope established Gilliver and Wright in business, although there is no absolute proof.[66] It is certainly clear that Pope dominated the relationship between himself and his publishers. In 1732, for example, he and Gilliver signed a contract under which Pope granted Gilliver the right to print such of Pope's poems as Pope permitted for a period of one year after their entry in the Stationers' Register, in return for a payment of £50 per poem.[67] In this remarkable document, Pope, in effect, retained all the rights, and merely granted Gilliver a very limited and rather expensive licence. This was indeed a potent demonstration of the power of a famous and successful author.

Pope did not, however, confine himself to the privacy of contracts in protecting his rights. He also went into the broad daylight of the courts. The most famous of several cases is that in which he tried to protect *The Dunciad* against piracy, through a suit in the Court of Chancery.[68] In his submission to Chancery, Gilliver, as plaintiff, stated that he had bought *The Dunciad* on or about

1 March 1729, and had entered it on the Stationers' Register on 4 April in the same year.[69] That Gilliver was slightly wrong is less important than the legal arguments which were then developed out of his initial statement. In effect, Gilliver based his claim to the rights in the copy on the fact of entry in the Register, 'pursuant to the Act',[70] that is, the 1710 Copyright Act, which does indeed state that:

> . . . nothing in this Act contained shall be construed to extend to subject any Bookseller, Printer, or other Person whatsoever, to the Forfeitures or Penalties therein mentioned, for or by reason of the Printing or Reprinting of any Book or Books without such Consent, as aforesaid [from the proprietor of the copy], unless the title to the Copy of such Book or Books hereafter Published shall, before such Publication be entred in the Register-Book of the Company of Stationers . . .[71]

This clause was to provide a number of difficulties throughout the rest of the century and beyond.

In the present case, the defendants, James Watson, Thomas Astley and John Stagg, replied in two ways. First, they argued that the Gilliver edition was published before the copy was entered in the Register, and therefore that the conditions in the Act had not been met. This was apparently straightforward, and, if true, irrefutable. Unfortunately, it was actually as uncertain as almost everything else in this affair.[72] This was also the case with their second, and rather more obscure, line of defence, which was that they did not know that Gilliver had bought the rights, and that in any case he was not qualified to enter them in the Register. Despite all the difficulties, Chancery did actually grant the plaintiff an injunction to prevent the distribution and sale of the pirated edition.[73] The general significance of *Gilliver v. Watson and others* is that it seems to be the first time that the 1710 Act was cited in court to support a case for breach of copyright.

Pope used the Act again on at least three other occasions. One was in 1743 when he sued Bernard Lintot, who claimed a one-third share in *The Dunciad*,[74] and a second in the same year, when he sued Jacob Ilive for pirating part of the same work.[75] A third occasion was in 1744, when he sued the engraver George Bickham for an edition of the *Essay on Man*.[76] The first of these is the most interesting, since, once again, it raises questions about the meaning of the 1710 Act. Gilliver had sold a one-third share in *The Dunciad* to John Clarke, who subsequently sold it to John Osborne, who, in his turn, sold it to Lintot. Lintot bought this share in January 1740, and in December 1740 he bought the remaining two-thirds from Gilliver. On that basis he printed an edition, but Pope sued on the grounds that under the Act the rights had reverted to him, as author, when fourteen years had elapsed after publication, that is, at the end of 1742. In his response, Lintot simply denied that Pope had any residual rights. There the matter rested; it was still undetermined when Pope died in 1744.

Pope's cases are of interest in themselves, because they begin to highlight some of the key issues which arose out of the 1710 Act. At the same time, they remind us that authors were becoming more assertive, and that relations between authors and publishers were changing. By the middle of the eighteenth century, it was possible to make a decent living from writing, certainly if that writing included regular work for the newspapers and magazines.[77] Patronage was no longer essential even to literary authors, and the idea of the author as a participant in commercial activity was beginning to be accepted.[78] At the same time as authors were becoming more overtly mercenary, there was also developing a more elevated idea of the author as artist or creator. The very concept of 'originality', in the sense of an 'original work' of art or literature, is an eighteenth-century idea.[79] It is perhaps most famously located in Edward Young's *Conjectures on Original Composition*, published in 1759, but Young was actually giving popular expression to ideas that were in fairly widespread circulation in literary and intellectual circles.[80] Such ideas inevitably had consequences for the business of literature, and for the commercial relations between authors and the book trade. Those relations were defined, in legal terms, by the law of copyright, since it was the rights in the copy which were the subject of the commercial transactions. As ideas of authorship changed, so too did ideas about copyrights.

Some authors tried to circumvent the conventional channels of the trade, as indeed Pope had done by finding himself tame booksellers and printers. Subscription publishing, which was also used by Pope, was one method, and was fairly common for certain kinds of learned books, or books of local or particular interest.[81] Some authors came together in a sort of cooperative in the 1730s to form the Society for the Encouragement of Learning, a name which clearly reflects the 1710 Act, but the venture was short-lived.[82] It failed, according to one contemporary, because the trade refused to distribute the books which it produced.[83] Frustrated by the complexities of the law, one author, Samuel Buckley, even obtained a private Act of Parliament in 1734 to protect his edition of Thuanus's *History*,[84] but this was clearly not a practical proposition for the majority. Authors were exhorted to take their affairs into their own hands; Ralph wrote: 'Combine! And perhaps you will need neither Patrons nor Establishments.'[85] But this was an impossible dream for so long as the booksellers controlled the trade through their stranglehold on copyrights, production facilities and distribution. Even the provincial booksellers were unable to compete with them, except on a very local basis.[86]

Despite this, however, the status of authors did change, at least in a monetary sense, for the better. Professional authors were reasonably well-paid by the middle of the century. At one end of the scale, Samuel Johnson, although sometimes short of cash, was able to survive entirely by his pen, and to attain the utmost respectability while doing so.[87] At the other, the hacks employed by John Nourse in the 1750s and 1760s received modest but adequate rewards for their labours. Sometimes they received a single payment for the copy, sometimes they were paid by the printed sheet, sometimes they shared in the profits, and occasionally they were paid in kind with free copies of the book. Sometimes they had to agree to undertake revisions for subsequent editions without extra payment, and in one or two instances other conditions were imposed. In general, however, the author sold his copy outright to the publisher, who then did with it as he wished. These agreements seem to be fairly typical of the middle of the century.[88]

The dependence of authors on publishers was frustrating; equally frustrated were those in the book trade who were not involved in the business of the publishing and distribution of books. The trade sales ensured that the most profitable copies, however much they might be subdivided, remained within a comparatively small group of owners. The copy-owning booksellers effectively controlled the wholesaling and distribution system, even though the congers had vanished as organized operations. Authors whose books were not published through the usual channels of the trade could expect neither wide distribution nor, more importantly to many of them, an adequate income. In the same way, members of the trade found it extremely difficult to break into the national distribution system unless they were allowed to do so by those already engaged in that part of the trade.

This was particularly irksome for those who worked in the two other flourishing centres of the book trade in the British Isles, Ireland and Scotland. The Dublin booksellers were, indeed, in a comparatively favourable position. The 1710 Act did not apply to them, and they could reprint as much as they liked provided they did not attempt to sell in Great Britain. Some did so, as was pointed out in 1735,[89] but others worked in a rapidly expanding domestic market, or exported their books to North America.[90]

The Scots, however, were in a far less satisfactory position. The Act did apply in Scotland, so they could not even reprint for their domestic market. They did indeed print for export, both to North America and to continental Europe, but the real prizes were to be won at home, and by the late 1730s Scottish booksellers and printers were beginning to flout the law and to justify their actions on patriotic grounds.[91] Inevitably, this led to attempts at retribution by the London trade, whose incursions into the Scottish legal system were eventually to precipitate one of the most significant developments in the history of British copyright law.

The early cases heard in Scotland concerned the reprinting in Edinburgh or Glasgow of copies claimed by London booksellers. In most cases, the reprints were of copies whose protection had apparently expired under the terms of the 1710 Act. The Scots courts were uncertain about the Act, and reluctant to reach decisions, but their very indecisiveness exacerbated the situation. By the middle of the 1740s, Scottish reprints were widely sold throughout the north of England, as well as in Scotland itself, and there seemed to be little that could be done about it.[92]

In 1743, however, a case began which was indeed to reach a momentous resolution. Daniel Midwinter and other London booksellers sued a number of Scottish printers and booksellers for reprinting Ephraim Chambers's *Cyclopaedia*, which they had first published in 1728, and other books. The suit was brought under both the 1710 and 1739 acts. The case was that the reprints were protected by copyright, and that in any case their import into England was illegal. The defence was, essentially, that the copyrights had expired under the time limits imposed in the 1710 Act.[93] To counter this, the plaintiffs (the London booksellers) argued that the Act imposed time limits on the penalties for breaches of its provisions, but not on the existence of the copyright itself, a point which had, indeed, been made in 1735 when new legislation was being discussed.[94] Eventually, the Court of Session reached a decision which, in effect, represented victory for the defendants. It held that the 1710 Act did not apply at all in this case, because the book had not been entered in the Stationers' Register.[95]

The Scots were even more successful in a related action in which Millar and others sued Alexander Kincaid and a large number of

Edinburgh and Glasgow printers and booksellers for reprinting Locke, Burnet's *History of the Reformation*, Fielding's *Joseph Andrews* and other books.[96] This time, the verdict in the Court of Session was devastating for the London trade. The Court ruled that no action could be brought under the 1710 Act when more than ten months had elapsed after the offence; that actions depended upon entry in the Register; and that damages could not be awarded. The plaintiffs then appealed to the House of Lords, and the defendants published a full version of their case.[97]

This document lays out in detail the arguments of the Scottish trade, both commercial and legal. The commercial case was essentially that the Londoners were merely using the cover of the law to protect their own monopoly 'now that by cheapness of Work, and great Diligence, the *Scots* Printers are gaining Ground upon them . . .'[98] The legal arguments turn on two points. First, recalling no doubt the earlier views of the Court of Session, the defendants point out that unless copies are entered in the Stationers' Register, they are not protected at all, precisely the case that had been made in *Gilliver v. Watson and others* in 1743.[99] Because the Act is specific on that, they argued:

> . . . there must be established a *praesumptio juris et de jure*, that every new Book which is not thus entered in Stationers Hall is abandoned to the Publick, and a lawful Subject of Commerce for every man to deal in . . .

Secondly, they point out that the Act confers rights for a limited period only. It was the first of these arguments which had indeed convinced the Lords of Session, in their declaration that 'no Action lies upon the Statute, except for such books as have been entered at Stationers Hall'.[100] The House of Lords found for the Scots in 1751, although on technical grounds, which left open the possibility of further actions on the main issues of copyright.[101]

Despite the failure to reach an absolute legal resolution, these two cases were a major blow for the London trade. It was clear that the Scottish courts would do nothing to protect them against the Scottish reprinters. The Scots were rapidly gaining in confidence. In 1754, Robert Foulis, the Glasgow printer who had been one of the defendants in both cases, wrote to the Attorney-General complaining of:

> . . . the new doctrine by which Authors are supposed to be vested with a property, not only antecedent to all acts of parliament, but even such

a one as claims indefeasibility, and refuses to be limited by the highest national Authority.

With this, he enclosed that opinion of an Edinburgh lawyer, Ronald Craufurd, to the effect that the copyright '. . . is only personal, to the Author himself, but not to his Executors or Assignees'.[102] Such views as this, if they were to be upheld in the courts, would undermine the whole basis of the London trade, for this was a challenge not merely to the law of copyright as it was embodied in the 1710 Act, but to the protection of the rights in the works of all dead authors.

Such an extreme argument was never accepted, but there can be little doubt that the London trade was seriously rattled by what had happened and by the continued activities of the Scots. The London trade now tried another tack, by turning their attention to the English provincial booksellers who were the main channels of sale for the Scots reprints south of the border. In April 1759, the leading London booksellers subscribed over £3,000 to enable them to take action against the sale of the reprints. One of their number, John Whiston, then wrote an open letter to John Merill, a bookseller in Cambridge, intended for wide circulation, in which he stated their intention to prosecute, under the 1739 Act, any English bookseller whom they found to be selling Scottish reprints. Once again, Millar actually lay behind this initiative, despite the fact that it was in Whiston's name.[103]

In fact, the letter exposed the fundamental weakness of the position of the London copy owners. They demanded that the provincial booksellers should hand over to them any Scottish or Irish reprints in their shops, but they offered to replace them with the authentic London editions. In itself, this would probably have absorbed much of the £3,000, and was clearly something which could not be done on a regular basis. The truth was that the Londoners had no way of policing the provincial trade, and were unable to prevent the penetration of their markets by the reprinters. All the evidence, from the 1730s to the 1750s, suggests that Scottish and Irish reprints were widely sold in the provinces, especially, but not solely, in the north of England.

This episode cannot be seen in isolation. In the following year, another attempt was made by the London trade to have the law clarified in the courts. In 1760, Jacob Tonson sued Benjamin Collins, a bookseller in Salisbury, for selling a Scottish reprint of *The Spectator*. The case is surrounded with suspicion, for Collins was an eminently respectable tradesman, closely associated with the London trade, and one of the few provincial booksellers with substantial shareholdings in London copies.[104] Following, as it did, the 1759 letters and the verdicts in *Midwinter v. Hamilton* and *Millar v. Kincaid*, it seems more than likely that the action was brought in collusion between the plaintiff and the defendant, in an attempt to get an authoritative decision on the state of the law.

The case came on in King's Bench in 1760, with Lord Chief Justice Mansfield on the bench.[105] The question was: 'Whether copy-right subsists in authors, as a valuable property, independently of the Stat. 8 Ann.' In the lower courts, the jury had been unable to reach a verdict, and it was now for King's Bench to resolve the issue. For the plaintiff, it was argued that 'The words "for fourteen years and no longer", extend only to the accumulative remedy by penal action'. The point was directly refuted by the defence; in the event Mansfield reserved his judgment.

The significance of this first hearing of *Tonson v. Collins*, however, lies as much in the general thrust of the arguments as in the specific legal points. The plaintiff's counsel, Alexander Wedderburn, based his case largely on the common law of property, arguing that the law is the 'guard of property' and that copyright is a property like any other which the law can and does protect. He employed a certain amount of historical ingenuity in showing that copyright had been recognized since the sixteenth century, but eventually admitted that the precedents were unhelpful, partly because they all related to privileged copies or the English Stock, and partly because they were badly reported. Defence counsel, Edward Thurloe, took his stand on different ground. He revived the old argument about the public good not being served by a monopoly, and then argued, in very simple terms, that the 1710 Act limited the time during which the monopoly could subsist in the case of copyrights. Under the Act, no author can assign a copy for longer than 14 years, and therefore at that point the rights cease to exist. Like Wedderburn, he rejected precedent, but he was more specific, concluding that 'This is the first action ever to be brought upon this head of property.' Strictly speaking this was not true, for Pope's cases also seem to have been based upon it, but they never came to court, or were not reported.[106] Two conflicting views of copyright were now clearly emerging; on the one hand, there was the view that it was a simple property with a permanent existence, while on the other hand it was held that, although it did exist, it did so in terms of the limitations of time imposed in the 1710 Act.

The case returned to King's Bench in the following year, when Wedderburn was replaced by Blackstone as counsel for the plaintiff.[107] Blackstone made the case for perpetual copyrights on two grounds: first, the common law of property, and secondly, unlike Wedderburn, historical precedents. On the first ground, Blackstone argued that the plaintiff's case was 'founded in reason', by which he meant the law as it related to the ownership of property. He argued that in buying a book, the purchaser does not buy the right to copy it, any more than he can copy an opera ticket which he has bought, or make a copy of a coin. Turning then to the other pillar of his case, Blackstone argued that perpetual copyright was 'supported by law'. He cited a number of cases, both before and after 1710, to lend weight to his contention that the courts had generally recognized the permanent rights of the legitimate owner of a copy. He referred to a series of cases from the 1730s which, he claimed, established the legality of perpetual copyrights.

In rebuttal, Joseph Yates said that this so-called property could not be shown to exist, that the very act of publication made it impossible to restrict the ideas and words thus published, and that the law depended upon the 1710 Act which tried to protect those ideas and words for a limited period of time. The positions seemed irreconcilable. Mansfield adjourned the case to Chambers, and refused to reach a verdict because he suspected collusion designed to establish a precedent, but the editor of the official report believed that 'in so far as the Court had formed an opinion, they all inclined to the Plaintiff'.[108]

Despite the failure to reach a resolution, *Tonson v. Collins* is a case of some significance. The lines of argument which were deployed very clearly expose the nature of the debate about copyright which was taking place in mid-eighteenth-century Britain. The case for perpetual copyright was that the rights in a copy were simply as a piece of property like any other, whereas the opponents of that view took the line that the statute law over-rode this common-law approach. The legal and constitutional implications were wide-reaching, and the lawyers dug deep into their armoury of both law and precedent to support their cases.

The understanding of the law of property was of particular importance, and underlies much of the argument in court both in *Tonson v. Collins* and in other cases. The general view, and one which was broadly endorsed by Blackstone, was that the property derived from natural rights, having originally been created by the labour of its owner. This theory had been developed during the seventeenth century, and reached its fullest expression in the works of Locke, who allied it to his theory of the contract between the state and the people which was, to him, the foundation of civil government. Blackstone broadly followed this view, including its logical rider that individuals (including writers) could create new property by their own efforts, although he also inclined to the view that the state could abrogate or extend property rights as part of the contract between governors and governed.[109] All the key writers who had developed the natural law theory of property – Grotius, Selden, Pufendorf and Locke – were cited in support of perpetual copyright.

To some extent, the natural rights theory conflicted with the traditional English concept that all property was vested in the Crown and derived from it. This was, in the eighteenth century, the normal conservative line, to be found, for example, in the writings of Hume and Paley, and, at the end of the century, in Burke.[110] It was this theory which had generally been applied by the courts in the seventeenth-century copyright cases, and which sustained the defence of the privileged copies and the English Stock. By the middle of the eighteenth century, however, the courts were taking a far less inclusive view of the royal prerogative. In one of his interventions in *Tonson v. Collins*, Mansfield dismissed the relevance of the precedents relating to the privileged copies on the grounds that 'The Crown has no rights over books in general; therefore the patents could have no effect [as binding precedents]'.[111]

The gradual exploration of the meaning of the concept of copyright was therefore caught up in a wider debate about the nature of property itself. On the one hand, there was the prevalent view that property was a natural right, partially ceded to the state, which could be created and, having been created, existed in perpetuity. On the other, there was the view that all property derived from the Crown, and was therefore subject to the authority of the Crown and its agents, including laws made by the Crown-in-Parliament.

If *Tonson v. Collins* were indeed a collusive action designed to establish unambiguous precedents, it had failed miserably; it had, however, helped to clarify the issues in legal as well as commercial terms. It was perhaps inevitable that the courts had not heard the last of the matter, which was eventually brought to a head by an act of deliberate provocation. The provoker was Alexander Donaldson, an Edinburgh bookseller who had built a large and profitable business on reprinting. He was far from satisfied with his Scottish and northern English market, and was determined to break into the book trade in London. In 1764, he fired his opening salvo by accusing the London trade of terrorizing the provincial booksellers, and publishing the 1759 letters to prove his case.[112] He concluded that the London trade had entered into an 'illegal conspiracy' to protect its own interests, a view supported by an eminent Scots lawyer, Lord Dreghorn, who cited *Midwinter v. Hamilton* to sustain his opinion that 'after a certain Number of Years was elapsed . . . any Person might print who had a mind'.[113] In 1769, Andrew Millar once again went to law to prove that Dreghorn was wrong.

In *Millar v. Taylor*,[114] heard in King's Bench on 20 April 1769, the plaintiff sued Robert Taylor for printing an edition of James Thomson's poem, *The Seasons*, of which he claimed to own the copyright. Taylor had printed an edition in 1766, when the 28-year term expired, and Millar immediately entered his suit. The case reached King's Bench, for what was apparently to be a landmark verdict. As the official reporter put it, this was an 'old and oft-litigated question . . . [of which this case was] . . . the first determination which the question ever received, in this Court of King's Bench'.[115] The judgment was delivered by Mansfield and three other justices, Willes, Aston and Yates, the last now elevated to the Bench.[116]

Willes, the junior Justice, was the first to speak. He reviewed at length the history of copyright cases both before and after 1710. He noted in particular that Chancery had continued to uphold copyright on the basis of pre-1710 common law, and that it would 'have been in error, if the whole right of an author in his copy depended upon this positive Act, as introductive of a new law'.[117] He concluded that it was not, that even the 1662 Printing Act 'supposes an ownership at common law',[118] and that 'there is a common-law right of an author to his copy . . . not taken away by the 8th of Anne'.[119] He found for the plaintiff.

Aston, who spoke next, concurred, although on different grounds. He based his argument on the theory of the natural origin of property, defining property as anything which can be assigned in law to a lawful owner, which is clearly the case with copyright. He accepted, therefore, that the author created the property at the time of writing, but he also argued that the property only took on a value, and therefore became defensible, when it was published, for 'without publication, 'tis useless to the owner . . . [Publication is] necessary . . . to render this confessed property useful . . . and profitable'.[120] He concludes from this that the property, by definition, cannot be renounced by publication, since publication is the essential act of completing its creation. The 1710 Act merely prescribed methods for protecting the property and means of securing redress against those who infringe on it.

The case was formidable, but Yates, who had been counsel for the defence in *Tonson v. Collins*, dissented. He admitted to some difficulty with the theory, but argued that the author changes the nature of the property by the act of publication. He did not really pursue whatever logic suggested this to him, but turned, perhaps with some relief, to historical and statutory issues. First, he dismissed the Stationers' Company's private practices as having become irrelevant in 1710,[121] and then came to the nub of his case:

> The Legislature may indeed make a new right. The Statute of Queen Ann. has vested a new right in authors for a limited time: and whilst that right exists, they will be established in the possession of their property.[122]

He added that 'There is not one clause, one expression . . . that hints at a prior exclusive right in authors to an eternal monopoly'.[123] In effect, Yates rejected the natural rights theory which sustained the case for perpetual copyright, in favour of an updated version of the conservative view, which vested the right to create forms of property in the Crown-in-Parliament. He found for the defendant.

Both Yates and Aston were attempting to define a concept which still had no name, but which would later be called intellectual property. They both recognized, although reaching different conclusions from their recognition, that what an author created had to be distinguished from the form in which it was disseminated, and that ownership, if any, was vested in the creation and therefore the creator. The difference between them was about the moment at which that ownership was made manifest, and how it was to be secured. Neither, however, doubted the existence of such property, or the fundamental ability of the English law to deal with it.

Mansfield engaged in no such speculations. He took a firm historically based view that all the precedents, both in Chancery and in King's Bench, supported the existence of property rights before publication. He concluded from this that the property continued to exist after publication, since if it did not, it would not have been property in the first place. So far as he was concerned, the 1710 Act was irrelevant to this, since it dealt only with a limited range of temporary protections for a permanent right. Thus by a majority of three to one, King's Bench decided the point which the London copy owners claimed they had never doubted: that rights in copies were merely a form of property, and like all property they existed for ever. An appeal under a Writ of Error was rejected, and the final injunction against Taylor was granted to Millar in the early summer of 1770.[124]

It was at this point that Alexander Donaldson resumed his career as a *provocateur*. He reprinted Thomson's *Seasons*, the very copy for which Taylor had been injuncted, and put it on sale in his bookshop in London, under the noses of Millar and the other copy-owning booksellers. The latter, now led by Thomas Becket, filed a Bill of Complaint in Chancery on 21 January 1771, elaborating the history of the shares in the copy, and asking for an injunction to prevent Donaldson from selling his present edition or printing any more. Chancery, not surprisingly in the light of its own precedents and that newly established in *Millar v. Taylor*, granted the injunction on 16 November 1772.[125]

Donaldson had to respond. The whole position of the Scottish trade was becoming impossible in the aftermath of *Millar v. Taylor*. The authoritative verdict of King's Bench had already been cited as a precedent by at least one Scottish judge in hearing a case in the Court of Session, with the rider that there was no conflict in the matter between English and Scots jurisdictions.[126] If that were to stand, and there was no obvious reason why it should not, the Scots would lose everything which they had won in *Midwinter v. Hamilton* and *Millar v. Kincaid*, for the courts in Scotland would have to recognize perpetual copyright just as the English courts did. Donaldson therefore appealed to the House of Lords, which, at last, reached a fully authoritative verdict on the 1710 Copyright Act and the place of copyright in English law.

Donaldson's lawyers had based their case in Chancery on several points, all of them familiar, although with differences of emphasis. First, they argued that natural-law property rights are assumed to exist as a matter of 'public Utility', but in the case of copyright they would create a commercial monopoly, which was never the intention. Secondly, they rejected the historical precedents. They dismissed the relevance of the private arrangements of the Stationers' Company, and all Chancery rulings before 1710, on the grounds that they were superseded by Act of Parliament. It was argued that the 1710 Act was 'not declaratory of the Common Law, but introductive of a New Law . . .'[127] This was intended to protect authors and their families, and they cited the parallel example of the protection afforded by Parliament to engravers in 1735. They asserted that all the alleged precedents for injunctions for breach of copyright were within the 28-year term, with the single exception of *Millar v. Taylor*. This was both learned and ingenious, although somewhat flawed, especially in the last part. Many cases, including, for example, *Pope v. Lintot*, had been argued on the basis of the 14-year term of copyright, rather than 21 years, and it was going to be very difficult to evade the arguments of three out of the four judges in *Millar v. Taylor*.

Counsel for Becket seems to have been confident. He rehearsed the natural law theory of property, accepting it, and arguing that in 'Reason and Natural Justice' there is an 'implied agreement' not to reprint a copy when it is owned by someone else. On the historical front, he contented himself with the argument that Parliament has recognized such rights, that they were also embodied in the crown patents and the English Stock, and that the 1710 Act merely provided some support for the booksellers by imposing penalties on the perpetrators of unauthorized reprints under certain conditions.

When the case came to the House of Lords, the same arguments were repeated. Thurloe, for Donaldson, argued that the 1710 Act was a new and quite specific law giving protection for a specific period of time and for no longer. He largely avoided legal theory, but he did argue that only property which could be defended could have an existence, and that this could not be done with literary property, because, having no physical existence, it could not be occupied. Finally, he returned to the firmer ground of precedent, and invited the House to consider the verdict in *Midwinter v. Hamilton*, commending the common sense of the Court of Session in trying to 'emancipate . . . [the booksellers] . . . from such an odious Oppression'. Thurloe's junior, Sir John Dalrymple, was more blunt. He argued that the 1710 Act created a new right and vested it in authors and booksellers; there was nothing to suggest that it was confirming existing rights, or that the rights which it created subsisted beyond the periods of time specified in the Act.

The Lord Chancellor now put three questions to the twelve judges,[128] to which Lord Camden successfully moved the addition of two more. The five questions were:

1. Whether at common Law, the Author of any Literary composition had the sole first Right of printing and publishing the same for Sale,

and could bring an Action against any Person for publishing the same, without his consent?
2. If the Author had such right originally, did the Law take it away upon his printing and publishing the said literary composition, or might any Person reprint and publish the said literary composition, for his own Benefit, against the Will of the Author?
3. If such Action would have laid at Common Law, is the same taken away by the statute of Anne? Or is an Author precluded by such Statute from any Remedy, except on the foundation of such Statute?
4. Whether the Author of any literary Composition, or his assigns, had the sole Right of printing and publishing the same in perpetuity by the Common Law?
5. Whether this Right is in any way impeached, restrained or taken away by the 8th of Anne?

Camden's two questions (the last two) encapsulated, as they were meant to do, the whole problem, for it was they which dealt with the central issue of the rights of authors and the meaning of the 1710 Act.

The eleven judges then gave their views on these five questions, and, not surprisingly, they were neither unanimous nor unambiguous. The actual votes varied considerably between questions (see Table 3.1) and on the crucial issue of the existence of perpetual rights (Question 4) they were equally divided with one abstention besides Mansfield. On the other questions they were somewhat clearer. There were clear majorities both for the creation of rights by the author (Question 1) and for the partial loss of those rights on publication (Question 2), and a majority also for the view that the author can only seek legal redress under the 1710 Act (Question 3),[129] so that the Act was indeed held to change the nature of the author's rights.

Table 3.1
Becket v. Donaldson: the Law Lords' opinions

Question number	Yes	No
1	8	3
2	7	4
3	6	5
4	5	5
5	4	7

Source: *The Case of the Appellants* (see note 125), modified from Rose, The author as proprietor (see note 80).

In fact, the judges were rather more decisive than some of the more ambiguous responses might suggest. In general, all agreed that the 1710 Act superseded whatever common law might have existed before that time. All agreed, again in general terms, that authors had rights, although there was a genuine division of opinion on the extent of those rights. There was also, however, some very sensible understanding of the background to the case, and a recognition that the House was dealing with a commercial as well as a legal issue. This became almost explicit in the views of Lord de Grey, the Chief Justice of Common Pleas. He held that even though Chancery had never actually managed to decide what the law was (he did not refer to *Millar v. Taylor*, a King's Bench case), in fact the Act was quite clear about it. It made no reference to existing rights, and must therefore be presumed to have created new ones, which it then proceeded to limit to 14, 21 or 28 years according to circumstances. De Grey, however, thought he detected a reason for all the legal activity of the previous forty years; he said, 'The truth is the Idea of a common Law Right in Perpetuity was not taken up till after that Failure [in 1735–37] in procuring a new Statute for the Enlargement of the Term'. In that he was absolutely right, and he discerned the very essence of the problem: the almost frantic desire of some members of the London book trade to protect their investments in copies.

A debate followed, in which Camden argued passionately against confirming what he regarded as a monopoly. Mansfield, to the surprise of many, remained silent. At the division, the House overwhelmingly supported the reversal of the Chancery decree. Donaldson had won. Perpetual copyright was ruled not to exist, and the 1710 Act to mean what it said.

The case had aroused a good deal of interest in literary circles and in the press. Indeed, in the minds of some writers, including Catherine Macaulay, it raised far larger issues of the freedom of the press; she saw copyright as simply another means of restricting the circulation of ideas.[130] More generally, however, the public resolution of the copyright issue lent support to those writers who wanted to make strong claims for their rights. Most famously, perhaps, Samuel Johnson pronounced that 'The Judgement of the Lords was . . . legally and politically right'.[131]

If the decision was generally welcomed in literary circles, the same was not true of some members of the London book trade.

When the case was over, the trade made an attempt to restore what they had lost. On 28 February 1774, only six days after the Lords' decision, the booksellers petitioned the Commons against the 'hardship' which would be caused to them by the verdict. In effect, they were seeking an Act which would reverse the verdict by giving unambiguous statutory authority to perpetual rights in all copies, both new and existing.[132] A Committee was appointed to look into the petition, and it reported its findings to the House on 24 March.[133] The Committee heard two witnesses on behalf of the London trade. The first was William Johnson, who had been in business since 1748, and was a large-scale owner of copies. He testified that he had invested his money on the understanding that he was buying a piece of perpetual property, and that he had never seen a contract or assignment in which fourteen years was mentioned. He argued that if a new law were not passed, the value of copies would be reduced, and the market flooded with cheap reprints which would devalue existing stocks of books. John Wilkie, the second witness, who had served for many years as the clerk at the trade sales, testified that at least £50,000 had changed hands in buying and selling copies since 1755.[134]

The very real fears of the trade were exposed here, especially by Johnson. The effect of the verdict in *Becket v. Donaldson* was to open the market to unlimited reprinting of any copy more than 28 years old, and perhaps of any copy not entered in the Stationers' Register. Even the former would be bad enough, for many of the shares bought and sold at the trade sales were in copies far older than that. There was a vast collectively owned *corpus* of 'rights' in the standard works which sustained the London trade, and which was now thrown onto the open market. The trade was convinced that ruin was staring it in the face, and so perhaps it was.

These arguments had some force. Leave was given to bring in a Bill, but it provoked a storm of protest. The Edinburgh booksellers, not surprisingly, were in the forefront of this, arguing that the Bill would damage their trade, and that, in any case, Scots law had never recognized perpetual copyrights.[135] This was followed by a further petition from English provincial booksellers and some of those members of the London trade who were not in the inner circles of the copy owners,[136] and from Alexander Donaldson himself.[137] The copy owners went into action, but their arguments were difficult to sustain. In *The Case of the Booksellers of London and Westminster*,[138] they tried to maintain that the Lords had taken away common-law rights which the 1710 Act had carefully sought to maintain. This astonishing piece of effrontery was easily refuted.[139] Some of the trade's other arguments were equally ill-conceived, even if they were more accurate. When a group of major copy owners published their accounts to show how much they had spent on the encouragement of learning, it was inevitable that the response was along the lines that however many thousands they had spent on improving books, they had made thousands more by selling them.[140]

The trade lobbied hard for this Bill, spending some £1,500 in promoting it, including over £1,000 raised by the Stationers' Company from a general subscription.[141] The Bill had no hope, however, and never proceeded any further in the Commons. No further attempt was made to assert the claim to perpetual copyright.

The book trade was transformed by *Becket v. Donaldson*, in a way which was, in part, intended by the reprinters and their supporters. The opening up of the trade copies to all comers created a new trade in low-priced reprints, while the copy owners were forced to find new books to publish, and to exploit them to the full during the limited term of copyright which now existed. This gave authors a far stronger position *vis-à-vis* the trade, and enabled them to begin to make new demands. No longer satisfied with outright sales of their newly defined rights, authors began to look for profit-sharing arrangements, or even for income related to the number of copies sold. Out of this there emerged two recognizably modern groups: publishers and professional authors.

Publishers, firms which specialized in the publishing of books, and which were not involved in the retail book trade (or only marginally so), were a product of the last quarter of the eighteenth century, and developed because of the need to exploit the market for new books rather than for old ones. Publishing could no longer depend on the safety of reprints, but became the high-risk entrepreneurial enterprise which characterized the book trade of the nineteenth and twentieth centuries. In this more overtly commercial environment, authors too could assert their rights, for they were now established as the creators of the products from which the publishers were making their profits. Both the book trade and the relationships within it were fundamentally and irreversibly changed by the chain of events which began in the House of Lords in February 1774.[142]

In the immediate aftermath, the trade was unpopular, and the accumulated resentment against the monopolistic copy owners came quickly to the surface. The law patent came under attack, and so too did the almanac monopoly, which was now the mainstay of the English Stock.[143] The almanacs had been the subject of piracy throughout the century, and it was increasingly difficult for the Stationers' Company to police its claim to a monopoly of all almanacs, new and old, throughout Great Britain. Thomas Carnan, a well-established and successful London bookseller who had strong provincial connections, deliberately flouted the Company's claims for many years, and finally provoked them into action in 1773. The timing of *Company of Stationers v. Carnan* could not have been worse. It came to Chancery for determination in May 1775, and it was, inevitably, decided in Carnan's favour. The almanac monopoly, and with it much of the income of the English Stock, vanished at a stroke. The truth was that the age of the book trade monopolies was over. In only one matter did Parliament agree to protect perpetual copyrights; an Act which protected those belonging to the universities, Eton and Winchester colleges and Westminster School received the Royal Assent on 22 May 1775.[144] That was all that remained of two hundred years of continuous attempts, by the Stationers' Company and by less formal groups of booksellers, to establish a monolithic control over the publishing of books in London.

After these tumultuous events, a period of comparative quiet followed, as the trade settled down to new ways of working. Yet the issues which arose out of the 1710 Act had not yet been fully resolved. After *Becket v. Donaldson* there could no longer be any doubt about the legal basis of copyright as a property, or about the time during which it subsisted, but many others remained, and new issues emerged as the book trade became more complex and more capitalistic, and as modes of publications became more varied. Indeed, some of these issues had already arisen. As early as 1766, King's Bench had determined in *Tonson v. Waller* that Thomas Newton's notes on *Paradise Lost* were the subject of a separate copyright from that in Milton's poem.[145] In the nineteenth century, this was cited as the authority for sustaining copyright in an edition of a text in public domain.[146] The equally tricky question of abridgements had also been addressed in the eighteenth century,[147] with the courts reaching the view that an abridgement was a 'Work of Judgement', and therefore had its own copyright.[148]

Even more fundamental was the beginning of an attempt to define copyright as a concept rather than simply as a piece of property. The key case here was that of *Trusler v. Murray*, in which the author John Trusler sued John Murray the publisher for alleged breach of the copyright in his *Chronology: or a concise view of the annals of England*, first published in 1769, and many times reprinted.[149] Trusler's case rested on the fact that Murray had published a chronology very similar to his, but the court held that the facts contained in the chronology were not protected by the law, and that, provided the form of presentation had not been substantially followed, no offence had been committed. A basic rule thus began to emerge towards the end of the century: that piracy occurred only when the words were reproduced in such a way that a book was, in effect, a copy of a previous book by another author.[150]

By the end of the eighteenth century, copyright was well-established, and reasonably well-understood. It depended, however, upon the 1710 Act, which, despite clarification by the courts, was still the same fundamentally unsatisfactory piece of legislation which it had always been. British copyright still betrayed its dual and conflicting origins as an exercise of the royal prerogative and as a commercial monopoly. The procedures of the law had been used to some effect to sharpen the definition of the law, but practice had far outstripped the law itself. Changing relationships between authors and book trade, and changing perceptions of the very nature of authorship, could no longer be contained within an early eighteenth-century statute designed to embody late seventeenth-century practices. Moreover, new ideas of copyright were in the air, blowing from revolutionary America and revolutionary France. They were not to appeal to the British Parliament for so long as France was an enemy, but when copyright again became a matter of political and public concern in the second decade of the nineteenth century, new men and new ideas were to make a new law.

4 The Legal Deposit of Books

By the beginning of the nineteenth century, British copyright law was thoroughly unsatisfactory. The law had always lagged behind practice, but now there was an accumulation of statute, precedent, trade practice and cultural assumptions which was becoming extremely difficult to use at all. The need for reform and codification would soon become apparent, but before that could be undertaken, there was a strange episode in the history of copyright law which was, in theory, wholly separate from it, and yet delayed the reform of the law by perhaps as much as twenty years.

The 1710 Act had dealt with three separate and largely unrelated issues: rights in copies, the regulation of book prices, and the deposit of copies of certain books in specified libraries. By the end of the eighteenth century, the courts had gone a long way towards defining rights in copies, and significance of those parts of the Act which dealt with them. The attempt to control book prices had been predictably futile, and was quietly abandoned in the Import of Books Act of 1739, apparently without ever having been enforced.[1] There remained, however, the question of the libraries.

The presence of legal deposit clauses in the 1710 Act was an historical accident, arising out of the Printing Act of 1662. That Act had required that copies of all new books, or new editions of old books, should be deposited in the Royal Library, in the Bodleian Library at Oxford and in the University Library at Cambridge. The copies were to be sent to Stationers' Hall, and thence, by the Clerk, to the libraries.[2] Like everything in the 1662 Act,[3] the intention was to promote the control of the press; there is no evidence of benevolence towards the libraries.

There were a number of precedents for this legislation. In England, there was no example in law, but in 1610, Sir Thomas Bodley had negotiated an agreement with the Stationers' Company under which a copy of every new book printed by a member of the

Company had to be sent to Oxford for the use of the Library. The idea had originated with Thomas James, the Librarian of the Bodleian since its foundation in 1598, but it was the influence of Bodley which secured the consent of the Stationers. The deed was sealed in Congregation at Oxford in February 1610, and received by the Court of Assistants in March.[4] After various experiments with sending the books to Bodley's own house in Fulham, and thence to Oxford, it was agreed that the Clerk of the Stationers' Company should receive them, and be responsible for their onward transmission. Although the agreement was by no means universally respected by the London book trade, a very considerable number of books were indeed sent to the Bodleian under this arrangement, which, in theory, subsisted until it was superseded by the 1662 Act.[5]

This English precedent was an unofficial private arrangement between two private corporations, the Stationers' Company and the University of Oxford. There were, however, continental examples of the deposit of books being required by law, the earliest being that of 1537 in France, under which all French printers were required to deposit a copy of each book they produced. The books went to the Bibliothèque Royale, partly certainly to augment its holdings, and perhaps in part to ensure that they were duly licensed and published.[6]

The 1662 Act was, however, a new departure in English law; although it was to prove difficult to enforce, it did have some effect. There was, however, a serious administrative problem; the law required the books to be sent to Stationers' Hall, but made no arrangements for their onward transmission to the libraries. This was corrected in the 1665 renewal of the Printing Act, which also introduced fines for failure to deposit, the first time that such penalties had been imposed.[7] The Stationers' Company was actually in a very difficult position. The Court of Assistants seems to have been assumed to be responsible for the effective operation of the deposit clauses, but all it could actually do was remind members to send books to Stationers' Hall. This it did on several occasions in the 1660s and early 1670s, often under pressure from the libraries. In November 1663, the Royal Library complained that it was not receiving its books, and the Vice-Chancellor of Oxford wrote a letter to the same effect in February 1664.[8] The Court reminded members of their obligations, but could do little more. Both universities experienced endless difficulties in claiming their books, and even joint efforts between them often led nowhere.[9]

When the Printing Act lapsed between 1679 and 1685 and again after 1695, the deposit clauses obviously lapsed with it. In November 1695, Oxford tried to revive the original agreement between Bodley and the Stationers' Company but the attempt, perhaps inevitably, failed.[10] Richard Bentley, Librarian of the Royal Library, had complained in 1698 of the difficulty in obtaining his deposit copies;[11] at that time, of course, he had no such right, but perhaps did not understand the implications of the lapse of the Printing Act.

In 1707, however, when there seemed to be a realistic hope of some new book trade legislation,[12] libraries in Oxford and elsewhere tried to find a way to take advantage of it. In particular, there was a small group of men gathered around Arthur Charlett, Master of University College, Oxford, from 1692 to 1722, who were interested in attempting to restore the Bodleian's deposit privilege.[13] They had already persuaded a few booksellers to make voluntary donations to the Library, but clearly a legal obligation would be far more effective in the long run.[14] Charlett himself never had a formal connection with the Bodleian, but the Librarian, John Hudson, was a Fellow of University College, and had been one of Charlett's strongest supporters when he had been elected to the mastership. This link was to prove of vital importance, for Charlett conducted a vast correspondence, not least with the University's two M.P.s, Sir William Whitelock and William Bromley.

On 17 March 1707, Bromley wrote to Charlett, enclosing a copy of the Bill then before the Commons, in which there was a deposit clause. He hoped that the Bill would be:

> . . . to the Satisfaction of those learned Bodies and answer the Desires of our Librarian so far as I have understood them from the Applications he has made to others, which however I have endeavoured to accommodate.[15]

From this, it seems that Hudson had been lobbying other M.P.s, as well as his own University representatives, and had done so to some effect. Oxford was not alone in such activities. A reliable tradition records that Thomas Tenison, the Archbishop of Canterbury, was instrumental in having Sion College added to the list of deposit libraries, and that one of the City of London M.P.s had put the alternative case for the Library of St Paul's Cathedral.[16]

Alas, these efforts were all in vain, for as Thomas Hearne, another supporter of Bodleian deposit privilege, noted in his diary on 20 March: 'Sir William Whitelock and Mr Bromley have written to Dr Hudson signifying the Miscarriage of the Bill for Printing.'[17] That, however, was not the end of the matter. When the next Bill came to Parliament in 1710, the deposit clauses were still there. Originally, these made arrangements for Oxford, Cambridge and the Royal Library, but, during the committee and report stages, Sion and the five Scottish universities (St Andrews, Glasgow, Edinburgh, and King's and Mareschal Colleges, Aberdeen) were added to the list. When the 1710 Act received the Royal Assent, there were thus nine deposit libraries in the United Kingdom.[18]

In the first few years after the passage of the Act, most of the libraries made some attempt to obtain their books. The Bodleian was assiduous at first, as might have been expected,[19] and so was Edinburgh University.[20] Glasgow University was forced to look for a new building to house the books thus obtained, but in fact the flow of books into the Library was very limited in the early eighteenth century.[21] Others, however, were either less fortunate or less persistent; it was estimated that the books sent to Sion College were worth barely five pounds a year.[22] All these efforts, however, were short-lived, and the London trade was distinctly uncooperative.

By the end of the eighteenth century, the Bodleian was receiving almost no books at all, and, incidentally, failing to catalogue almost all of those which it did receive.[23] At St Andrews, there had been a few rumblings of discontent in the 1760s because so few books were being sent down from London, but nothing was done to remedy the situation.[24] Evidence from Glasgow suggests that claims were rarely made, and when they were they were often late,[25] while, by the 1760s, Edinburgh was obtaining almost all of its books from other sources.[26] The deposit clauses were a dead letter. When the 1801 Act added Trinity College and King's Inn, Dublin, to the list of deposit libraries, not a voice was raised in protest.[27] After the summer of 1801, therefore, there were eleven deposit libraries, none of them particularly interested in exercising their rights.[28]

This complacency was soon to be shattered. The troubles began in Cambridge. In 1805, Basil Montagu, a Cambridge graduate and a barrister, discovered that the University Library did not have a recent volume of law reports which he wished to consult. Annoyed by this, he wrote a pamphlet in which he called for a stricter enforcement of the law, aiming his criticism principally at the apparent indolence of the University Library itself.[29] In the following year, the same cause was taken up by another barrister who had also been frustrated by the inadequacy of the same Library. Edward Christian, who was apparently an indifferent lawyer and seems to have been personally rather unpopular, was Downing Professor of the Laws of England at Cambridge. Like Montagu, he found the University Library's holdings of recent law reports to be deficient. In 1807, he too went into print on the deposit question, in a pamphlet which marks the real beginning of the long campaign for the enforcement and reform of the law.[30] Christian argued, much as Montagu had done, that the law conferred unambiguous rights on the universities, but that these rights were also obligations, and that they were ignoring these obligations to the detriment of their members. He also, however, adduced another important legal argument, which was to prove of critical importance. In *Beckford v. Hood (1798)*,[31] King's Bench had held that an author could sue for breach of copyright even if the pirated book were not entered in the Stationers' Register. The immediate intention was to clear up yet another ambiguity or omission of the 1710 Act. It had, however, another effect, according to Christian. The Act could be read to mean that only books entered in the Register were liable for deposit, and indeed the 1801 Act was specific on the point in relation to the Irish libraries. Christian, however, claimed that the 1801 Act was based on a misunderstanding of the law, as clarified in *Beckford v. Hood,* and that that case supported the contention that all books had to be deposited, whether they were entered or not. To round off his argument, Christian added that the law applied to revised and augmented editions as well as to new books. If nothing else, he had raised issues which clearly needed to be clarified.

On 16 June 1808, the House of Commons gave permission for a Bill to be brought in which would indeed clarify the law.[32] The main proposal in the Bill dealt with the mechanisms of legal deposit. It required that copies of all new books and reprints should be sent to the Warehouse Keeper of the Stationer's Company before publication, so that he could send them to the libraries. This was to be done regardless of whether the book had been, or was intended subsequently to be, entered in the Stationers' Register. Almost as an afterthought there was also a clause which extended the term of copyright.

After a brief debate, this Bill was given its Second Reading on 17 June,[33] but when it reached its Committee Stage serious differences of opinion began to emerge. The Committee ignored the rather sensible suggestion that the Bill should be divided into two separate measures, one dealing with the term of copyright and the other with legal deposit. Indeed, the two issues were almost inextricably linked, partly because Christian thought that he had persuaded the sponsor of the Bill to reach an agreement with the book trade. An amendment was accepted which extended the term of copyright to 28 years,[34] which, as Christian understood the position, meant that the trade would not oppose the deposit clauses. In fact, something had gone wrong. The Bill's sponsor was John Charles Villiers, M.P. for Queenborough, a Tory reformer who was disillusioned with Pitt and later a strong supporter of Canning.[35] Not for the last time, the whole issue took on a political complexion dictated by the wider political interests and reputations of those involved in it.

The misunderstandings between Villiers and Christian were about the discussions which the former had had with the book trade. Christian believed that there had been an agreement that the trade would not object to the proposed deposit arrangements provided that the term of copyright was extended. That was certainly Christian's recollection some ten years later,[36] but, even if his memory was accurate, he may have misunderstood Villiers at the time, or Villiers himself may have been confused. Whatever the explanation, it was the deposit clause which aroused the most serious opposition in the debate of 22 June, and the trade lay behind this. C. W. Williams Wynne, M.P. for Montgomeryshire, said bluntly that the trade objected to the deposit proposals, and that the Bill ought to be withdrawn. Sir Samuel Romilly gave whole-hearted support to the extended term of copyright, but regarded deposit as being objectionable on principle, as an infringement on the property rights of the publishers. Both men were supporters of reform, Romilly actively so.[37] In their objections we can see Whigs of various shades, together with some moderate Tories, beginning to question the propriety of interfering in the freedom of trade and the inviolability of private property by taking books from their 'rightful' owners. The proposal to divide the Bill into two parts was a ploy by Villiers to rescue something from this debacle, but it came to nothing. The Bill never reappeared in the House, and was lost at the end of the Session.

If there had been some negotiations with the trade, Wynne was certainly right to claim that they had not led to unanimous support for the Bill. Two or three days after the debate in the Commons, an anonymous pamphlet was published which laid out the details of the objections of at least some publishers, and possibly a considerable number of them.[38] The author based his case on two arguments. The first was an appeal to the House's sense of fair play. The Bill, he wrote, had been brought in late in the Session, without warning and without proper preparation or discussion: '[The Bill] was never heard of by many of them [the book trade] till the day before.'[39] It was argued that the matter was not urgent, and that if the Bill were to be delayed valid and important arguments could be mustered against it.

The writer's second point was both more substantial and potentially more damaging. He argued that, although the Bill was designed to help both authors and libraries, in practice it helped neither. So far as the libraries were concerned, the works 'thus to be extorted from their proprietors' would include many which the universities could not possibly want such as school-books and similar trivia.[40] The danger to authors is less clearly explained, but it is suggested that publishers will be less willing to publish expensive books if eleven copies are to be extracted from them for the eleven libraries. An example is given; John Sibthorp's *Flora Graeca*, then in course of publication, would eventually cost 200 guineas a copy, a cost to the publishers of £2,310 for the deposit copies. In such circumstances, it is argued, such books will not be published at all. The Postscript expands on the point; while authors will not really benefit from the extension of copyright, but the proposal 'would eventually injure the Printers'.[41]

The themes which run through the anonymous *Strictures* of 1808 were to become very familiar during every discussion of the issue until it was resolved in 1837. On the one hand, the libraries would be overwhelmed with rubbish; on the other, authors would not be helped by an extension of the term of copyright. Moreover, both developments would harm the publishers and printers. It was, of course, this rider which was the real concern of almost all of the objectors, and which provided them with their most potent political argument. The anonymous pamphleteer of 1808 said bluntly that deposit was a 'violation of private property', and to a parliament of property owners that was a very forceful argument indeed.

The failure of this Bill did not deter Christian or other would-be reformers. He pursued the matter further through the courts, and at last persuaded the authorities at Cambridge to join forces with him in a matter which was, after all, in their interest as well as in his. After some abortive attempts, in 1811 the University began proceedings against Henry Bryer for failing to deposit a copy of a book which he had recently printed for the publishers Johnson and Ridgeway of London. The London book trade formed an *ad hoc* committee to assist Bryer in his defence, for they too recognized the importance of what was happening. The test case of *Cambridge University v. Bryer* came to King's Bench for an authoritative ruling in November 1812, and was unanimously decided in favour of the University.[42] As in *Beckford v. Hood*, the court held that entry in the Stationers' Register was irrelevant, and that the 1710 Act applied whether or not this had been done. Christian had been vindicated in full, but the trade was faced with a very serious problem.

A committee of London booksellers and printers took action in December 1812, by petitioning Parliament to ask for legislation which would neutralize the effects of *Cambridge University v. Bryer*. Specifically, they wanted expensive books and books published in very small print runs to be exempt from the deposit requirements. According to the petitioners, some publishers would lose thousands of pounds a year if the law were not changed, and once again it was argued that this would be a deterrent to publishing certain kinds of books, a discouragement to learning.[43] Nothing happened immediately as a result of this petition, but on 11 March 1813 the matter was revived by a petition from the printers of London and Westminster, supporting the publishers' petition of the previous December, and asking for a 28-year term of copyright to encourage both authors and their assignees.[44] The arguments of 1808 were emerging once again, and once again it was the question of legal deposit which was to dominate the debate.

The printers' petition was presented to the Commons by Davies Giddy, M.P. for Bodmin, who was to be a key figure in the parliamentary history of copyright in the next few years. He was a friend of Wynne, the opponent of the 1808 Bill, but, unlike him, was an active supporter of the Liverpool government and therefore a man with rather more political influence than either Wynne or any of the other members involved in the events of 1808.[45] This influence was indeed to be critical. When he presented the printers' petition to the House, Giddy moved that a Select Committee be appointed to examine both the petition itself and copyright law in general. He argued that recent decisions in the courts had created a situation which was unfair to the publishers, and arose out of the lack of clarity in the 1710 Act. The time had come, he argued, to investigate the whole subject.

There was some debate after Giddy's speech, including contributions from Wynne and Romilly. The latter supported a 28-year period of copyright, but the whole question of copyright was now being swamped by the deposit question. Wynne bluntly described it as a tax on publishers, and, like Romilly, supported the establishment of the Select Committee. J. H. Smyth, one of the M.P.s for Cambridge University,[46] who had doubtless been briefed by some of his constituents, tried to suggest that an extension of the term of copyright was a reasonable *quid pro quo* for the confirmation of the law as it had been interpreted by King's Bench in *Cambridge University v. Bryer*. This evoked no response at the time, but a Select Committee was indeed established along the lines suggested by Giddy.[47]

The Select Committee met on ten occasions between 24 March and 16 June 1813, hearing witnesses at six of those meetings. Nearly all of the witnesses were from the trade. The first of them was Henry Parry, speaking on behalf of the petitioners and other publishers.[48] His key point was that book prices would rise by an average of 5 per cent if eleven copies were required of every book which was published. This statement was supported by some statistical information. Essentially, Parry based his conclusion on two grounds: first, that eleven copies represented a disproportionately high percentage of the print run of small editions; and secondly, that slow-selling books would not be profitable in a reasonable period of time if eleven copies had to be given away.

The first part of this was easily demonstrated; the eleven copies were one-quarter of 1 per cent of an edition of 5,000, but 22 per cent of an edition of 250. The second point, depending as it did upon a negative, was less easily proved. The example which was offered was interesting and pertinent, but the argument somewhat specious. Isaac Reed's edition of Shakespeare had, according to Parry, cost £5,875 to produce when it was published in 1803. It took nine years to sell the edition, and this had yielded a net profit of £375. 16*s*. 0*d*.; if eleven copies had been deposited, this profit would have been reduced to 6*s*. 0*d*. From this Parry argued that the book could not have been published except at a much higher price than its actual one. He concluded by suggesting what presumably seemed to him and his fellow publishers to be a compromise solution. The important point was to reduce the number of deposit copies (although he was not specific about numbers), but he also suggested that for those which remained there should be a small charge (of say one-third or one-quarter of the retail price), that expensive books and books printed in editions of less than 250 should be exempt, that copies on cheaper paper should be acceptable to the libraries, and that copies should only be deposited if they were demanded.

Not all of this was to prove very helpful to the trade, as became clear during the examination of the next witness, Thomas Norton Longman.[49] Longman was the head of a firm which was already almost a century old, and which had been one of the most successful in adapting to the new ways of publishing in the late eighteenth century. By 1813, Longmans was one of the giants of the book trade, dominating large parts of the market in school-books, as well as publishing a vast range of both fiction and non-fiction.[50] Longman could speak with massive authority, as a successful publisher. No longer was the trade represented by committees, and certainly not by its historic guild, but by such men as him, who were wealthy, influential and substantial businessmen.

Longman was with the Committee for the better part of two days, during which he gave them an elementary, but immensely detailed, lesson in the economics of publishing.[51] Although he made some general statements about copyright, he concentrated almost entirely on the question of legal deposit. He first explained the general principle on which he based his case: some books take many years to go into profit, and sales would be further reduced if the prices of books were increased. This was particularly true of small editions, which might not be economic at all at a higher price; on the other hand, it was these which were 'conducive to the diffusion of literature', because the choice was between a small edition or no edition at all. Such arguments had indeed been heard during the eighteenth century, but they were now being presented rather differently. Longman made little pretence of concern for the encouragement of learning; he was interested in profits, and would publish only those books which were profitable.

The members of the Select Committee, however, were not passive auditors of all of this. Longman argued that giving eleven copies to the libraries would necessarily increase the price of the book and thus affect its sales; when he was challenged, however, he could not give an actual example of sales being reduced by higher prices, nor could he suggest what the effect might be of the 5 per cent increase postulated by Parry. He might have felt himself on rather more solid ground when he was pressed to explain why the price would increase if eleven copies had to be deposited, but even then he was not wholly convincing. He denied that printing the extra eleven copies (if that was what it amounted to, as the Committee tended to assume) merely entailed extra paper, but was unable to explain what other costs were involved. He was continually pressed on this issue, but could not explain the difference between selling 989 copies of a book and selling 1,000, or indeed how eleven copies could make such a vital difference in what everyone agreed was a very hazardous trade. In the end, he did indeed produce some concrete figures, but only to the effect that depositing eleven copies of every book he had published would have cost him £1,800 a year over the last three years.

The other trade witnesses added little of substance to what Parry and Longman had said. All argued, in one way or another, that a requirement to deposit eleven copies of every book they published would deter them from publishing certain kinds of books. Joseph Mawman claimed that books published for charitable purposes (of which he gave no examples) would be badly affected, as would learned works.[52] Richard Taylor said that it would badly affect the publication of translations of foreign works, and William Davies that it would affect exports of British books because prices would be higher.[53]

Some of the evidence was perhaps slightly more telling. John Nichols testified that some of the deposit libraries subscribed to his *Bibliotheca Topographica Britannica*, and that he would suffer serious losses if they did not do so and he also had to deposit the books in all eleven libraries.[54] The implication was that the libraries could afford the books which they really wanted. J. G. Cochrane, a partner in the long-established firm of White's in Fleet Street, also adopted a slightly different approach. He introduced himself as a publisher of expensive illustrated books (as indeed he was) to whom the cost of the eleven copies would be at least £300 a year, or £450 if copies on the best paper were required. In effect, he argued, some of these books could not economically be published if such a law were to be enforced.

To support his case, Cochrane produced a letter from an author who was compiling and publishing a major work of scholarship. The writer was Rogers Ruding, who was in the process of completing his *Annals of the Coinage of Great Britain* (3 vols., 1817–19 and subsequent editions), which he intended to publish by subscription. A prospectus had been issued,[55] but the project was now in doubt because of the uncertain state of the law. Ruding wrote to Cochrane that the decision of the House 'is of considerable importance to me, as upon it will depend *certainly* whether I shall print any large paper copies, or not; and *possibly* . . . whether I shall be able to print at all'.[56] Cochrane read this letter to the Select Committee[57] as evidence of how a deposit law would adversely affect scholarly publishing. According to him, in a letter to Ruding a few days later, it 'produced the strongest effect upon the minds of all the members'.[58]

Ruding was not the only author to support the publishers' case. The bibliographer, Thomas Frognall Dibdin, appeared before the Select Committee, in his capacity as a scholar who published his own books by subscription. He said that it would have cost him about £120 to deliver eleven copies of his *Typographical Antiquities* to the libraries, or £300 if large paper copies were required.[59] He did not add, as he might have done, that his profit on this book, published in 1810, had been about £600.[60] Dibdin also revealed that some of the libraries had subscribed to his *Bibliotheca Spenceriana*, but under questioning he was actually rather evasive when pressed to say whether he would have been deterred from publishing any of his books if he had indeed been obliged to deposit eleven copies.[61]

Parry, Longman and Cochrane, with the implicit support of the other trade witnesses, had argued that the deposit law was an unfair tax on the book trade, which would positively deter the publication of good books. In a pamphlet published in the late spring of 1813, Cochrane developed this point at length and also raised other important issues.[62] Perhaps the most telling of these, which had already been aired in 1808 and was to recur constantly, was that the libraries did not need all of these books, and that some of them did not even deserve a place on their shelves.[63] Cochrane also added, both in the pamphlet and in his evidence to the Select Committee, that the libraries had some funds for buying books, and should make use of these to buy selectively, not failing to adduce the examples of other libraries which had no deposit claims and were therefore obliged to use their own money.[64] This brought Cochrane to the nub of the matter as he saw it: the 1710 Act was intended to encourage learning, but he questioned whether this was achieved by taxing the book trade on behalf of a select group of libraries. This was merely using the law to take private property from its owner for the benefit of other private bodies.[65]

This line of argument was pursued by others, once Cochrane had suggested it. Richard Taylor, another of the Select Committee witnesses, wrote a pamphlet in which it was propounded at length.[66] Sharon Turner, the last witness to appear before the Select Committee, on 6 April 1813, also took up the point; both there and in a pamphlet, he argued that libraries encouraged learning by buying books, not by taking them from their rightful owners.[67]

It fell to Turner to lay the trade's requests systematically before the Select Committee. They were a judicious blend of demands and concessions. The trade agreed to five deposit copies, one each for England, Scotland and Ireland, and for Oxford and Cambridge; they would concede a greater number if any additional libraries would pay one-third or one-quarter of the retail price. They asked, however, for exemption from the deposit requirement if the author waived the copyright, if the book were for private circulation only, if it were printed in colour, if it cost more than ten guineas, or if it were published by subscription, and also for all prints, newspapers, music and reprints of foreign books. To protect the libraries' interests, they suggested that all books should be registered at Stationers' Hall, and to protect the authors, the term of copyright should be extended to 28 years.[68]

Turner's proposals make it clear that, whatever else it might concede, the trade was not going to succumb without a fight on the eleven copies, but when the Select Committee reported on 17 June, it was this very point which they had not accepted.[69] While admitting that there had been 'great changes . . . in the literary system of this country' since 1710, the Select Committee saw no reason to change the principles of the law. They did propose some modifications, but these were minor. All eleven libraries were to retain their deposit rights, but only the British Museum (as the 'National establishment') was to have a copy on the best paper, delivery was to be on demand only ('after due and proper notice . . . of the publication'), and editions subsequent to the first need not be deposited. That was all. On two key points, the Committee made no firm recommendations; they suggested that the House should consider the implications of the verdict in *Cambridge University v. Bryer* (which some might have felt to have been their *raison d'être* in the first place), and that the term of copyright should be extended beyond fourteen years (but without suggesting what this might be). When Giddy opened the debate, he tried to present the results as favourable to the trade, but his ingenuity was not equal to the task.

In fact, the trade had not lost as badly as it might. For the immediate future it was safe enough, because it was almost the end of the Session, and the House merely received the Report and took no action upon it. In the longer term, however, the book trade witnesses had actually contrived to shift the whole ground of the debate about copyright. By concentrating almost entirely on the principle and practice of legal deposit, they had distracted attention from copyright itself, and such potentially embarrassing matters as registration, terms of copyright and the rights of authors.

In the following year, the matter was raised once more, and again by Giddy, who introduced a Bill on 10 May 1814 which, as he said, dealt with the two problems of copyright and deposit. Copyright was to be extended to an unconditional 28 years, which cleared the ambiguity in the 1710 Act about the second 14-year term. On deposit, the eleven copies remained, and they had to be delivered to Stationers' Hall for distribution to the libraries within six months of publication; the only concession to the trade was that subsequent editions need not be deposited unless there were 'material additions'. The Bill was given its First Reading on 12 May.[70]

The Committee Stage began on 18 May, and was to drag on for the better part of two months. During its first two days, some very significant amendments were made to Giddy's original Bill.[71] The first was that all books were to be entered in the Stationers' Register within one month of publication, unless the author and publisher were willing to waive their claim to copyright, which would also, apparently, exempt them from the deposit requirement. Secondly, all the libraries except the British Museum were to be required to pay one-third of the retail price of their books. Finally, the libraries were forbidden to sell the deposit copies within seven years of receiving them. These proposals were far more favourable to the trade than anything recommended by the Select Committee of the previous year, but they underwent further change as the House considered them on Report Stage. The option to waive both copyright and deposit was accepted (on Giddy's own motion), provided that the British Museum was to receive a copy in any case. It was also agreed that the best paper should not be required. The Bill was recommitted for these changes to be incorporated.

The Bill's troubles, however, were only just beginning. At last the other libraries seem to have realized that Cambridge had been trying to defend and promote their common interests, and recognized that the Bill in its amended form was greatly to their advantage, unlike the original proposal from Giddy, or indeed the recommendations of the 1813 Select Committee. On 6 June, Trinity College, Dublin, petitioned for the privilege of giving evidence in favour of the Bill, followed by Edinburgh University and the

Faculty of Advocates on 13 June, Glasgow and St Andrews universities on 15 June, King's College, Aberdeen, on 20 June, and Cambridge itself on 24 June.[72] The flavour of all these petitions is doubtless conveyed by Glasgow's response to the booksellers' original petition in the winter of 1812–13, in which it was argued that deposit was beneficial to the nation as a whole, by preserving its literary heritage, and that the real cost of this to the book trade was minimal.[73] But the response was not unanimous. Oxford and Aberdeen both petitioned to be heard *against* the Bill when the proposal to make the libraries pay for their books became public, as Cambridge had done on the same grounds in the previous year.[74] In the meanwhile, the petitions from booksellers and authors in favour of the extended term of copyright was lost in the general mêlée about the libraries.[75]

By now the whole affair was thoroughly confused. During a further attempt to complete the Committee and Report stages on 12 July, Giddy actually offered to withdraw the Bill, now apparently hopelessly mangled and under assault from all sides, until the next Session, but was persuaded not to do so.[76] Behind this lay a personal tragedy. Giddy was severely depressed following the death of his son a few weeks earlier, and was showing little interest in any of his parliamentary business; the Copyright Bill was the principal victim of this understandable neglect.[77] The Bill survived, but it was by no means certain that it would pass.

Only two days after Giddy had agreed to continue, Sir Egerton Brydges presented to the House a petition from John Valpy, which was intended to revive all the arguments about deposit which the trade had presented to the Select Committee in the previous year. Valpy's petition informed the House that he had collected a subscription of £18,000 for a new edition of Estienne's *Thesaurus*, but that if he had to give eleven copies to the libraries, this would cost him £290 and delay publication while he raised the extra money. Brydges, who had served on the Select Committee in the previous year, and was a firm supporter of the trade in this matter, put the case perhaps too vigorously, for his speech was not well received by the House.[78] Despite this, however, Valpy's petition caused yet another delay, and another tissue of discourse in the growing confusion. Twice more, the Report Stage was resumed, but even when it was, at last, concluded on 18 July, there was still dissent about the deposit clauses. The opponents of deposit seem to have been determined to wreck the Bill, and up to the last minute were proposing schemes to undermine the effect of the deposit requirements.[79]

The Bill was at last sent to the Lords, by now in a thoroughly unsatisfactory condition. The peers made their own contributions to the rising tide of contradiction, by making amendments to the proposed term of copyright. The critical amendments were that there should be an additional fourteen years' protection for any book whose author died within fourteen years of publication, and that, if the author were still alive at the end of the 28-year term, the author or the assignees (that is, presumably, the publishers) should retain the copyright until the author's death.[80] There had been no real discussion of this, and yet it was a crucial innovation, linking the subsistence of copyright for the first time to the lifetime of the author. The Commons amended the detail, but accepted the substance.[81] The Bill received the Royal Assent on 29 July 1814.[82]

After this tortuous passage through Parliament, it is hardly surprising that the 1814 Copyright Act emerged as a thoroughly unsatisfactory law,[83] with at least as many ambiguities and inconsistencies as the 1710 Act which it was intended to clarify and partly replace. The authors had, at the last minute and largely by accident, done quite well out of it. Protection was to be for 28 years, or the lifetime of the author, whichever was the longer. The Lords had, in effect, transformed copyright from a publisher's right to an author's right, a matter which was to be of great significance in the future, although largely ignored at the time.[84] On the deposit question, the libraries had won: the eleven copies were to be sent to Stationers' Hall within a year of publication, and the only exemption was for unaltered reprints. All in all, the trade had not done well in its dealings with politicians between 1808 and 1814. Its main objective had been to persuade Parliament to reverse the verdict in *Cambridge University v. Bryer*, and this it had signally and conspicuously failed to do. Its evidence to the 1813 Select Committee, disingenuous as some of it may have been, had not been without some force, and yet had been completely ignored. The vested interests of the universities, the unfortunate indisposition of Giddy, and the passionate but foolish advocacy of Brydges meant that the battle of the 'library tax' had to be fought all over again.

The libraries, having been made more aware of their rights by the attempt to remove them, became more active in trying to enforce the Act. They also recognized that they had common interests. The Scottish universities jointly paid George Greenhill, the Warehouse

Keeper of the Stationers' Company, to collect their books and send them to Scotland.[85] More generally, in March 1816, the representatives of all the libraries met at Sion College, and agreed to work together for mutual benefit in enforcing the law.[86] This seems to have been the first time that the libraries had tried to cooperate in this way, so that in the immediate aftermath of the 1814 Act we can see the remote origins both of the employment of a London agent by the out-of-town libraries, and of their regular meetings to discuss matters of common concern. In fact, the flow of books to the libraries greatly increased after the summer of 1814, as indeed did the number of registrations at Stationers' Hall. From 1811 to 1814, only 1,235 books had been entered on the Register; from 1815 to 1818, there were 4,353 entries.[87] Between May 1816 and May 1817, some 1,500 items were sent to Cambridge, where many were rejected, and a similar number to Oxford, where almost everything was kept.[88]

It was inevitable that all this activity by the libraries should provoke a response from the trade. Once again, the publishers found their champion in Sir Egerton Brydges who, on 19 June 1817, moved in the House of Commons to amend the 1814 Act. His motion was lost by a single vote in a division of 115 members.[89] The closeness of this vote was, in itself, a danger signal for the libraries. Even more ominous, perhaps, was the line of argument which was beginning to be followed during the debate. Brydges had begun by repeating the oft-heard contention that the need to deposit eleven copies inhibited the publication of worthwhile books because it meant that many of them could not return a profit to their authors and publishers. He added, however, that he knew that he had 'a powerful and widely extended body to deal with',[90] an obvious reference to the lobbying power of the universities. The theme was taken up by another speaker, Henry Brougham, who had already made a name for himself as a promoter and supporter of radical causes.[91] He argued that the Act did nothing to encourage learning; it merely gave free books to 'rich and well endowed bodies'.[92] In fact, Brougham's interest in the matter was one of general political principle rather than a particular concern for the issue itself. He was a strong advocate of free trade, and also of the freedom of the press. He regarded copyright as being a limitation on both, and the requirement to give books to libraries as an intrusion on private property rights.[93] He was supported on all of these grounds by an even more radical free-trader, Sir Francis Burdett, who bluntly told the House that a man should be allowed to enjoy the 'fruits of his labour', and not have them stolen from him by the universities.[94]

Nothing further happened in 1817, but feelings were too strong, and the issues too contentious, for the matter to be forgotten. In March 1818, after various preliminary skirmishings in the House of Commons, Brydges was given leave to bring in a Bill. This he duly did on 16 March. It was concerned with deposit only, and simply proposed to reduce the deposit copies to a number not yet specified.[95] He now mounted a formidable campaign aimed at the vested interests of the libraries and the universities. Of course, he had the support of the trade, but he also attracted more overtly political interests by deploying to great effect some of the arguments which had first been heard in the previous year. Brydges, Brougham and Burdett between them contrived to link the deposit question to the freedom of the press, free trade and the inviolability of private property. Deposit was represented as being in conflict with all three. It was merely an outmoded and unwelcome survival of the attempt to control the press in 1662, in which the deposit of books had first been required by law. It was an invasion of property, by giving books to the universities which rightly belonged to others. It was a restraint on trade and on the market forces which, alone, should regulate it. The systematic statement and repetition of this position made a formidable case.[96]

The libraries swung into action. A petition was received from Oxford on 4 March, before the Bill had even had its First Reading, followed by others from Glasgow (16 March), Cambridge (6 April), the Faculty of Advocates (15 April), Sion College (28 April), Edinburgh (4 May), Trinity (13 May), Aberdeen (14 May), St Andrews (18 May) and another from Glasgow (19 May).[97] All were to the same effect. When Parliament had thoroughly discussed the matter in 1813 and 1814, it had reached the conclusion embodied in the 1814 Act and there was no need for any further consideration. This, however, was not a view shared by the trade. Almost all of the leading firms in the London trade were involved in petitions for reform, led by Longmans for the well-established publishers and Lackingtons for some of the more recent firms on 6 April, and Cadell and Davies two days later.[98] Within a week, booksellers, printers, authors and engravers had all added their voices to the chorus calling for a change in the law, and on 13 April the House ordered that the Minutes of Evidence from the 1813 Select Committee should be reprinted.[99] The Bill was given its Second Reading on 17 April, but, before it could begin its Committee Stage, which had been scheduled for 27 April, a Select

Committee had been appointed to investigate the whole business yet again.[100]

The 1818 Select Committee was even more thorough than its predecessors of five years earlier. This time, however, the trade did not have the field to itself, and the libraries made a much more public case for the retention of their privileges. They had indeed good cause to be worried. The issue at stake was clear: it was deposit, and deposit alone, for copyright itself was not raised at any stage. The trade had assembled a formidable case and formidable supporters, and had Brydges to help them to present the former and to orchestrate the latter.[101] The petition from Lackington and his partners set the tone. They gave six examples of books 'of which they are engaged in the publication' and of the cost of depositing eleven copies of each of them, which they claimed would be £2,454. 7*s*. 6*d*. The examples were very carefully chosen. All were learned works of the very kind which the 1710 and 1814 Acts were allegedly designed to encourage. To refer to Philip Bliss's new edition of Wood's *Athenae Oxoniensis*, which had been appearing since 1813, was a particularly cruel blow aimed at the universities.[102]

The Select Committee began its work on 27 April,[103] and even its composition seemed to favour the trade over the libraries. Of the 21 members, three, Brydges, Wynne and Giddy [now Gilbert], had been advocates of reform since 1813 or even 1808. Others could be relied upon to support them and therefore the trade. Joseph Butterworth was no radical, but since 1793 he had been the proprietor of the publishing house which had inherited the remains of the law patent; he was a major force in legal publishing, and also active in the public affairs of the trade.[104] Across the political spectrum was the Whig author, Sir James Mackintosh, a regular contributor to *The Edinburgh Review*, an outspoken defender of press freedom and a man with a wide range of literary interests.[105] In addition, there were at least five others who, from a generally Whig or radical stance, might be expected to support the publishers' case if it were reasonably well-presented.[106] One of them, John Lambton, was close to Brougham, and had important links with the press as one of the intermediaries between the Whig leadership and the London newspapers, and it was indeed he who presented the booksellers' petition to the House on 9 April 1818.[107]

On the other hand, there were some hard-line Tories who opposed change of any kind as a matter of principle,[108] but also, crucially, six men with direct links with the libraries. Henry

Bankes, M.P. for Corfe Castle, was a Trustee of the British Museum.[109] There were no fewer than five university members on the Committee: William Scott and Robert Peel (Oxford), Lord Palmerston and J. H. Smyth (Cambridge), and William Plunkett (Trinity).[110] Smyth had been active in the cause of Cambridge University Library in 1813–14, but the most politically significant among them was Peel, who had already made his name as Chief Secretary for Ireland. Clearly the trade was not going to have an unchallenged passage.

Most of the first five days on which the Committee sat were taken up with hearing witnesses from the book trade. Their well-presented evidence had clearly been coordinated in advance. Much of what they said was familiar, merely adding to the examples adduced in 1808, 1813 and 1814 yet more cases of expensive and learned works whose profitability had been, or could have been, fatally affected by the deposit laws. They concentrated on the effect of the 1814 Act which, they claimed, had made matters worse.[111] A more original reinforcement came from the antiquary, Samuel Lysons, a distinguished scholar of Roman Britain who, among other achievements, published the first adequate account of the site at Woodmanchester.[112] His masterpiece, however, was *Reliquae Britannico-Romano*, originally published in two volumes in 1801 and 1817, with a three-volume edition published between 1813 and 1817. This lavish and elaborately illustrated book was published in only 50 copies, at a price of £48. 6*s*. 0*d*.[113] Lysons testified that several libraries had subscribed before 1814, but that now the book had to be deposited they no longer did so. As a consequence, he proposed to have the large-paper copies printed abroad so that he did not have to deposit them and thus lose income.[114] At last the trade seemed to have produced a witness who could actually prove that he had lost money because of the legal deposit laws.

A whole succession of witnesses laboured the same point, although less convincingly. Specialist publishers in fields as different as law and architecture claimed that their businesses had been damaged, and it was argued that the trade in general had suffered very badly since 1814. The case seemed formidable, assuming that it was possible to ascribe all of these undoubted ills to the 1814 Copyright Act in general and to legal deposit in particular. The trade's position was eloquently summarized by Brydges: '. . . this Tax then is a blight to production. It nips the most valuable fruits of literature in the bud.'[115]

The libraries, however, did not neglect their own defence, and they were able to benefit from their experience of working together since 1814. Their arguments were as predictable as those of the trade, although slightly less familiar since they had not formally presented them in 1813. In general terms, they claimed that good libraries were a benefit to the public in general and scholars in particular. William Webb, Vice-Chancellor of Cambridge, Thomas Gaisford, Regius Professor of Greek at Oxford, and H. H. Baber, Keeper of Printed Books at the British Museum, all played variations on this theme.[116] All of them took some trouble to prepare their cases; Oxford discussed the matter with Peel, and Webb even went into print to recall the alleged agreement between the trade and Villiers in 1808, a recollection which Villiers confirmed in his evidence to the Select Committee.[117] Several library witnesses emphasized the extent to which the libraries were used, and the deposited books therefore useful to scholars and the general public. None of this really answered the trade's case, except perhaps in making public statements that the libraries appreciated the books, and that they were indeed used. The latter point was supported by a few independent witnesses, one of whom was Edward Christian who, in a sense, had started the whole affair.[118]

Christian, the last witness, was heard on 8 May 1818, but it was not until 5 June that the Select Committee took its Report to the House. It was not the definitive and conclusive document which might have been expected after such a detailed investigation; indeed, it reflected rather the fundamentally divided membership of the Committee itself.[119] There were three straightforward recommendations. First, deposit was not to be required if copyright were waived by the author and the publisher. Secondly, plate books (that is, books consisting wholly or largely of engraved plates) need be sent only to the British Museum. Thirdly, printers were no longer required to keep the copy formerly required under the Seditious Societies Act of 1799. None of this, of course, addressed the central issue of the eleven deposit copies, and when it came to consider that matter the Select Committee was unable to make a single recommendation. Instead, it suggested alternatives. It was proposed either that only the British Museum should be a deposit library, and the other libraries should receive an annual grant instead of their books, or that deposit should be limited to the British Museum, the Bodleian, Cambridge University and Trinity College, Dublin. The Select Committee had been hopelessly and irreconcilably divided. Smyth revealed during the subsequent debate in the House that all of the resolutions had been carried by small majorities, and one by Chairman's casting vote.[120] The elephant had laboured to bring forth a mouse. The House received the Report and then ignored it completely.

The fiasco of 1818 is perhaps more significant for the long delay which it probably caused in the reform of the law of copyright than for its place in the history of legal deposit. To those in the book trade who truly believed that the 'library tax' was a serious inhibition on their businesses, the Report was, no doubt, a devastating blow. On the other side, the libraries could take little comfort; they had almost certainly been saved by influence rather than by the strength of their case. Bad relations between the two sides continued. In 1819, the Booksellers' Committee, the representative body of the leading members of the London book trade, was unsuccessful in its attempt to persuade the House of Commons to reopen the matter,[121] and had to content itself with harassing the universities about their printing privileges.[122] The 1826 Royal Commission on the Scottish universities suggested that it would be to their advantage to accept money instead of books, but nothing was done.[123] Great issues were in hand, and these matters were of little general importance.

By the mid-1830s, however, the political climate had changed. Apparently immutable institutions, including the House of Commons itself, had been reformed, and the most venerable of bodies were no longer exempt from the pressure for change. The English universities, in particular, with their accumulated wealth and apparent power, were well within the purview of the reformers. In 1836, the House of Commons once again turned its attention to the question of legal deposit. Again, the initiative came from the radical side. The motion to introduce a Bill was proposed by James Silk Buckingham, M.P. for Sheffield, one of the seats created in the Reform Act of 1832. He was a social reformer and a temperance advocate; he was also strongly identified with the cause of the freedom of the press and with the long campaign to abolish the stamp duties on newspapers.[124] In raising the question of legal deposit in the House on 28 April 1836, Buckingham linked it with the other 'taxes on knowledge', not yet abolished but drastically reduced just a few weeks earlier. He urged complete abolition of legal deposit, arguing that the nation was 'rich enough to buy the books it requires'. Opposition was feeble. Spring Rice, the Chancellor of the Exchequer, gave his support for a scheme to offer financial compensation to the libraries. A Bill was brought in and given its First Reading.[125]

The first version of the Bill did indeed abolish legal deposit altogether, and this provoked some protests. It was duly amended in Committee, but still emerged as a fairly radical measure.[126] The amended Bill preserved the deposit privileges of the British Museum and the English universities, but abolished those of the other libraries. By way of compensation, each library was to receive an annual sum equal to the average annual value of the books which they had actually received in the years 1833 to 1836.[127] After some minor problems with the compensation clauses, there were no further difficulties in Committee. The Faculty of Advocates and Trinity College, Dublin, were, however, restored to the list of deposit libraries during the last days of the Committee Stage. It was thus in this form that the Bill reached the Lords, who dealt with it in three days.[128] It received the Royal Assent on 20 August 1836.[129]

The 1836 Act set the pattern for British legal deposit for the future, and also cleared the way for a serious reconsideration of the law of copyright itself. The last phase of the battle of the library tax was as quiet as the earlier phases had been noisy. In 1836, the trade was, apparently, silent, while the universities were supine. This was not indolence. Buckingham argued the case on grounds which were fundamentally different from those put forward in 1808, 1814 or 1818. The 1836 Act is merely one part of the whole process of the reform of the British state in the middle decades of the nineteenth century. Even the British Museum and the English universities were not ultimately to escape from these changes. For the radicals, the reform of the law of legal deposit was one small part of a far larger campaign for political, social and economic change.

In theory, there was no reason why legal deposit should not have been treated as a separate issue from copyright since 1836, and indeed to a large extent it has been. Traditional associations were strong, however, and when the law of copyright was, at last, reformed in 1842, legal deposit was, without controversy, confirmed there, and incorporated into the Act.[130] Throughout the rest of the nineteenth century, the issue rarely surfaced. When it did so, it was always in the context of the further reform of the law of copyright. This was especially so during the sittings of the Royal Commission on Copyright in 1875, and subsequent events.[131] In its Report, the Commission actually recommended that deposit privileges be withdrawn from all the libraries except the British Museum, but when the abortive Bill to give force to the Commission's recommendations appeared in 1878, all five libraries had reappeared thanks to effective lobbying.[132]

By that time, although there was still some resentment from publishers, for the most part legal deposit was widely accepted and generally obeyed. In the early 1850s, Sir Anthony Panizzi, the formidable Director of the British Museum, made a serious and sustained effort to enforce the Museum's rights under the 1842 Act, and was largely successful.[133] Support came from the Bodleian,[134] and all the libraries eventually benefited from the vigilance of these two. Shortly afterwards, the Copyright Agency was established with the help of Panizzi, so that the other four libraries had a permanent representative in London as a channel for obtaining their books.[135]

Despite the apparently smooth operation of the system during the second half of the nineteenth century, and the comparative ease with which the spectre of abolition had been vanquished in 1875–78, the libraries (other than the British Museum) were always in a slightly vulnerable position. Whenever copyright law was under consideration, the whole question of legal deposit might be raised again. This happened in 1910–11, when the proposals which became the 1911 Copyright Act were under discussion.[136] The problem arose out of the anomalous position of the National Library of Wales which had been established in 1907, and for which the deposit privilege was now claimed by its Trustees.[137] Sydney Buxton, the President of the Board of Trade, who was responsible for the Bill, was unsympathetic, but a long memorandum argued the case in detail.[138] The issue of the National Library of Wales reopened the whole question of legal deposit, and some of the publishers leapt upon it. The Joint Copyright Committee of the Publishers' Association, the Society of Authors and the Copyright Association objected specifically to the addition of a sixth library,[139] but others went further, and it was only after active lobbying from both Oxford and Cambridge that a revived proposal to remove the privilege from all the libraries except the British Museum was defeated.[140]

Under the 1911 Act, which is substantially unamended in this respect and is the basis of the current legal deposit law in the United Kingdom, the British Museum has an absolute and automatic right to a copy of every new book, or revised edition, in the 'best' version (i.e. on the best paper, with coloured illustrations, etc. where relevant), to be delivered within one month of publication.[141] The other five libraries must claim their copies within six months of publication. Until the late 1970s, as a result of a compromise reached in 1911, the National Library of Wales could only claim material in Welsh or of Welsh or Celtic interest. The most striking anomaly is that Trinity College, Dublin, is still a U.K. legal deposit library, despite the fact that it has not been part of the United Kingdom since 1922. By way of reciprocation, Irish publishers are obliged to deposit copies at the five U.K. libraries.[142] Some minor modifications have also been made about the kind of material covered by deposit law, but otherwise it has remained substantially unchanged. Two historic names have, however, vanished. The first was in Edinburgh. After the National Library of Scotland was established in 1926, it took over the deposit privilege of the Faculty of Advocates (except for law books) partly because the Faculty could no longer afford to maintain its library on such a scale.[143] The second change was in London. When the British Library was formed out of the library departments of the British Museum and various other libraries in 1973, it took over the deposit privilege which the Museum itself had inherited from the Royal Library on its own foundation in 1754.

For a few years in the early nineteenth century, legal deposit was a critical, although negative, factor in the development of copyright in Britain. From 1808 to 1836 it occupied the centre of the stage whenever copyright was discussed in the press or in Parliament. By an historical accident the two were linked, and the link has never been entirely broken. Deposit was, however, never again to be the major issue which it became during the first three decades of the nineteenth century. Once it was settled, it was possible to turn to the ever more urgent matter of devising a law of copyright which was appropriate for a prosperous industrial society with a world-wide empire and an international language. It was that task to which the legislators turned when the battle of the library tax was, effectively, brought to an end in 1836.

5 The Reform of the Law 1800–1842

At the beginning of the nineteenth century, the United Kingdom had a pragmatic, but ambiguous, law of copyright. In the ninety years which had elapsed since the only substantive piece of copyright legislation had been approved by Parliament, a series of decisions in the courts had established a body of precedent in the interpretation of the law which made it broadly acceptable to most of those involved with it. The general understanding of copyright was that it was a means by which the owner of a piece of property could protect that property from the depredations of anyone who sought to steal it. It was also understood that, although copyright was created by an author, it was normally exercised by a publisher to whom the author had granted the right to do so in return for payment. In one respect only did copyright differ from other property rights: it ceased to exist when 14, or in some circumstances 28, years had elapsed from the first publication of the work, and then became common property which could be freely used by anyone.

The conservative legal position, however, has to be put in a broader context. The decision of the House of Lords in *Becket v. Donaldson* was more than merely a landmark in legal history.[1] It reflected a growing awareness of the author as the creator of 'literary property' and as a partner with the publisher in the ownership of it. Nevertheless, it is the social role of the author, and the social usefulness of literature, which is constantly emphasized. The 'encouragement of learning' may have originally been little more than a blanket of respectability to cover the naked commercialism of the late seventeenth- and early eighteenth-century booksellers, but it had become the core of the argument about literary property by the mid-1770s. Even so, copyright remained, as it had always been, an important property right because of its commercial value. The changes in the book trade in the late eighteenth and early nineteenth centuries merely emphasized that importance, and made authors more aware of their role in the creation of valuable properties. As authors became more powerful, they too began to take an interest in copyright matters.

In the eighteenth century, a few authors had indeed exploited the law.[2] They were exceptional, but far more writers began to benefit from the exertions of these few, as the relationships between authors and publishers changed. By 1800, the mutual dependence of authors and publishers was recognized on both sides, for in the aftermath of *Becket v. Donaldson* the publishers needed a constant stream of new books if they were to continue to make profits from works protected by the law. At the same time, the phenomenal growth of circulating libraries, the further development of a nationwide network of bookshops, and the continuing growth of newspapers and of the periodical press created a huge market from which authors and publishers alike could benefit. Moreover, publishers could take advantage of, and indeed had to exploit, wide-ranging technological developments both within and beyond the book trade. The harnessing of steam power to printing, which began in the second decade of the nineteenth century, was a major influence in reducing the price of books while vastly increasing their numbers. At the same time, machine-made paper became available in huge quantities, and at prices far lower than its hand-made predecessor. From the 1830s onwards, like all distributive trades, the book trade was further transformed by the opening of the railway network, and the infinitely greater ease of both distribution and travel which that allowed.[3] As the book trade became more prosperous, authors sought their share in its prosperity.[4]

Even the legal theorists recognized the justice of the authors' claims. Robert Maugham, lawyer and legal journalist, was the author of one of the first English books to deal with the law of copyright.[5] His *Treatise on the Laws of Literary Property*, published in 1828, took a very conservative view of both law and practice. Maugham could see no reason to distinguish between literary property and any other kind, and regarded the decision in *Becket v. Donaldson* as an unwelcome innovation.[6] When he comes to 'the principles of the laws', this conservatism becomes even more overt. His premise was that copyright was in words, not in ideas, a point already accepted by the courts.[7] But common ownership must be carefully defined, for which he used a homely metaphor: 'The wells of literature are open to all, but no one has the right to use the bucket of another.'[8] While conceding the need to allow reprinting of old books which are in constant demand, Maugham could see no reason for depriving authors and their families of income for the sake of a legal theory: 'Authors are not a peculiar race of men able to live on the air.'[9]

By the time that Maugham wrote those words, the law had already accepted the role of the author in the creation of literary property. The Copyright Act of 1814 had extended the term of copyright to 28 years or the lifetime of the author, whichever was the longer, and thus put the author at the very centre of the whole arrangement.[10] Because this change had been buried in the seemingly endless and introspective arguments about legal deposit, there had never been a full public debate on the principles involved, and it was perhaps inevitable that there should be.

By the mid-1830s, there were those who felt that the time had come to change the law, and that the general climate of opinion would favour such changes. There was, indeed, some evidence for that. In 1833, the Dramatic Copyright Act had, for the first time, given protection for the performance as well as for the publication of a text.[11] The basic provision was that the owner of the rights (the dramatist or other legal owner) had to give permission, and by implication receive payment, for every performance which took place within 28 years of the first performance, or during the dramatist's lifetime, whichever was the longer. The derivation of the Act from the 1814 Copyright Act is obvious and was deliberate. In effect, it created a second set of rights in a play, for the author could now sell the performing rights to a producer as well as the copyright to a publisher. The Act had passed, with little opposition, within a year of the first formal proposal.

The relatively easy acceptance of the Dramatic Copyright Act of 1833 is an important reminder that the *principle* of attaching copyright to the author, and indeed to his lifespan, was no longer questioned. The issue was a rather different one, which extended yet further the principle that authors had a right to enjoy the fruits of their labours. Even the conservative theorist, Maugham, implied this, although it was in an example upon which he did not expand:

> The author's and bookseller's interests are inseparable . . . Archbishop Tillotson died in mean circumstances, and if it had not been for a copy of his sermons sold to the booksellers, his family might have been under the necessity of perhaps applying in vain for relief to their country.[12]

Maugham's implication was clear: it was a case for the posthumous survival of the author's rights, perhaps as close as he dared to come to making a case for the restoration of perpetual copyrights for which he seems to have hankered.

Posthumous rights were first proposed in 1837, and became the central issue in the debate for the next five years. The campaign was publicly opened by T. N. Talfourd, M.P. for Reading, who, on 18 May, was given leave by the House of Commons to bring in a Bill to extend the term of copyright. The proposed extension was radical indeed. There were two elements in it. The first was that all new books, and all existing books by living authors, were to be protected for the author's lifetime and for 60 years thereafter.[13] The second proposal was perhaps even more radical, for it was that the copyrights in books by living authors which had been assigned to others (normally, of course, a publisher) were to revert to the author after the expiry of their 28-year protection under the 1814 Act, and thereafter to be protected as other books were now to be, that is for the author's lifetime plus 60 years. Between them, these two proposals left no room for doubt that copyright was an author's right, and that it was a right for his family and heirs as much as for the author himself.

This was indeed a remarkable proposal, and it was the work of a remarkable man. Thomas Noon Talfourd was a lawyer who was successful enough in his profession to become a judge, but whose real passion in life was literature.[14] He was an author himself, and enjoyed a brief celebrity with his tragedy, *Ion*, in 1835. More significant in this context, however, was his admiration for Charles Lamb, which verged upon hero-worship. This brought him into Lamb's literary circle in the 1820s and 1830s, and thus into contact with many of the leading writers of the day. They respected him. By the time he became involved in the copyright question, he was already regarded by Carlyle as a 'most polite and humane man',[15] and by Wordsworth as 'my friend Serjeaunt Talfourd'.[16] These connections, forged through his work on Lamb's literary remains, were to prove crucial throughout the copyright campaign.

As an author and a friend of authors, Talfourd was surely aware of the growing concern about copyright in the literary world, a concern which was particularly marked in Wordsworth. Indeed, it seems likely that it was Wordsworth who was the immediate inspiration for the 1837 Bill and therefore for the agitation which followed. Certainly, he was a key figure in the events of the next five years.[17] Wordsworth's concern about the rights of authors was of many years' standing. As early as 1808, he had written that:

The law, as it now stands, merely consults the interest of the useful drudges of Literature, or of flimsy and shallow writers . . . real men of power . . . are deprived of all hope of their families being benefited by their exertions.[18]

The 1814 Act did not satisfy him; in 1819, he still felt that 'The wrongs of literary men are crying out for redress on all sides. It appears to me that towards no class of his Majesty's Subjects are the laws so unjust and oppressive.'[19] Others might have disagreed in the year of Peterloo and the Six Acts, but there was no doubting the strength of Wordsworth's feelings.

As he grew older, these feelings became even stronger, and even more overtly mercenary, as one expression of his general worries about financial matters and what would happen to his dependants after his death. Towards the end of 1836 he had written to his publisher, Edward Moxon, that 'the state of the commercial world does not leave me free from anxiety'.[20] Looking back on his own career, he was able to see how long it had been before he had an established reputation and a reasonable income. In 1835, nearly 40 years after the publication of *Lyrical Ballads*, his income from his books was just £200, although over the next three years this actually went up to about £500 a year. One of the reasons for not publishing *The Prelude* during his lifetime was that he wanted its posthumous publication to guarantee some income for his family.[21] The proposal for a 60-year posthumous term of copyright was a solution to the very problem which was of such concern to Wordsworth, and, given his association with Talfourd, it is impossible to believe that he was not privy to it. Indeed, when success seemed possible (fleetingly, as we shall see) in 1838, he wrote, 'I may claim some credit . . . for the pain which I have taken for many years, to interest men in the H[ouse] of C[ommons] in the extension of the term of copyright'.[22]

Certainly, when he introduced his Bill to the House, Talfourd concentrated in his speech on the very preoccupations which were of such pressing concern to Wordsworth.[23] First, he argued that the existing law, whose history he recounted at some length, was unfair to authors, because it prevented them from making proper provisions for their families, or even for their own old age. Talfourd, like Maugham, took a deeply conservative line on the theory of copyright law; he regarded the limited term, however extended the limitation might be, as an infringement of the natural rights of the property owner, what he called, in a revised version of the speech published shortly afterwards, a 'limitation of the ancient rights of authorship'.[24] Secondly, Talfourd argued that the law encouraged writers to go for short-term success rather than long-term merit, another matter about which Wordsworth was increasingly adamant. In the Preface to the published version of his speech, Talfourd was explicit about how he proposed to redress this grievance: '. . . one object of the Act is to secure to the descendants of authors . . . the benefit of their works beyond the subsisting term.'[25] If Wordsworth was seeking a champion, it seemed that he had found him.

Talfourd was later to claim that this Bill failed to become law only because of the unexpected dissolution of Parliament caused by the death of William IV on 20 June. This, he said, gave the opponents of his proposals time to muster their forces and marshall their arguments by the time that the new House returned to the matter.[26] This may have been a little disingenuous, for the opposition was already vociferous when the Bill was given its Second Reading on 28 June, just before the dissolution.[27] If it had been truly uncontroversial, it could have been rushed through in the dying days of the old Parliament, but the book trade had already gone into action, and it was clear that no such Bill could have an easy passage.

The first publisher who openly attacked Talfourd's Bill was Thomas Tegg, whom the supporters of copyright law reform were to come to regard as the symbol of opposition. Tegg was an interesting and successful, but by no means typical, publisher, who had built a business which could not survive the sort of extension of the term of copyright now proposed. He was a Londoner by birth, but was largely brought up in Scotland. He had tried various unsuccessful enterprises in the newspaper and book trades there, but returned to his native city, and established himself as a bookseller and publisher in Cheapside in 1805. In his new shop he built, at last, a successful business. He was a publisher of cheap and popular books, allegedly publishing some 4,000 titles during a long career.[28] His trade was particularly dependent on reprints and abridgements; the reprints were, in their turn, dependent on the existing law of copyright which allowed him to publish public domain copies while they were still of interest to the book-buying public. A massive extension of the term of copyright, and particularly the proposal for a retrospective *post mortem* term, would have killed the most lucrative part of Tegg's trade at a stroke.

Naturally enough, this was not quite how Tegg presented his case when he responded publicly to Talfourd's Bill in the early summer of 1837. In a pamphlet dedicated to Peel he put the case in terms of 'public advantage, not private reward'.[29] In essence, he argued that cheap reprints, such as those which he published, were generally beneficial, especially at a time when a more educated public was looking for more reading matter. Coleridge and Wordsworth, and their like, he argued, were for the 'enlightened few', not the masses whom he and others sought to serve.[30] He could see no evidence that the existing law was in any way inhibiting creativity, or indeed the publishing of new books. Certainly, he wrote, no one had complained to him that there were not enough new books being published, despite the alleged discouragements to literature in the existing copyright law. Talfourd may have been supported by a few authors, but he 'was not backed by petitions from Circulating Libraries and Book Societies, complaining of the paucity of new books'.[31] The mild irony emphasized the strength of his case. Talfourd's proposal is 'a great injustice to all booksellers',[32] who carry all the risks of publication, and are now to find their investments taken from them by authors.

It was good polemic, and not without force, but the dissolution of Parliament meant that Talfourd did not have to reply at once. By the following year he was, perhaps, better prepared to face the mounting opposition to his proposals.

When the new Parliament met, Talfourd was, in due course, given leave to bring in a new Bill on copyright. This he did on 14 December 1837.[33] In its main provisions, it was the same as the Bill which had been lost in June, although it was now confined to books, and no longer concerned itself with plays, engravings and other printed matter. This point, for some reason, particularly commended itself to Peel, who was one of the speakers in the subsequent debate.[34] The essence of the Bill was, however, unchanged from 1837. The key point was that copyright in both new and existing books was to subsist for the author's lifetime and 60 years thereafter. If a copyright were assigned by the author to someone else, the assignment was for the author's lifetime or for 28 years, whichever was the longer. There was one important, if complicated, new proposal: five years after the author's death, or five years after the expiry of the 28 years if the author were still alive, anyone could apply to the Court of Chancery for permission to reprint the work. Talfourd never explained the purpose of this, but it was presumably intended to answer those critics who argued that the effect of the reversion of copyrights, and of the 60-year term, was to restrict the reprinting of books which were in demand and thus increase their prices. Other clauses confirmed the existing deposit laws, made rules for registration at Stationers' Hall, provided for penalties against the import of foreign piracies, brought performing rights into line with the copyright proposals by conferring them for the writer's lifetime plus 60 years, and extended British law to all British overseas dominions.

The debate in the House cannot have been much to Talfourd's liking. His own arguments were, of course, much as they had been in the previous summer, but another issue now raised its head which was a complicating factor. Two members, one of whom was the novelist Bulwer-Lytton, spoke of the need to prevent the import of French piracies of British books, a matter of considerable concern to both authors and publishers at this time. Indeed, it was quite possibly of greater general interest in both the trade and in the literary world at large than was Talfourd's proposal to extend the term of domestic copyright. The need to restrain such piracies was to lead to legislation in the following year, with none of the difficulty which attended the reform of the domestic law. It was a matter in which Talfourd had little interest.[35] The support for his Bill, meanwhile, was only a little more helpful than these foreign diversions; Peel was, at best, ambiguous, and Disraeli, the only other speaker, although he was inordinately proud of his speech, still carried little weight as a politician.[36] Nevertheless, leave was given to bring in a Bill, and it was given a formal First Reading on 28 February, with the Second Reading fixed for 11 April;[37] it was not an impossible timetable.

Long before April, however, the whole proposal had run into very serious difficulties both inside and outside the House. The book trade took concerted action to oppose the Bill in every particular. As the date of the Second Reading approached, the House found itself confronted with a number of petitions against the Bill, and they continued to come in throughout April and May. Almost all of them were from printers, both masters and men, and they came from all over the country. Printers from London, Wolverhampton, Carlisle, Leicester, Glasgow, Edinburgh, Sheffield, Aberdeen, Worcester, Liverpool and Oxford were among those who contributed to this torrent of paper. On the day of the Second Reading, postponed eventually to 25 April, came the largest of all, from dozens of London and provincial printers.[38]

The outpouring of opposition from the printers was no coincidence. It was carefully coordinated lobbying designed to kill Talfourd's proposal once and for all. On 5 April 1838, the committee of the Association of Master Printers met under the chairmanship of Andrew Spottiswoode to prepare and sign a petition to the House. This Association was of recent origin. It had been formed in 1836, largely for the purpose of negotiating with the newly founded London Union of Compositors about rates of pay for journeymen. Nevertheless, it included among its objectives 'the purpose of protecting the general interests of the trade', and proved a useful vehicle for opposing the Bill at a time when the publishers had no comparable body of their own.[39]

The Association's petition, which was that tabled on the day set for the Second Reading debate, denied that any reform of the law was needed. The law, according to the Master Printers, was intended to encourage the publication of good books, and this Bill would actually inhibit that objective by causing the increase in prices which is the inevitable consequence of any monopoly. The extension of the term in the 1814 Act is dismissed as a mere device: 'an attempt (though an unsuccessful one) by the Universities to reconcile the London booksellers . . . to the contribution of eleven copies'.[40] The perception is more important than the historical fact, for it allowed the petitioners to argue that the existing period of protection was adequate, and already twice as long as that for inventions. From this, they concluded that the Bill would merely create an expensive monopoly, which would, in turn, cause unemployment in their trade, without conferring any benefit on authors.

This, at least, was the public presentation of the printers' case. Privately, they were less circumspect. In a document circulated to members of the Association with the text of the petition, the case was amplified and presented rather differently.[41] There is little pretence of public interest. In the view of the writer, the Bill is fundamentally unjust, giving 'an additional endowment to Authors' at the expense of publishers, printers and booksellers. This, he says, has happened at a time when the printing trade is under great pressure. Technical innovations, especially machine printing and stereotyping, have changed the economics of printing, to the disadvantage of printers, but 'from these inventions . . . the Public reaped immediate and much advantage', presumably because of the cheaper books which they made possible. He puts the case for competition rather than monopoly:

The judicious and proper publication of any one particular book is as much a personal invention as the manuscript of the book itself; and if two or more Publishers can compete in their inventions, will not the Public reap the benefit?

He concludes that if Talfourd's Bill passes in its present form, many of the cheap reprints and abridgements will be illegal, 'thus sadly reducing the number of cheap and really readable books'. There was a good deal of self-interest here, but also an element of truth. Books had indeed become significantly cheaper in the last few years, largely as a result of the new technologies to which the anonymous author referred.[42] It was, no doubt, tactically wise not to publish this document more widely, but it vividly illustrates the fact that strength of feeling was not confined to one side as the issues in the copyright debate were adumbrated during the next four years.

The opposition to Talfourd was not confined to the printers. Various lines of argument were deployed. Robert Mudie, a hack writer who was to die destitute,[43] argued that great writers did not write for money, but for the sake of literature, and, more pertinently, that a book was worthless to an author until he had found a publisher to publish it for him. This, he claimed, invalidated Talfourd's claim for the natural rights of authors, for those rights cannot exist until he has sold the manuscript. In effect, Mudie wrote, Talfourd was proposing the transfer of a monopoly from one group of people – the publishers – to another, the authors.[44] It is possible, of course, that Mudie was put up to this by the publishers for whom he worked, but nevertheless his argument is not without interest. It is a variation on a theme which had already been played in the House of Commons in 1837: that Talfourd was being driven by a handful of literary authors, whose concerns were quite different from those of the vast majority of writers who produced the books which appealed to large numbers of readers.

Mudie's case was certainly thought worthy of refutation. The author of *Areopagitica Secunda* substantially accepted Talfourd's argument, and which was also Wordsworth's contention: '. . . the *trial* of the merits of a book, which is eight-and-twenty years, is much too short for the attainment of the ends of literary justice.'[45] An anonymous 'Friend to Authors' went much further. He countered Mudie by arguing that authors were obliged to use publishers whether they wanted to or not, and that proper protection for them and their families will encourage the writing of books. The 'Friend' indeed goes rather further than Talfourd was ever prepared to do in public, by advocating the restoration of perpetual copyright, so that his work, too, reveals some of the more extreme parameters of the developing discourse.[46]

The political dimension of this discourse was also being revealed more clearly than it had been in 1837.[47] Talfourd was aware of the growing partisan opposition to his proposals, and of the source of it. He wrote to Wordsworth as early as 21 March 1838 that 'the Doctrinaire party are inclined to support' the book trade.[48] The 'Doctrinaire party', the free traders and radicals, were indeed to be consistent opponents of the extension of copyright. The mainstream Whigs, however, were also under pressure. Yet another anonymous pamphlet from 1838 was explicit on this point.[49] It was dedicated to Lord John Russell, and begins by arguing that since the Bill will create a new monopoly, the author is surprised to find such reforming Whigs as Spring Rice, the Chancellor of the Exchequer (who had seconded Talfourd's motion in the spring of 1837), supporting it. The free trade case is made forcefully and without disguise:

> The descendants of authors can have no right to reclaim any successful authorship which may have been produced by a deceased relative, and formerly sold at its marketable value, and published at the expense and risk of another.[50]

The rights of property owners and the claims of authors were, once again, presented in conflict with each other.

It was against this background of mounting opposition, public and private, commercial and political, that Talfourd approached the Second Reading. Wordsworth had been quietly confident during the winter, although not inactive. In a letter of 4 January 1838,[51] he acknowledged that Bulwer-Lytton and others had identified a genuine problem about the foreign piracies, and says that he has indeed spoken to some M.P.s about this, including Peel. It was, however, his view that piracy could wait until the extension of the term of the domestic copyright had been dealt with. This lordly complacency was not punctured for some time. In a postscript to a letter to his publisher, Edward Moxon, on 5 February 1838, he wrote, almost casually: 'Have you any reason for believing that Sergeant Talfourd's motion will meet with any opposition in the House – at all formidable.'[52] Moxon may or may not have known the answer to Wordsworth's question, but after receiving Talfourd's letter of 21 March, Wordsworth himself can have been left in no doubt.[53] On 23 March he wrote to two other M.P.s seeking their support. One was Gladstone, still a Tory at that time, and the other was Sir William Gomm, an influential army officer with a wide range of connections in both the literary and the political worlds.[54]

By mid-April, Wordsworth was, at last, aware of the enormity of the storm which he and Talfourd had unleashed. Perhaps unconsciously echoing his earlier letter to Moxon, he wrote to Dorothy that there was 'formidable opposition' to the Bill, adding, perhaps a little petulantly, that 'if other persons . . . had done half as much as I had, it would be carried to a certainty'.[55] The same petulance can perhaps be detected in a letter to Peel, a supporter, if a lukewarm one, at about the same time: '. . . if the bill do not pass . . . I shall be aggrieved in the most tender points.'[56] That letter was written on 18 April, between the original and newly set dates of the Second Reading, and by that time the dangers were only too obvious. Even so, Wordsworth drew back from what might have been thought to be the obvious course of action: to petition Parliament himself. What he did do was to make his views public through the medium of an open letter, printed first in *The Kendal Mercury*, and then reprinted as a separate pamphlet as *The Law of Copyright*.[57]

Wordsworth was actually responding to the printers of the newspaper, who were themselves opposed to the Bill.[58] In an open covering letter to Talfourd, he explained that he was working on behalf of all authors, not merely himself, and that this is why he has been reluctant to make 'this public declaration of my judgment'. He now does so because of the importance of the issue. He points out that Coleridge died a poor man, that even Southey has made little money, and that he himself is not rich. He admits that 'the profits of a season' are probably all that most authors can hope for, and indeed are all that most books deserve. On the other hand, books of real worth deserve more than 28 years of protection, and authors and their families have a claim in natural justice to enjoy the profits, such as they are, of their works. The tone is unashamedly élitist; it is little wonder that, in a letter to Southey two weeks later, Wordsworth admitted that he had little desire to 'fall prey to Mr Tegg'.[59]

When the Second Reading debate was finally held on 25 April, the worst fears of Talfourd and Wordsworth were not immediately realized. This was undoubtedly partly because, for once, Talfourd made a good speech. In general, he was not a particularly inspired speaker, and it seems that he rarely commanded the full attention of the House, but in 1838, he rose to the occasion which he had created. He argued the case, as he always had, on the grounds of natural justice, and in doing so revealed yet again his inherently conservative approach to copyright law. He did, however, make some concessions to the rising tide of opposition inside and outside Parliament, by trying to present the Bill as an attempt to introduce greater equity into the relationship of publishers and authors, by sharing profits between them. At the core of his argument, however, was the need to help authors: 'The question is not one of reward – it is one of justice . . . On what principle is Mr Tegg to retain what was denied to Sir Walter?'[60] He found a number of supporters, including Peel and Disraeli, but there was the inevitable opposition. As Talfourd had predicted, the most virulent came from the 'Doctrinaire party', led on this occasion by Joseph Hume, M.P. for Aberdeen, who argued that authors were well-rewarded already, and that there was no reason to favour them more than inventors. His view of Wordsworth was little short of contemptuous; dismissing him as 'indolent', he could not resist referring to his other source of income as a Distributor of Stamps for Westmorland, the poet as tax collector.

Hume's economic argument, for such it was, was not generally deployed. The real debate centred around the legitimacy of the monopoly apparently conferred by copyright. This certainly worried Disraeli, although he convinced himself that, while this was indeed a monopoly, it was a legitimate one if it protected authors. The present law, he argued, merely protected publishers, and thus he supported Talfourd's Bill. Disraeli's somewhat convoluted logic commanded little assent. One member dismissed literary property as 'fictitious', and therefore needing no law, new or old; perhaps more authoritatively, the Attorney-General opposed the Bill on the grounds that copyright was a commercial monopoly, and that, even in Talfourd's version, it protected owners rather than authors. Gladstone, despite Wordsworth's request, did not speak. He did, however, vote for the Bill, one of 39 who did so. This was a very close division indeed; 34 voted against, and the subsequent motion to send the Bill into Committee was only slightly better received, passing by 38 to 31. The danger was clear, both in the closeness of the divisions and in the small number of members who troubled to vote at all. The Bill had aroused little general interest; it had few enthusiastic supporters, and some very determined enemies.

Talfourd and Wordsworth had few reliable allies, and not all of these were particularly desirable. Chief among them was Sir Robert Inglis, teller for the ayes in the divisions on 25 April. Inglis was one of the members for Oxford University, and an extreme reactionary. He had opposed Catholic relief in the 1820s and parliamentary reform in the 1830s. Later he was to oppose the removal of the civil disabilities of Jews, church reform in both England and Ireland, public funds for Irish education and the repeal of the Corn Laws. Such a man was hardly likely to convert the 'Doctrinaire party', but that was probably impossible in any case given the way in which they saw the issue. Inglis had, however, made for himself a more serious enemy. In 1829, he had felt so strongly about Catholic emancipation that he had taken the Chiltern Hundreds so that he was free to stand against Peel in the latter's attempt to be re-elected for Oxford University. He took Peel's seat from him by a majority of nearly 150 in a poll of 1,364 electors.[61] Little wonder that Peel's support for Talfourd's Bill was apparently reluctant, when its promoter had such friends as Inglis. Within days of the Second Reading, Peel's doubts were becoming stronger; he had not voted in the division on 25 April, and by 3 May Wordsworth was worried. He wrote to Talfourd that 'we have cause to fear about Sir R. Peel', who had written to him taking up Hume's point to the effect that it would be fair to treat authors and inventors in the same way.[62] Wordsworth wrote to Peel himself on the same day, trying to answer this very point. He argued, perhaps somewhat speciously, that many people *might* have invented a particular article, but that only one person could write a unique work of literature.[63] Peel was unconvinced. The Bill had lost its most senior and potentially most influential supporter, and had lost him, moreover, on a point of political and economic principle.

Wordsworth was now desperate; the high hopes of the winter had vanished. He wrote to everyone he could think of to solicit support, but he admitted to Lockhart that he feared that the Bill would indeed be lost because the Utilitarians (who 'do not deserve the name') are putting pressure on M.P.s to vote against it.[64] This was particularly poignant for Lockhart, for he had written to Wordsworth some weeks earlier, to say that 'unless [Talfourd's] Bill is carried he considers the emancipation of Abbotsford all but hopeless'.[65] It does not seem surprising that on the same day, Mary Wordsworth wrote to her friend Isabella Fenwick that the household was 'fully occupied in the Copyright cause',[66] for Wordsworth himself admitted that his 'mind was full of the subject', and his claim that he had written 'scarcely less than fifty letters' seeking support seems only too credible.[67]

The Bill went into Committee on 9 May, but even that was achieved only after another division; the vote (116 to 64) was perhaps a little healthier, but procedural manoeuvring by the Bill's opponents, which is what it was, was hardly the best start.[68] To make matters worse, on the same day, the House received a petition from 'persons interested in . . . literature and science' in Dublin, who were opposed to the Bill.[69] In the debate on the motion to commit, Thomas Wakley moved the adjournment of the Committee for six months, which, if carried, would have been the end of the matter. He argued that the smallness of the House for the Second Reading, and the closeness of the division, indicated that there was no real approval for it. He then reiterated some of the arguments: the Bill interferes with natural property rights, it will make books more expensive, and there is, in any case, no evidence that authors need any more help. The only other significant contributor to the debate was another radical, Henry Warburton, who gave notice that he intended to question every clause.[70]

Wakley and Warburton were typical of the political opposition which Talfourd's Bill was now attracting. Wakley was a prominent man. A physician by training, he founded *The Lancet* in 1823, and, as M.P. for Finsbury from 1835, he was a committed supporter of reform at every level. He sought to alleviate the iniquities, as he saw them, of the Poor Law of 1834 and the workhouses which it created. He was an outspoken supporter of trade unions and of the Tolpuddle martyrs. He was favourable to most of the demands made by the Chartists.[71] Two years earlier, he had been one of the most fervent advocates of the repeal of the newspaper duties, and had shared a public platform with Hume and with George Grote, both of whom had spoken against the Copyright Bill on its Second Reading.[72] He was an exceptional man, but the many political traits which he showed typified much of the radical opposition: copyright was seen as an entrenched right, a commercial monopoly, and, worst of all, restrained the freedom of the press.

The opponents led the Bill into a procedural jungle, and there it was lost. The first meeting of the Committee was duly reported to the House, and it was agreed to reconvene the following week. A few minor amendments had been made, but there was no real progress.[73] In fact, on 15 May, the date which had been arranged, the meeting of the Committee was postponed, and no date was fixed for its resumption.[74] With the Session drawing to its close, it was becoming clear that the Bill was lost. On 20 June, Gladstone 'suggested the postponement of the Copyright Bill',[75] and Talfourd bowed to the inevitable. Both he and Wordsworth analysed the failure, trying to learn some lessons from it. Both men now saw Gladstone as the key figure. Wordsworth wrote to thank him for his support, and to ask him to try to win back Peel for the cause.[76]

Talfourd too was learning a lesson in political reality. He wrote to Gladstone on 8 July:

> I have some idea of printing in a compact form my speeches on the Copyright question – the Act as it will be introduced next Session with notes shewing the object and reason of each of the clauses – and some communication from Wordsworth on the subject – to distribute before the next Session. Should I do so, will you permit me the honor and gratification of inscribing it to you?[77]

In seeking to dedicate his proposed book to Gladstone, Talfourd was hoping to link his name indissolubly to the cause of copyright law reform.

On 12 February 1839, Talfourd was given leave to bring in yet another Copyright Bill, which duly received its formal First Reading; it was identical in all essentials with the amended version of the Bill which had been lost in the previous Session.[78] Neither Wordsworth nor Talfourd had been inactive during the autumn and winter. Wordsworth was now very anxious indeed, appreciating at last the extent of the opposition which the proposals had aroused; his letters have a pessimistic tone. He wrote to Moxon in December 1838, apparently close to despair: 'If Sergeant Talfourd's bill should not pass I know not what will come of poor Authors and their Works.'[79] At least Wordsworth now realized that his role had to be public as well as private. By 28 January, he had his own petition to the House in draft, and showed it to Henry Crabb Robinson. Robinson, however, was not completely happy about it; he found it rather egotistical, suggesting (in the privacy of his diary) that Wordsworth: 'is too desirous to express his own impressions and cares too little about the impressions it will excite in others'.[80] No doubt he was still making distinctions between writers of great literary merit like himself, and those for whom 'the profits of a season' were the just and reasonable reward. A few weeks later, Robinson, according to his own account, 'took charge of Talfourd's Copyright Petition' and organized the signatures of large numbers of authors.[81]

In the meanwhile, Wordsworth, presumably oblivious of Robinson's opinions and welcoming his help, continued to solicit help from his other friends. These included Southey, who shared both Wordsworth's concern about copyright and his reluctance to petition Parliament. In December 1837, Southey had written to Sir Henry Taylor, a utilitarian contributor to *The Quarterly Review*, to explain his own position, which was, in its way, even more precarious than Wordsworth's:

> Were I to die before Talfourd's Bill passes, the greater part of my poems, and no little part of my prose, would be seized immediately by some rascally booksellers . . . It is true that . . . I secure a new term of copyright by the corrected edition . . . But those fellows would publish from the former copies.[82]

Despite this, he was reluctant to make a public statement, not least since his name had so often been mentioned in the debate, and he did not wish to be thought to be acting simply in his own interests. In any case, he had some doubts about the precise form of the proposals in the 1838 Bill, and felt unable to support them in their entirety.[83] Wordsworth's persuasion worked, for Southey was, in due course, one of the authors who petitioned the House.

The Second Reading was scheduled for 27 February, but neither Wordsworth nor Talfourd achieved all that they had planned before that date. Talfourd seems to have been uncertain about his best course of action. Gladstone had agreed to be dedicatee of the proposed pamphlet explaining the Bill, but it remained unwritten on the advice of some other supporters, as he explained to Gladstone in early February:

> The hope which you permitted me to cherish, when I last saw you, of associating my humble efforts in Cause of Literature with your name, has been deferred in consequence of the opinion of some of the more practical of my supporters that it would be injudicious to cause discussion by a publication previous to the renewal of the struggle in the House of Commons; but I still look forward to the time – 'when the battle's lost and won' – when I may record some of the attempts which have been made to obtain justice for the noblest aims of industry and genius, under your auspices. I purpose to move for leave to bring in the Bill at the earliest convenient day; and hope, before the second reading, to obtain Petitions from those who also much need and much deserve such a measure, in its favour.[84]

The petition, despite Wordsworth, and largely thanks to Robinson, was indeed prepared, and was tabled on the day of the Second

Reading.[85] This long-expected document was signed by a large number of authors, including Carlyle, Harrison Ainsworth, G. P. R. James, Douglas Jerrold and H. H. Milman, but Robinson had actually been only moderately successful; no doubt this was partly because he was short of time, but some people whom he had approached, including Arnold, had refused his request for help.[86] Some authors sent their own petitions, including Wordsworth himself. His was indeed typical, in arguing that almost all of his copyrights will be in public domain by the time that he dies, and that he wants to protect the interests of his family and heirs.[87]

The others were along much the same lines, and there can be little doubt that there had been a coordinated campaign, presumably organized by Wordsworth, Robinson and Talfourd himself. They revolved around two essential points: the need for long-term protection to justify the expense in works of learning, and the need to protect the families of dead authors. The Scottish historian, Sir Archibald Alison, for example, revealed in his petition that his *History of Europe During the French Revolution*, published in ten volumes between 1833 and 1842, had cost him £4,000 to write over a period of twenty-five years.[88] To his publisher, Alexander Blackwood, Alison wrote privately that 'if Sergeant Talfourd's Bill passes it may . . . prove the same benefit to you and your heirs as it will to me and mine'.[89] Other academics joined in this chorus, including professors from Glasgow and St Andrews.[90] Like the general petition of the English authors organized by Robinson, it was an impressive display of support, which at least showed that Wordsworth was not isolated and that Talfourd was arguing a real case, but it was unlikely to convince anyone to whom the same arguments had been unconvincing only twelve months earlier.

So indeed it proved. Talfourd moved the Second Reading, and Hume opposed it. The former said that the opposition arose from self-interest in the book trade; the latter countered that, although authors might indeed deserve some protection, the extension of the term was meaningless for most of them. This did indeed shift the ground a little, and suggested a possible way forward, for if the objection was to the length of the term, rather than the principle of *post mortem* copyright, there might even be room for compromise. The point was taken up by the Solicitor-General, who perhaps justified Wordsworth's earlier reluctance to become publicly involved, for he argued that the poet's case was a special one because of his longevity, his current eminence and his early literary history, and should not form the basis of a new law. Eventually in a division of 110 members, the Bill was given its Second Reading by a majority of 36.[91]

The real victors were torpor and indifference. Far less passion was aroused than in 1838. The trade, perhaps aware of the strength of the political opposition to the Bill, which had defeated its predecessor, did little. There were two isolated petitions against it, and another in its favour, during March and April, but no more organized lobbying by the book trade.[92] The authors were not entirely inactive, and Talfourd was still looking for support in the literary world. Dickens, through the agency of John Forster, persuaded Carlyle to petition the House in his own name, as well as signing the general petition.[93] Carlyle was reluctant,[94] but he did eventually relent: 'Here, after all, is a Petition, since you have set me on it; of a very wonderful nature, for which you are responsible.'[95] The 'very wonderful nature' of this document can only be conveyed in Carlyle's own prose, perhaps at its most characteristic when he writes that he is asking the House:

> . . . to forbid all Thomas Teggs and other extraneous persons . . . to steal from him his small winnings, for a space of sixty years at shortest. After sixty years, unless your Honourable House provide otherwise, they may begin to steal.[96]

This document, along with one from Hartley Coleridge and others from other writers, was tabled on 1 May.[97]

That was the date set for the Committee Stage of the Bill, which had been postponed from 10 April. The events on that occasion were ominous indeed, for the House had been inquorate, as Gladstone recorded in his diary: 'We failed in making a House for the Copyright at 4 – only 28 present.'[98] This was a humiliation, and Wordsworth knew it; he told Talfourd that he was 'mortified . . . you should have had so much trouble and made such a sacrifice, to meet so unworthy a House of Commons'.[99]

The House was only a little more worthy on 1 May, for, once again, the opponents of the Bill used every possible procedural device to obstruct it. The business was not reached until late in the evening. When it was taken, Warburton, who had threatened to oppose every clause in the previous year, moved to defer it yet again. This motion was lost on a division by 127 to 24.[100] The House then went into Committee, but Warburton, seconded by Wakley, immediately proposed the adjournment. This was lost by 9 votes to 132, a further motion by Warburton to defer the Committee Stage was defeated by 7 to 119, and a second adjournment motion failed by 9 to 91. By now it was far into the night, and Warburton and his small group of radical allies had succeeded both in wasting precious time and in ensuring that the House was thinning out as members went home, thus once again raising the spectre of inquoracy. When the Committee at last reached the substantive business, there were no fewer than fourteen divisions on various motions and amendments. Although, as Gladstone, who faithfully supported the Bill throughout these weary hours, noted in his diary, 'the majority triumphed',[101] it was all very time-consuming. Some of the votes, moreover, were alarmingly close, and betrayed some divisions of opinion even among the Bill's supporters. The 60-year term of copyright was approved by a majority of 12, and by that time the House was down to 82. The Committee adjourned as dawn was breaking, having dealt with just four out of more than twenty clauses.

In the circumstances, this was little better than outright failure. Subsequently, the Committee Stage was deferred on twelve occasions, without any progress being made. The Bill had few active supporters other than Talfourd himself; its opponents, equally small in numbers, were simply better organized in the House. It was this which wrecked Talfourd's efforts; all his petitions from the luminaries of British learning and literature counted for nothing in the face of the unreformed procedures of the House of Commons. When the Committee Stage was deferred again, for three months, on 8 July, the Bill was dead.[102]

It is difficult to see what more Talfourd could have done. He had learned one lesson from his earlier failures, and had mobilized the support of the literary and learned worlds. But he had not, and perhaps he could not, overcome the political opposition of the 'Doctrinaire party'. The issue was a marginal one, even to many authors, and Talfourd carried too little political weight to force it through the archaic procedures of the House of Commons. The failure of 1839, after all the efforts which had been made, had broken the spirit of many of Talfourd's literary supporters. Even Wordsworth, although he retained a strong interest in the matter, was never again to be so active a campaigner. Yet Talfourd would not admit defeat.

In the next Session, he tried again. He was given leave to bring in a Bill in February, and the delaying tactics started again; no fewer than 228 petitions were tabled from the printers and publishers against the Bill. Failure was inevitable.[103] If anything, this was worse than the failures in 1838 and 1839, for there had not even been a proper debate on the issues involved. Talfourd's attempt to arouse public support by publishing the book which he had postponed in 1839 had precisely the opposite effect, as he had feared, of provoking opposition from the trade.[104]

Talfourd, however, was nothing if not persistent. In 1841, he once again moved for leave to bring in a Bill, this time on the first day of the Session, and, following a division on the inevitable motion of opposition from Warburton, was given leave to do so.[105] After so many failures, Talfourd was, at last, beginning to learn some lessons and to make some concessions. In his speech on the Second Reading, he took up a point which had been raised two years earlier, and suggested that the 60-year term was not, in itself, essential; what he sought was an endorsement of the principle of extending the term of copyright, and, by implication, that of *post mortem* protection.[106]

That display of reason and compromise on Talfourd's part might have been successful, had it not been for the eloquence of a new and formidable opponent of the Bill in its present form. This was Macaulay, addressing the House on this subject for the first time. Macaulay was dismissive of theoretical arguments. He swept aside the idea of natural rights, as being something which could be expressed in the law in many different ways. For him, this was a practical issue, and he simply thought that 60 years was too long, and would impose a 'tax on readers for the purpose of giving a bounty to writers'.[107] In any case, he considered that it would be publishers, not authors, who benefited from the extended term. Not surprisingly, Talfourd was hurt and angry; even Macaulay's official and adulatory biographer noted that 'Talfourd, in the bitterness of his soul, exclaimed that Literature's own familiar friend, in whom she had trusted, and who had eaten of her bread, had lifted up his heel against her'.[108] It was certainly not Macaulay's finest hour; his speech lacked in logic, and actually concealed his view that there was a case in principle for *post mortem* copyright; it was the length of time to which he objected, not the concept itself. Harriet Martineau certainly thought that Macaulay had been talking nonsense, and said so.[109] Whatever the quality of Macaulay's argument, however, there was no doubt of the rhetorical quality of his speech. He did indeed, as his biographer wrote, 'induce a thin House to reject the bill by a few votes',[110] deferring the Second Reading for six months by 45 to 38.[111] As had been the intention, and Macaulay's objective, it was never seen again.

This disaster was Talfourd's swan-song in his efforts to reform the law of copyright; indeed, it was his swan-song in the House, for he lost his seat in the General Election of 1841, and thereafter concentrated on his legal career. Why had he failed? Primarily, he was a limited and inexperienced politician in every sense. He was unbending when compromise was needed. He was innocent of the ways of the House of Commons. He was a poor and unconvincing speaker in an age when the House could be swayed by oratory, and expected to hear it. This was not all, however. There were conflicts of principle, of which copyright law was a small and insignificant part, and they consumed all Talfourd's efforts to reform the law.

Justice for authors was, no doubt, a battle cry which was appealing to Wordsworth and his friends. Indeed, as Maugham had argued, natural law and natural justice were regarded by legal theorists as the basis of the legal concept of copyright. Such theories, however, were no longer universally accepted, especially by the radicals. Talfourd's most committed political opponents belonged to the one faction in the House of Commons in the 1830s which was reasonably well-organized, and had a more or less consistent political philosophy against which they tested individual measures and proposals. This was the 'Doctrinaire party' which he had, quite rightly, identified at a very early stage as being his main problem. Talfourd was sitting in the first two parliaments elected under the 1832 Reform Act, and, although the social composition of the House was not unlike that of its unreformed predecessor, it was nevertheless changing. The new influx of Whig, liberal and radical members in the 1830s had brought into the Commons men who took their duties seriously. The radical free traders, in particular, the core of the 'Doctrinaire party', were close to being professional politicians in the modern sense. Their mere presence made party divisions more marked, and tended to give a political dimension to every issue. The radicals soon learned how to exploit the unreformed procedures of the House to their own advantage. Talfourd was one of their victims.[112]

The radicals disliked Talfourd's proposals on two theoretical grounds. First, it could be argued that copyright restricted the free operation of the market, and was therefore inimical to free trade, to which they were wholly committed. Secondly, it could be argued to be a constraint on the freedom of the press, to which they were equally strongly committed. Neither of these points was ever really answered by Talfourd and his supporters, despite the fact that they were the factors which motivated their principal opponents. Even

Macaulay, an old-fashioned Whig rather than an advanced liberal, subscribed to both views in his own way.

The discourse had moved away from the literary into the political arena, and Talfourd was unable to pursue it there. He laboured under three disadvantages. First, there was his inexperience and ineptitude. Secondly, his supporters in the House of Commons were neither so well-organized nor so wholly committed as his opponents. Thirdly, his supporters outside the House were not always as helpful as they might have been to his (and their) cause. Talfourd's own political failings could have been overcome if he had had more help, but Gladstone, the only major politician who consistently supported him, was already marked out for greater things, and had many other preoccupations. Talfourd was a Tory in a House which never had a clear Tory majority, and frequently had a Whig one, and he simply could not command it. What was worse was that his supporters sometimes gave comfort, unwittingly, to his enemies. Wordsworth was easy enough to portray, as Hume had done, as a curmudgeonly old reactionary looking to his bank balance under the pretence of supporting literature. It was only too easy to suggest that the cause of copyright law reform was a Tory cause, a reactionary cause, a cause which did not deserve the support of the growing liberal consensus of early Victorian England.

When Talfourd lost his seat in the summer of 1841, he was disillusioned, and perhaps bitter. His last words on the subject with which he hoped to make his political name, and which had perhaps instead destroyed his political career, were in a letter to Leigh Hunt:

> I have no reason to feel grateful to [the Whigs]; for myself I desire nothing but justice & the Cause of Literature which I had undertaken; and I found nothing but hollow profession or bitter and unfair enmity.[113]

To the very end, Talfourd did not understand the power, or even the nature, of the forces which he called up against himself.

It is not clear whom Talfourd was accusing of 'hollow profession', although Peel has to be one possibility. Certainly, it cannot have been Gladstone, who never wavered on the matter, and despite all the other calls on his time, studied it carefully. In February 1840, he had read John Lowndes's newly published *Historical Sketch of the Law of Copyright*, an authoritative work of history which concluded with the case for extending the term of copyright to at least forty years.[114] Another consistent supporter was Lord Mahon, son of the fifth Earl Stanhope, who had served in government in 1834.[115] Both men were safely returned in the 1841 election, and they now sat on the government side of the House following the Tory victory. Indeed, Gladstone was to join the Cabinet for the first time in 1843, as President of the Board of Trade. Both, but especially Gladstone, were in a far stronger position personally than Talfourd had ever been. Politically, too, they had far more influence than they could have had in the Whig and radical dominated House of the late 1830s. The new House was not only Tory; it was perhaps more reasonable and better disciplined than its predecessor.[116]

Mahon now took the initiative on copyright law reform. He was not only in a more favourable position than Talfourd, he was also temperamentally better suited to the task: he was willing to compromise. The opposition of the radicals might now work in favour of the reformers in a Tory-dominated House, and there seemed to be a very real hope of achieving some measure of reform. All that was needed was to find out what was generally acceptable, and then to settle for it. On 3 May 1843, when Mahon, supported by Gladstone and Inglis, introduced a new Bill, the spirit of compromise was already in the air.[117] The principle which underlay Talfourd's bills was still there: there was a term of *post mortem* copyright. Mahon, however, made provision for this to be 25 years, rather than the contentious 60.[118] Even Wakley, one of the most vociferous of Talfourd's enemies, did not reject this out of hand, although he did say that he expected to hear a good case made for any change at all.[119] When the Bill was given its First Reading on 4 March, both Wakley and Macaulay indicated that they were willing to discuss it in Committee on the basis that it might be acceptable to them.[120] The Second Reading debate, on 16 March, was equally calm when compared with the traumas of Talfourd's experiences. Lord John Russell, speaking for the Whigs, went out of his way to compliment Mahon on his willingness to make changes and to listen to reasoned arguments, and Mahon accepted the compliment gracefully.[121]

The Committee Stage began on 23 March, and a few minor technical amendments were made without difficulty.[122] When it was resumed on 6 April, there was a little more trouble. Wakley recanted on his earlier attitude, saying that he had not heard the convincing arguments which he had demanded, and that he would no longer support the Bill. Macaulay also opposed it in its present form, although for different reasons. He was not, he said, opposed in principle to *post mortem* copyright; this was true, although it may not have been apparent to all those who had heard his speech on the subject in 1841. He then proposed a period of 42 years from the date of publication, regardless of whether or not the author was still alive. This was accepted by Mahon, as were associated proposals which had the effect of giving the same term if the author died within 7 years of publication, and protecting the rights of assignees in a limited way. All these amendments were accepted by the House on substantial majorities.

Macaulay was triumphant. His nephew recalled that 'he enjoyed the satisfaction of having framed according to his mind a Statute which may fairly be described as the charter of his craft . . .'[123] Carlyle took a less charitable view of Macaulay's conversion: '. . . Mr Macaulay too finds that his last year's excoursion was on the wrong tack; that even at the risk of smelling of the shop he had better take the common one . . .'[124] Macaulay's own description of the events, and of his part in them, is in a letter to Macvey Napier, written the day after the debate:

> We had a field-day in the House of Commons yesterday. The question was . . . the Copy right Bill. I succeeded in modifying Mahon's plan to a great extent: and I really hope that you will be of the opinion that what I proposed is a far greater boon to literature than his measure would have been. I am really inclined to think that we shall settle the matter to general satisfaction.[125]

He was not seriously exaggerating what he had done. In 1841, he had killed the reform of the law of copyright; in 1842, he had made it possible.

Macaulay did indeed, in the same letter, pay tribute to Mahon's willingness to compromise (and, incidentally, added that it was 'lucky that both Talfourd and Warburton are out of the way'), and thereafter it was plain sailing. There was a brief debate at the Committee Stage in the Lords on 26 May, when Brougham tried to shorten the term of copyright, while not objecting to any of the principles involved. He found no support.[126] The Lords did, however, make one amendment of some significance, which had the effect of giving longer *post mortem* protection in many cases. If the 7-year term expired before the end of the 42-year term which would have subsisted had the author still been alive, there was to be protection for the full 42 years from the date of publication.[127] This and some other minor amendments were accepted by the Commons, and on 1 July 1842, the Copyright Bill received the Royal Assent.[128]

The Copyright Act of 1842[129] was to remain the basis of British copyright law until 1911, and was to exercise immense influence throughout the world. The impetus to reform the law had begun with an elderly author seeking to protect his descendants, and that wish was, to a large extent, satisfied. At the same time, the book trade was not alienated, for the law was indeed a compromise which both protected investments in copyrights and opened up the possibility of reprints of public domain copies when they were still of interest to the public.

The basic term of copyright was built around Macaulay's compromise figure of 42 years. Normally, copyright would subsist for the author's lifetime, and for 7 years thereafter. If, however, 42 years had not elapsed since publication when the author died, the full term of 42 years could apply. Copyrights assigned to members of an author's family enjoyed exactly the same rights as if the author had retained them. This was an exception, for rights assigned to anyone outside the family enjoyed the first period of protection only, that is for no more than 7 years after the death of the author. Thus, if an author published a book in 1842, it was protected until at least 1884; if the author were still alive in 1884, it continued to be protected until 7 years after his death. Under no circumstances, whoever owned the rights, could the work be in the public domain before 1884. This was the effect of Macaulay's compromise and the Lords' amendments, and it produced a law which commanded general acceptance.

Other parts of the Act were less contentious. All copyrights had to be registered at Stationers' Hall, and no action would lie under the Act if this were not done. For books which were properly protected, there were penalties for both domestic piracy and the import of foreign reprints. Not only books were protected; similar protection was afforded to contributors to periodicals, encyclopedias and collectaneous works. Finally, automatic deposit was required only at the British Museum; the other libraries had to claim the books which they wanted.

Much of this detail served to clarify and rationalize the law. For the first time, there was a statute which precisely defined the term of copyright and the means of obtaining it. The law was based on the clear assumption that copyright originated with the author, but that, because the author could only use the property thus created if it were shared with a publisher, the publisher was also afforded some protection. The public good was served by ensuring that a book of enduring value did not become a permanent commercial monopoly after its creators and publishers had had a reasonable opportunity to recoup their investments of time and money.

All this was clear, but problems remained. The law was still essentially a law about books, despite the provisions about contributors to magazines and the like. It did not deal with dramatic or musical performances, or with works of art, industrial designs and similar matters. It was still clearly derived from a law promoted by the book trade over a century earlier in its own interests, which essentially protected commercial rather than intellectual property. The rule that ideas could not be copyright was still there; only words were protected, and, very largely, words as they appeared in printed books. Ideas expressed in graphic or diagrammatic form, or as a theatrical performance or musical notes or steps in a dance, were wholly outside the province of the law.

The 1842 Copyright Act gave reasonable satisfaction to those who had promoted it. It offered protection to the authors of books in the United Kingdom, and some protection to their families. It did not infringe too far on the historic privileges of the book trade. But it could be argued to have done nothing to address the issues of the mid-nineteenth century, new media, new commercial relationships, and a new concept of creativity and authorship.

6 Copyright in Britain and the World

The protection afforded to British authors and publishers by the 1842 Act was, for both parties, a marked advance on the previous position. By the time that Mahon's Bill was enacted, however, the issue which Wordsworth had raised and which Talfourd had so stubbornly pursued was beginning to fade into the background. The authors who took the lead in pressing for domestic copyright law reform in the 1830s were primarily the writers of an older generation, Wordsworth himself, Southey and the heirs of Scott and Coleridge. All had started their careers slowly, all had made their name as poets, and all their families or dependants were or would be affected by the loss of copyright after their deaths. The writers of a new generation, emerging at the very time of the copyright agitation of the late 1830s, were in a very different position.

The most important of these was Dickens, established by the publication of *Pickwick Papers* in 1837 as the leading novelist of his generation, and already a best-selling author with everything he wrote by the time that the 1842 Act was passed. He was always aware of the importance of the copyright campaign; *Pickwick Papers*, in the 1837 edition, was dedicated to Talfourd, as:

> . . . a slight and most inadequate acknowledgement of the inestimable services you are rendering to the literature of your country, and of the lasting benefits you will confer upon authors of this and succeeding generations, by securing to them and their descendants a permanent interest in their works.[1]

Dickens's real involvement with the issue, however, lay elsewhere; even the Act of 1814 gave adequate protection to a young man whose books sold in huge numbers. His interest was in editions from which he could make no profits at all: editions published in the United States. The American piracy of his books concerned and indeed infuriated Dickens almost from the very beginning of his career, and intermittently throughout his life.[2] Indeed, he was to become closely identified with the campaign to persuade the governments of both the United Kingdom and the United States to take action against the problems which piracy posed.

Foreign piracy of British books was not a new issue in the early nineteenth century, but it was becoming more acute. During the seventeenth century, Dutch printers were infringing the patents of the King's Printer by printing the English Bible for import into England, an activity in which they were helped by rebel members of the London book trade like Michael Sparke.[3] In the decade leading up to 1710, there were many complaints about piracy, although the legal position was uncertain, and most of the pirates were in London rather than abroad.[4] The 1710 Act, for all its imperfections, went some way towards clarifying the position, but neither it, nor the Import of Books Act of 1739, could prevent unscrupulous booksellers from bringing in reprints from Ireland and the continent.[5] Scottish 'piracy' was brought under control, by recognition of its legality under the 1710 Act, in 1774,[6] and reprinting protected copies became illegal in Ireland when that country was incorporated into British copyright law in 1801.[7] At the beginning of the nineteenth century, therefore, the position was comparatively clear. No book which was protected under the 1710, 1801 or 1814 Act could be reprinted in the United Kingdom, or imported into the United Kingdom if reprinted abroad, without the permission of the copyright owner. In other words, such protection as the law afforded to authors and publishers was domestic, and did not extend outside the United Kingdom itself.

Towards the end of the eighteenth century and into the first decades of the nineteenth, three developments introduced new factors into this situation. First, the English language came to be more widely known on the continent, and more English people travelled there. This created a demand for English books in Germany, Italy and France, which was largely met by local printers reprinting fashionable English works.[8] The market for English-language books in continental Europe was small, but it was a development of great significance for the future.

Secondly, the American market underwent important changes. Until the 1820s, the United States, like the colonies from which it had evolved, imported British books on a large scale, but, as the population grew and scattered, the economic base of the American book trade was enlarged. The demand for British books was now large enough to justify reprinting them in America rather than importing the British edition. This entailed the partial loss of a significant export market for British publishers;[9] more significantly, however, it also presaged the continuous growth of the American market for books by British authors.

Thirdly, in the aftermath of the French and American revolutions, other countries developed copyright laws of their own to protect their own citizens. Until 1789, such copyright protection as existed in France and in most other continental countries derived from mechanisms originally developed to control the press. In France and in many German states the licence to print was not unlike that in early seventeenth-century England. The licence to print was a privilege granted in the name of a particular printer or publisher who thereby acquired the 'rights' in the book. This usually represented the only form of protection open to authors and publishers. It was thoroughly unsatisfactory, especially in the multitude of German states,[10] where it afforded no real protection at all. After their respective revolutions, however, both the United States and France developed copyright laws of their own. In the United States, this was largely based on current English practice, although it did give the specific recognition which was still denied in Britain to the role of the author. The first U.S. Copyright Act, passed in 1790, enlarged on the general provision in the Constitution by giving citizens and residents a copyright for fourteen years, renewable for a further fourteen if the author were still alive. Although clearly based on the 1710 British Act, American law went further in specifically recognizing the rights of the author.[11] In France, successive laws and constitutions gave firmer recognition to copyrights, protecting authors and at the same time recognizing the social utility of their works; the latter was the revolutionary equivalent of the encouragement of learning.[12]

The effect of these social, political and legal changes was twofold: first, the market for English books was greatly increased, and with it the potential income of British authors and publishers; and secondly, the idea of copyright protection came to be incorporated in the jurisprudence and legal practice of many of those countries where that market existed. It was the first factor which created the recognition of the need for some sort of protection for British books outside the United Kingdom, and the second which made it possible. The problem was how to develop and enforce such laws. The crisis developed, almost simultaneously, in relation to both France and the United States.

When the long war between Britain and France ended in 1815, for the first time in a generation the continent was open to British travellers and indeed to British cultural influence. A number of Paris publishers, most notably Galignani, Baudry and Baillière, became deeply involved in the reprinting of English books, which they did on a large scale.[13] At first, Galignani, who was the most active of the three, was principally intending to sell his books to British travellers in France, but during the 1820s both he and his competitors widened their horizons. The French reprints were exported to the United States in some quantity. Individual copies were, inevitably, brought into the United Kingdom by returning travellers. The latter was perhaps of little significance, but the American sales were damaging the export potential of British publishers, at the very time when American publishers were beginning to compete in their own domestic market.

Even that, however, was of little importance when set beside the sale of the French reprints in London and elsewhere in Britain, which began to happen in the mid-1830s. In 1830, Baillière, one of Galignani's principal Parisian competitors, opened a branch in London, through which he imported foreign books; in itself this was a perfectly legal branch of the book trade.[14] By 1834, however, the London branch of Baillière was also engaged in importing French reprints of English books, a distinctly illegal activity which encompassed smuggling as well as breach of copyright.[15] The case which was pursued in the courts involved two novels, *Ayesha* by James Morier, and Maria Edgeworth's *Helen*. The British publisher and copyright owner, Richard Bentley, successfully sought an injunction from the Court of Chancery to prevent the sale of these editions, and, in due course, Baillière settled out of court.[16] Other cases emerged during the next few months, and were pursued with vigour by Bentley, who, as the major novel publisher of the period, was the principal victim of the pirates and smugglers.[17] His actions put an end to the immediate problem, but it helped publishers rather than authors.

Until this unfortunate episode, relations between some British authors and some of the French publishers had been good. Galignani, in particular, had made a serious effort to obtain the permission of British authors or publishers to reprint their works, and in some cases had even gone to the lengths of asking them to check the texts for authenticity. By the 1830s, Galignani was also regularly publishing French translations of new English books, including the works of G. P. R. James and the early novels of Dickens. Some authors were paid for this. Theoretically, the

British authors could register for French copyright, but in practice few, if any, chose to do so. They were, therefore, dependent on the goodwill of their French 'publishers' for any recompense for the reprinting or translation of their works, a position which could easily break down under strain.

The same situation applied in other European countries. After 1815, the long-established practice of reprinting English books in Germany was resumed, especially at Leipzig in Saxony. In the 1820s, the Leipzig firm of Zwickau reprinted Byron, Scott and other English authors, and from the mid-1830s onwards Zwickau had competition in the city from the house of Fleischer, which included Bulwer-Lytton, Dickens and Marryat in its list.[18] There is no evidence of the export of these books to Britain or the United States on a commercial scale, but they, too, were eating into the small, but potentially lucrative, market for English books on the continent. Neither Zwickau or Fleischer seems to have troubled to contact British authors or publishers. The Leipzig rival of these two firms, and the future doyen of the whole continental trade in English books, was more ethical. This was Christian Bernhard Tauchnitz, who began to publish his celebrated *Collection of British Authors* in 1841, and within a year was consistently seeking the permission and cooperation of those whose works he reprinted.[19]

The continental reprinting of British books, developing rapidly during the twenty years after the end of the Napoleonic War, posed a real problem for both authors and publishers. So also did the parallel growth of similar practices in the United States, for by 1830, the practice of reprinting British books and periodicals was widespread in the American book trade. The market there was far larger than that in Europe, and the book trade itself perhaps more competitive than in Paris or Leipzig. Some American publishers, notably Carey and Lea of Philadelphia and Harper Brothers of New York made *ex gratia* payments to British authors, but there was certainly no legal obligation to do so.[20] Where there was some sort of arrangement with the British copyright owners, the normal practice was to send copies of the printed sheets of the book to America, where they were then reprinted. In the 1840s, this practice was gradually replaced by sending either stereotype plates or the moulds or flongs from which they were made. Whatever the method used, rapid publication of new British books in the United States depended upon either a degree of cooperation between the British and American publishers, or some surreptitious agent in Britain acting on behalf of the American firm.

Respectable firms like Carey and Lea or Harper Brothers were, however, only a part of the problem, and not the most important part. Although the British authors did not gain financial benefits on the scale which they might have expected from the extent of their American sales, they did at least get some income, and they had some control over what was actually printed. This was not so with the genuinely piratical reprints which abounded in the late 1830s as the American book trade tried to survive a depression which ravaged it as much as it did other parts of the American economy. One consequence of this desperation was a proliferation of cheap magazines and newspapers which indiscriminately reprinted books by foreign authors without even the pretence of acknowledgement.[21] There was, in law, no reason why any American publisher should seek permission to reprint a British book. It is important to recognize that the reprinters, despite the fact that British authors and publishers always referred to them as 'pirates', were not acting illegally in their own country. Some American reprints were imported into Britain, which was illegal, but the scale of the operations was very small.[22] For British authors and publishers, the American problem was similar to the continental problem: perfectly legal reprinting was eating into potential profits, by virtually eliminating major export markets and thus depriving them of potential income from the foreign sales of the legitimate British editions. Moreover, it should be added that some British publishers were equally unscrupulous in reprinting American books without permission, a trade in which George Routledge was deeply involved. Some American authors, notably Washington Irving, Harriet Beecher Stowe and Joel Harris, lost a great deal by this when their books became popular in Britain. Some tried, in vain, to obtain British imperial copyright by moving to Canada.[23] The whole position was thoroughly unsatisfactory.

The only redress in English law was against smugglers and British booksellers who dealt in the smuggled piracies. The customs officers did their best, but there was systematic evasion, which led to deep suspicions among the British book trade about the efficiency and perhaps even the probity of the officers. But, in general, the perception was that foreign publishers were trying, illegally, to compete in Britain.[24] A book trade newspaper in 1842 opined that 'It is a notorious fact that Foreign editions are printed *purposely for the English market*; the Foreign demand alone being far too limited to repay the cost'.[25] Whether any of these suspicions was justified was of less importance than the general belief in widespread underhand dealings. There was a growing feeling that there was a real need for some sort of regulation of international transactions in the book trade, based upon a law of copyright which would protect British books outside the United Kingdom.

That was easy to say, but far less easy to achieve. In the late 1830s, Talfourd's attempts to reform domestic copyright law had run into serious parliamentary and political trouble, and had aroused radical opposition to the whole idea of copyright.[26] International law, however, might be different. It could be presented as a matter of patriotic pride and duty rather than a restraint of trade, and as a means of preventing the exploitation of British genius by two recent ex-enemies, the United States and France. This was precisely the line which was taken, and the comparative ease with which the first international copyright law was passed by the British Parliament stands in stark contrast to the appalling problems confronted by Talfourd and his supporters.

Significantly, the proposal which came to the House of Commons on 20 March 1838 was from the government, not from a private member. Indeed, it was to be a characteristic of all subsequent British law on international copyright that it was regarded as a matter of public policy rather than private interest. The Bill was presented by C. E. Poulett Thomson, the Whig member for Manchester, who was President of the Board of Trade.[27] In introducing the Bill, Poulett Thomson cleverly presented it as a moderate but nationalistic proposal. First, he distanced himself from Talfourd, by simply saying that he did not wish to enter into the question of domestic copyright at all. The government's objective was simply to give some assistance to British subjects, so that authors could be protected as inventors already were. There was, in his view, an urgent need for this. It was, he said, 'a matter of notoriety that works were pirated abroad as soon as they made their appearance at home'.[28] He was well-primed with examples; Frances Trollope's *Travels in America* had been printed in Paris in an edition of 15,000 copies 'without the slightest benefit to the author', and he had 'been informed, that there was not a village of 2,000 inhabitants in the United States in which several copies of a pirated edition were not to be found'. Poulett Thomson was also, however, careful not be too overtly anti-American. He argued that an Anglo-American copyright agreement would be of benefit to American as well as to British authors, citing Noah Webster's sufferings from the depredations of British pirates who had reprinted his *Dictionary*.[29]

The Bill which Poulett Thomson introduced in this way was indeed a modest and sensible measure. Above all, it recognized that because the law varied so much between different countries, it was essential that any British law would have to be as flexible as possible if it were to offer the greatest possible protection for British authors. The key proposal, therefore, was to authorize the government to act by Order-in-Council to make reciprocal agreements with countries which were willing to give copyright protection to British authors under their own domestic law. This was important, because other countries were moving in the same direction. In the previous summer, Prussia had enacted a very similar law, under which foreign works were protected there if the state of origin of those works gave similar protection to works of Prussian origin.[30] At about the same time, the British and French governments had entered into negotiations on the possibilities for reciprocal copyright laws.[31] Most important of all, perhaps, the United States Congress was considering a proposed law which would give copyright protection to foreign nationals.[32] In effect, Poulett Thomson's case was that the British government should position itself so that it could respond to these or any other initiatives by foreign states, as well as taking initiatives of its own.

There was some opposition. No one who had followed the tortuous recent history of copyright legislation could have been surprised that Warburton, Wakley and Hume all spoke against the Bill. All three of them concentrated on the monopolies allegedly enjoyed by the publishers, and on their exploitation of the public through high prices. Warburton particularly laboured this point, not failing to play his own patriotic card by adding that if Talfourd's bill passed (he obviously could not resist the side-swipe) foreign authors would be better protected in Britain than would British authors abroad.[33] Hume was also suspicious of the publishers, saying that:

> . . . there were certain matters in the book trade and the mode in which it was conducted which must be inquired into before any means could be adopted to remedy the defects in the law of international copyright.[34]

Wakley favoured a Select Committee to investigate the whole matter before the Bill was even formally brought to the House, because he would 'like to learn what literary man had ever lost anything, or had complained that his interests had suffered, by his works having been pirated'.[35] In the circumstances, Wakley's claim to ignorance was unconvincing; it was merely a delaying tactic.

The radicals were in a minority. Other speakers were more concerned about the practical difficulties of enforcement. Sir

Robert Inglis and Lord John Russell both argued that the government ought to negotiate bilateral treaties rather than make a general law, and Henry Goulburn, a Tory, also foresaw difficulties, although he does not seem to have been against the principle involved.[36] Even Lord Mahon, the man who was eventually to carry the reform of domestic copyright law in 1842, saw the lack of international agreements as a greater problem than the lack of British legislation.[37] In replying to the debate, Poulett Thomson acknowledged the problems, but argued that they ought at least to try to address them.[38] His view prevailed, and the House gave leave for the Bill to brought in. It was subject to no further debate in either House, and received the Royal Assent on 31 July 1838.[39]

The International Copyright Act of 1838 attracted little attention or disagreement as it went through Parliament, in contrast to the various proposals to reform the domestic law. It proved modestly useful. Its basic principle was a very simple one, expressed in the preamble:

> . . . it is desirable to afford protection . . . to the Authors of Books first published in Foreign Countries, and their Assigns, in Cases where Protection shall be afforded in such Foreign Countries to the Authors of Books first published in her Majesty's Dominions . . .

This was to be achieved by the Order-in-Council to validate such agreements with foreign countries. Thereafter books from such countries, provided they were registered at Stationers' Hall and copies were deposited at the British Museum, would be protected in exactly the same way as a British book under the 1814 Act then in force. The Act, however, did no more than provide an enabling framework. Agreements still had to be negotiated with foreign states, and this, as speakers in the debate in the Commons had predicted, was no easy matter. Monckton Milnes had probably identified the root cause of the problem: 'Everyone knew that the circulation of English books in France was much more extensive than that of French books in England . . .' This was true, but the prophecy was to prove less acute than the analysis, for he added that 'He was of the opinion that the experiment should be first made with some such country as America, because there, there could be comparatively no difficulty to contend with'.[40] The 1838 Act provided a basis for action, but, in itself, had no effect.

The American troubles, so lightly dismissed by Monckton Milnes, were only just beginning. The late 1830s and early 1840s were the high-point (or the low-point) of American reprinting of

British books as the book trade there tried desperately to combat the effects of the depression.[41] It could not have been a worse time to try to enact a new copyright law designed to protect foreign authors, and yet that is exactly what was attempted. American copyright law was based on the principle of protecting both citizens and residents. The provision for protecting foreigners resident in the United States was comparatively generous, but it did not protect anyone not living in the U.S.A. In the late 1830s, an attempt was made to extend the provisions of the law to protect non-resident foreign writers.

The initiative came from a group of British authors, led by Harriet Martineau, who, in the autumn of 1836, prepared a petition to Congress asking for a law to protect their interests. Their cause was taken up by Senator Henry Clay of Kentucky, who presented it to the Senate in February 1837 and arranged for it to be presented to the House of Representatives at the same time.[42] A Bill was introduced, but it aroused great opposition from some sections of the American book trade, although there was also some support.[43] In an attempt to circumvent that, Clay introduced a provision which was to bedevil the American position in international copyright for the rest of the century and beyond. Clay's new proposal made the granting of copyright to foreign authors dependent upon their books being manufactured in the United States. Even this was not enough to satisfy the opposition. Clay encountered opponents as stubborn as those encountered by Talfourd in Britain, and despite persistent attempts, he never succeeded in persuading Congress to enact a law.

This was the situation when Charles Dickens arrived in America for the first time on 13 February 1842. In retrospect, this can be seen as the beginning of what is perhaps the most famous episode in the history of Anglo-American dealings on copyright, although by no means the most important.[44] There is no doubt that Dickens had suffered from the pirates, and that he felt very strongly on the subject. Indeed, one of his motives for this first visit was to make trouble about the copyright issue.[45] Later in the year, he was to write to one of his new American friends, John Pendleton Kennedy:

> . . . I have always felt, and do always feel so keenly the outrage which the existing piracy inflicts upon writers – the flagrant injustice which Law Makers suffer to be committed upon them . . . that I *cannot* . . . discuss the question as one of expediency, or reason it as one of National profit and loss . . .[46]

Indeed, it was precisely Dickens's inability to be rational on the subject which was to be such a problem. He contacted Clay and others in Washington, but he found he had little influence. Worst of all, he completely failed in his efforts to interest American authors in the cause.

Dickens's own view of the effects of his public intervention in American politics was rather more optimistic. In a letter to Forster in February 1842, he wrote that:

> The effect of all this copyright agitation has at least been to awaken a great sensation on both sides of the subject; the respectable newspapers and reviews taking up cudgels as strongly in my favour, as the others have done against me.[47]

In a sense, this was a reasonable assessment, although it seriously underplays the importance of five years' work by Harriet Martineau and Henry Clay. What is certain, however, is that Dickens did not help his cause when he abandoned the comparative privacy of letters and lobbying and assaulted the American book trade, and indeed the United States, in print. Anti-British sentiment always played some part in the political opposition to changes in copyright law, and Dickens probably exacerbated it.[48] *Martin Chuzzlewit* and *American Notes*, both published in the aftermath of this first visit to the U.S.A., reflect the frustration and anger which Dickens felt at what he saw as the theft of his work by 'the vagabonds', as he described the pirates in the same letter to Forster. Almost as soon as he had returned home, Dickens had issued a printed Circular, entitled *To British Authors and Journals*,[49] in which he called upon both to boycott the American pirates. The trouble was that he made little attempt to distinguish between the vagabonds and the rest of the trade, an omission which inevitably alienated potential American sympathizers.

Despite this, however, some American publishers and authors continued in their efforts to persuade Congress to introduce some sort of international copyright law. In particular, William C. Bryant, editor of the *New York Evening Post*, one of the 'respectable newspapers' to which Dickens referred, took up the cause. He was one of the founder-members of the American Copyright Club, which was formed in 1843 to lobby Congress and indeed to attempt to influence the book trade, which was still generally opposed to any change in the law. Nothing was achieved, however, despite nearly a decade of repeated attempts, partly because so few American authors would lend their names and their weight to the Club.[50] By the end of the 1840s, efforts to change the law of copyright in America seemed to have come to a dead end.

From the point of view of British authors and publishers this was, in practice, less catastrophic than it might have been. An increasing number of American publishers were indeed willing to pay for the right to publish the first American edition of new British books. By what was known in the United States as the 'courtesy of the trade', American publishers, or at least the respectable ones, did not pirate each other's British books once they had been acquired and published from British publishers. This was, at best, a tenuous arrangement, and not a satisfactory permanent solution. The real answer, if some protection were to be given to foreign authors, lay in the possibility of bilateral agreements, but that required an American equivalent of the Act passed by the British Parliament in 1838. There was no indication that Congress would ever agree to such a proposal. Other means therefore would have to be sought if international copyright protection were to be strengthened.

In the meanwhile, during the late 1840s and early 1850s, the 1838 Act was proving itself to be quietly useful in Europe. It was slightly amended in 1844 to bring it into line with the new domestic law of 1842.[51] The principal change in the 1844 Act was that it incorporated all the other rights which were a part of the 1842 Act, such as performing rights and the rights in the dramatization of novels. It also extended its application to the whole of the British Empire. Under this Act, the British government signed conventions with a number of German states, beginning with Prussia in 1846. Similar conventions were soon being negotiated all over the continent, between Austria-Hungary and Sardinia, for example, and between France and The Netherlands.[52] The interaction of these various conventions meant that there was gradually developing a network of reciprocal copyright protection which covered much of Europe.

One outstanding issue, however, was that between the United Kingdom and France, which had, in a sense, first brought the whole issue into the public arena. There had been negotiations between the two countries even before 1838, and indeed the progress of these negotiations had been one of the reasons given by Poulett Thomson in urging the House of Commons to support his proposed international copyright law. The negotiations, however, came to nothing in the 1830s, and seem to have fallen by the wayside during the 1840s. The stumbling-block was precisely the problem stated by Monckton Milnes: there was far greater demand for English books in France than for French books in Britain, and there was no intention of including translations (which *were* in demand in Britain) in the 1838 Act. Consequently, there was no incentive for the French government to pursue the negotiations seriously. Meanwhile, piracy continued, although after 1844 the British customs were assiduous in seizing any which were being imported into the United Kingdom, and it was rather easier to prosecute offenders.[53]

It was not until 1851–52 that the Anglo-French situation was finally resolved. Once again there was a Whig–Liberal government, keen to complete the work of giving Britain a free trade economy. The President of the Board of Trade, who was responsible for this, was Henry Labouchère, who had briefly succeeded Poulett Thomson in the office in 1839 when the latter had gone to Canada as Governor-General.[54] In 1847, Labouchère returned to the same post in the newly formed government; he instituted a series of major reforms in Britain's commercial legislation, dismantling the last remnants of mercantilism and protectionism. It was in this spirit that he renewed negotiations with the French about a copyright convention, and in November 1851, agreement was, at last, reached.

The treaty took account of the all-important point about translations. The solution was complicated, but practical, and a compromise was reached between the blanket protection for translations demanded by the French and the distaste of the British for any such protection at all.[55] It was agreed that the author could reserve the rights of translation for five years after original publication, provided that the work was deposited within three months of publication, and that a declaration of the reservation of the rights was printed on the title-page. Registration was to be at the Bureau de la Librairie at the Ministry of the Interior in Paris as well as at Stationers' Hall in London. Apart from that, the Anglo-French Copyright Convention was like those signed between the United Kingdom and other countries, giving full reciprocal rights to all books first published in either country. In the following year, a French law unilaterally extended the benefits of its domestic copyright law to all works published abroad, even if France did not have reciprocal agreements with the country of publication, a far more generous provision than any in Britain.[56]

Indeed, no such generosity was even proposed in Britain, but the Anglo-French Convention did, nevertheless, necessitate a change in British law. This was because of the clause about translation rights, which had specifically been omitted from the 1838 and 1844

Acts. Labouchère introduced an appropriate Bill in February 1852, and it received the Royal Assent on 28 May.[57] At no stage, in either House, was there any opposition, and the measure was discussed only when Labouchère introduced it and asked for leave to bring in the Bill. He explained the need to modify the 1844 Act to accommodate the translation clause, describing it as a 'sort of complement to the measure of 1844'. Only one other member spoke, but it was wholly appropriate that he should. Lord Mahon, in what is apparently his last public utterance on copyright, welcomed the proposal:

> . . . he and Mr Justice Talfourd both felt [in 1837–42] they could not complete the subject in a satisfactory manner without the aid of a treaty respecting international copyright. He rejoiced to see that some progress had been made . . .[58]

The Anglo-French Convention was an important part of the jigsaw of agreements which now covered much of western Europe. A Franco-Belgian treaty later in 1852, and an Anglo-Belgian agreement in 1855, solved the problem of Belgian piracy of French books, which had been, for the French, a running sore as annoying as France had been for England.[59] Far to the east in Leipzig, Baron Tauchnitz was another beneficiary of the Convention, for his editions, authorized by their authors, and protected by the Anglo-Prussian agreement of 1846, to which Saxony had subsequently adhered, were now the only legal editions in France and much of Germany.[60] The web was almost complete.[61]

British law itself, however, was still far from ideal. The imperfections, inadequacies and inconsistencies of the 1842 Act were arousing more and more complaints in the middle decades of the century. Various efforts were made to consolidate the law, including international law, culminating in the Royal Commission on Copyright which sat from 1875 to 1878.[62] In the international sphere, two major outstanding issues (apart from the perpetual problem of American copyright) needed to be resolved. One related to the colonies, which, because these included Canada, became a part of the Anglo-American issue.[63] The second, more easily addressed, concerned the nationality of authors, and what became known as 'priority of publication'.

The question of the relevance of the nationality of an author was raised as early as 1839. In that year, Chancery held that a foreigner, resident abroad, 'is entitled to the protection of the laws of this country relating to copyright' provided that the book in question was first published in the United Kingdom, and that publication otherwise complied with British law.[64] This decision was taken under the 1814 Act, but was apparently confirmed in terms of the 1842 and 1844 Acts in due course. The leading case was *Boosey v. Purday (1849)*,[65] one of a complicated series of actions concerning the rights in the score and libretto of Bellini's opera *La somnambula*. The Court of Exchequer cited *Bentley v. Foster*, and held that 'A foreign author residing abroad, who composes a work abroad, and sends it to this country, where it is first published under his authority, acquires copyright therein'. The arguments that 'the legislature did not mean to confer a copyright on any authors but British subjects . . . ', and that 'The object of the legislature is not to encourage the importation of foreign books and their first publication in England . . . but to promote the cultivation of the intellect of its own subjects . . .',[66] patriotic as they were, were completely rejected.

The courts did, however, draw some lines around the right of foreigners. They refused to grant rights to the assignees of foreign authors, even if the assignee were resident in the United Kingdom at the time of publication.[67] Even so, the boundaries were generous, and there was no doubt that, by the middle of the nineteenth century, foreign authors could acquire British copyright by first publishing their works under the protection of the 1842 Act. That was to introduce yet another complication into Anglo-American copyright affairs, when American authors began taking day trips to Montreal![68]

These decisions showed that British law could accommodate change, but its failings were sharply exposed when the British government began to explore the possibility of joining with other countries in a general agreement on international copyright. By the early 1880s, the network of bilateral agreements was as complicated as it was comprehensive, and there was clearly a case for some sort of codification in a general treaty. The first impetus came from the authors themselves, working through their own international body, the *Association Littéraire et Artistique Internationale*, founded in 1879 to promote the interests of authors throughout the world. At its own conference in 1883, the *Association* drafted the text of an international multilateral Convention which would give reciprocal protection to authors in all signatory states.[69] The Swiss government was persuaded to take up the cause, and it duly summoned intergovernmental conferences in Berne in 1884 and 1885. These conferences eventually agreed a revised version of the original proposal, and produced a draft Convention which was politically acceptable while meeting most of the demands of the authors. In 1886, delegates from five European governments came together again in Berne to discuss the issues and possibilities. There was, however, a clear intention to ratify the agreement reached in the previous year. The five participants were Germany, France, Belgium, Spain and Italy; they were soon joined by the host country, Switzerland, and also by Liberia, Tunis and Haiti. Japan and the U.S.A. were present as observers.

The British government hesitated. The initiative was eventually taken by the authors, who apparently drew the attention of the Prime Minister, Gladstone, to the matter in January 1886.[70] Through the newly formed Society of Authors,[71] which already had links with the international *Association*, they were better organized than on many previous occasions. They sent a delegation to meet A. J. Mundella, the President of the Board of Trade, in March, and persuaded him, and through him Gladstone, that the United Kingdom ought to be involved in the Berne conference.[72] The government agreed, and British diplomats joined the delegations which gathered in Berne. Some modifications would be needed to British law before the government could agree to the proposals. A Bill to allow the United Kingdom to enter into the Convention was introduced in the House of Commons by Mundella on 29 March, and received the Royal Assent on 25 June.[73] It was largely a technical measure.[74] Almost the only discussion during its passage through Parliament concerned the implications for the colonies, but that was significant. In proposing the Second Reading, Mundella explained that the colonies could join the proposed Convention through an Order-in-Council, but only by their own consent. He also pointed out that, for the first time, there would be full reciprocal copyright within the British Empire for any colonies which did accede to the Convention.[75] With this matter apparently out of the way, the British delegation was able to go to Berne with plenipotentiary powers.

The Berne Convention was signed by all the states present, except the two observers, on 9 September 1886. It was to come into force on 5 December 1887, following formal ratification, which was duly given by all the signatories except Liberia.[76] The essence of the Berne Convention was that it gave copyright protection in any member state to the nationals of all the other member states on the same basis as it did to its own nationals. Some disagreements which had arisen in 1884 and 1885 were still apparent, however, in the final text. The initiative had originally come from the French authors who dominated the *Association Littéraire et Artistique Internationale*, and their demands regarding translations had not been fully met. They wanted full terms comparable with those for original works. In fact, protection for translations was closer to the British position of a limited period following a declaration of the reservation of the rights by the original author.[77] One other clause was to prove to be of great importance. The Convention required that copyright had to be acquired by the mere fact of authorized publication in any member state. The significance of this was that signatories could not require formal registration in order to obtain or confirm copyright, and that there could be no law which required authors to publish their works in a particular country in order to establish and protect their rights. This was inconsistent with American law, and, consequently, the United States was unable to sign the Berne Convention.

Indeed, the Berne Convention served to emphasize the isolation of the United States from the rapidly growing network of international copyright protection. Some Americans were aware of the anomaly of their country's position, but a political solution was still very difficult to find. From the British perspective this was still the problem which it had been since the 1840s, a position which was only exacerbated in the middle decades of the century by the development of mutual protection between European states. Trollope, for example, contrasted the American publishers ('dishonest beasts') with 'Tauchnitz who always buys my novels'.[78] The lack of copyright protection in the United States was a grievance among British authors and publishers of all sorts, from Trollope and Blackwood on the one hand, to Benjamin Jowett, the translator of Plato, and the Oxford University Press on the other.[79]

The root of the legal problem lay in the inherent conflict between the laws of the two countries. There were two essential elements in this conflict. Under the Copyright Act of 1842, copyright was acquired in the United Kingdom by the fact of authorized publication and subsequent deposit of a copy at the British Museum. Registration at Stationers' Hall was just a record of the fact of publication and deposit. It was significant because it was the only record which would be accepted by the courts in the event of a legal action concerning the rights in a work. Copyright, moreover, was assured by the same actions and records in all countries with which the United Kingdom had bilateral conventions, and, after 1886, in all signatory states of the Berne Convention. With some exceptions, the law also applied in all British colonies and self-governing dominions in the same way as it did in the United Kingdom. The fundamental principle of American law was quite different. Under the 1790 Federal Copyright Act, and its successor of 1831, copyright could only be acquired by registration, with the Register of Copyrights in Washington, before publication; this was achieved by the deposit of a copy of the title page with the Register, followed, after publication, by a copy of the book itself being sent to the Library of Congress.

The second area of conflict between British and American law concerned the nationality of the author. By 1840, the British courts had established that a resident foreigner who first published a work in Britain was entitled to the protection of the British law. This was not changed by the 1842 or 1844 Acts. The provision was extended to residents in a British colony by a ruling in the House of Lords in 1868.[80] The American courts took a far more limited view, regarding the rights of resident non-citizens as being limited to those who had formally applied for citizenship; even the recruitment of an American collaborator in writing or editing a work did not guarantee that copyright could be secured in the United States.[81] Against this legal background, and the long history of cultural conflict, suspicion, dispute and bitterness between British and American authors and publishers, it began to seem that no agreement would ever be reached between the two countries. In the event, some measure of Anglo-American amity on copyright matters was achieved by limited changes in American law, although these failed to meet the international norms embodied in the Berne Convention.

The story resumed in the early 1850s. There had, briefly, been some hope of a resolution of the issue at that time. From 1849 to 1851, the British Minister in Washington was Henry Lytton Bulwer, the elder brother of Bulwer-Lytton the novelist.[82] His nephew, Robert, the novelist's son, joined his staff in the autumn of 1850, and took up his father's interest in Anglo-American copyright. He also began to learn the devious ways of American politics. When Bulwer was forced by illness to resign in 1851, his nephew stayed on to work with the new British Minister, John Crampton, who became equally adept in the corruption of ante-Bellum Washington. Crampton realized that only by the exercise of influence through lobbying and bribery was there any hope of pushing an international copyright Bill through Congress. He and young Lytton set about this with a will.

Through their contacts among the Washington lobbyists, they persuaded Edward Everitt, the Secretary of State, to support the cause, and he, in turn, influenced President Fillmore. A group of leading American publishers was persuaded to offer their support, although others in the trade were still bitterly opposed. In 1852, Crampton was authorized by the Foreign Office to negotiate a treaty modelled on the Anglo-French Convention which had just been concluded. He and Lytton realized that large sums of money would be needed to ensure the continuing support of the lobbyists and congressmen without whom no legislation was possible. Lytton returned home, and his father tried to raise the money – said to be £2,000 – which would apparently be necessary to push the proposed treaty through Congress. Many of the British authors had moral scruples about this, quite apart from more practical considerations, but, in the meanwhile, a treaty was indeed negotiated.

This treaty was actually signed in February 1853. It was based on the same general principles as the Anglo-French Convention and the other bilateral agreements between European states: reciprocal recognition of the rights of each other's writers and publishers in each other's countries. It foundered, however, in the political shoals of Washington. Franklin Pierce, who succeeded Fillmore as President in March 1854, signed the treaty, and sent it to the Senate for ratification, but he had little interest in the matter and was certainly not committed to this initiative by the previous administration. The opposition from some of the publishers and booksellers was now fierce, and the bill to ratify the treaty never emerged from the committee to which it was sent by the Senate. Negotiations involving publishers, authors, congressmen and diplomats continued, but they were in vain. The treaty was never ratified, and with it died what was to be the last hope of an Anglo-American copyright agreement comparable with those which Britain was successfully negotiating with her European neighbours. The gap between the two sides was as wide as ever, and the grievances felt by both were equally strong.

Repeated efforts were made to revive the idea of a treaty both before and after the American Civil War. In 1867, Dickens and Trollope went to the United States to help in the business, and there were various petitions from British authors and publishers during the 1860s and 1870s. Failure followed failure. The American publishers were entrenched in their opposition to international copyright, and showed no inclination to change as the market for reprints of English books became ever more lucrative. It seemed that no progress was possible.[83]

The exclusion of the United States from the Berne Convention, made necessary by its own domestic law, finally provoked some American authors and publishers into action. The American Copyright League was founded in 1884 by a group of publishers to press for reform of the law, both domestically and internationally. It became more active after 1887, and began to lobby vigorously and effectively for changes. A succession of bills was considered by Congress between 1886 and 1890, but all fell to the opposition of the Democrats. Their supporters, especially in the south, were bitterly antipathetic to any measure which would open up American markets to foreign competition, or, coincidentally, increase the price of books, as many feared that it would. The opposition was not only political. The publishers of cheap reprint series were against it, and so too were the increasingly powerful trade unions in the printing industry who feared loss of work if the copyright in imported books were protected under American law. It was a concession on the last point which finally allowed a bill to pass, but the same concession caused the continued exclusion of the United States from the growing international consensus on copyright protection.[84]

The Chase Act of 1891, as it is known from the name of one of its sponsors, Senator Henry Chase, at last made some of the provisions for which British authors had been calling for half a century. Non-resident authors were now protected in the United States on exactly the same terms as residents, which, under the 1891 Act, was for 28 years, with a 14-year renewal if the author were still alive at the end of that time. Although this fell far short of the terms which were now common in the Berne Convention countries, it was an important advance, and was welcomed as such by British authors.[85] There were, however, some serious complications. Two were particularly disadvantageous to foreign authors, and both arose out of the concession which had had to be made to the printing workers' unions.[86] First, to claim copyright protection in the United States, a book had to published there no later than it was published in its country of origin. Secondly, it had to be printed in the United States, or printed from type set in the United States or from plates made from type set in the United States. The manufacturing clause had come back to haunt American international copyright affairs yet again, and resulted in the continuing absence of the United States from the Berne Convention.

From a British point of view, however, the Chase Act was better than nothing. British authors and publishers soon learned how to make use of the Act to secure their copyrights in the United States. The young Bernard Shaw had predicted in 1885 that 'if an International Copyright Treaty [i.e. the Berne Convention] be concluded . . . authors . . . will deal directly with publishers in America . . .'[87] He was wrong in two respects: the Americans did not sign the treaty, and, in general, British authors used their publishers to deal with American rights rather than doing so themselves. Indeed, Shaw himself told Grant Richards that he wanted 'to secure the American copyright' in *The Perfect Wagnerite* in 1898, which Richards proceeded to do by negotiating (at Shaw's suggestion) with the New York publisher, Herbert S. Stone.[88] Indeed, one of the unintended longer-term consequences of the Chase Act was that British and American publishers began to work together more closely. It was in the decade after the passage of the Act that we can first detect American capital beginning to be invested in the somewhat ailing British publishing industry.[89] While the Chase Act certainly did not solve all the problems of Anglo-American copyright, it did create a climate in which authors and publishers could cooperate across the Atlantic.

It also, however, brought to a head another issue which had been smouldering, with increasing intensity, for much of the time since the passage of the 1842 Act in Britain. This was the question of copyright in the British colonies and dominions. For the most part, this was uncontentious. After some minor modifications to the law relating to the Customs, books which were protected under the 1842 Act were protected throughout the British Empire. Some British publishers, notably John Murray, took advantage of this and began to issue 'Colonial' editions or libraries specifically for sale in the British possessions outside the United Kingdom.[90] The problems arose, however, in connection with Canada, which both legally and culturally was in a unique position. Legally, Canada became a self-governing dominion in 1867, with its own Parliament empowered to pass its own legislation. Culturally (and indeed economically), it was increasingly influenced by the United States, and was, for the latter country, a potential export market of great importance. From the perspective of an American publisher, Canada was an English-speaking market on the doorstep, where the writ of the British government did not entirely run.

As early as the 1840s, Canadian booksellers, and indeed the Canadian public, were looking for ways to buy cheap books from the United States rather than expensive ones from Britain. One solution was smuggling, and this certainly happened on a large scale. Another course of action was to change the law, and, remarkably, this also happened. In 1847, Gladstone, at that time Colonial Secretary, addressed the issue under pressure from the Canadians themselves. A Bill was introduced of which the effect was to suspend the 1842 Act in any colony which made adequate provision to pay British authors for books published or sold in that colony. The Act would come into force in a particular colony when an Order-in-Council was made to implement it, which, in effect, would happen when the British government (represented by the Board of Trade or the Colonial Office) was satisfied with the arrangements which had been made. This Bill passed through Parliament with no opposition and became law, as the Foreign Reprints Act, on 22 July.[91] The Canadians acted promptly to take advantage of this Act, which had slipped through the British Parliament without any opposition, and without even arousing the interest of British authors and publishers, who presumably did not realize its implications. They were to have their eyes opened. The first Canadian proposal would, in effect, have granted Canadian copyright to British authors only if their works were printed and published in Canada; this was squashed, but the agreement which was eventually reached was little better from the British point of view. In 1851, a Canadian Act was accepted as the basis for an Order-in-Council in terms of the British Act of 1847. The 1842 Act was indeed suspended in Canada. An excise duty, not exceeding 20 per cent, was to be charged on the import of books from the United States, of which the proceeds were to go to British copyright owners. The Act was a farce; no serious attempt was made to enforce it. British publishers received almost nothing, and cheap American reprints of British books were on sale throughout the British territories in North America.[92]

Worse was to come, from the British point of view. The leading case of *Routledge v. Samson Low*, determined on appeal to the House of Lords in 1868, was at the heart of the problem.[93] The Lords had held that the 1842 Act applied to foreigners resident in any British territory. They also decided, however, that where the 1842 Act had been suspended by an Order-in-Council under the 1847 Foreign Reprints Act, the copyright acquired by publication in that territory did not extend to the rest of the Empire. This conundrum was not even solved when the United Kingdom signed the Berne Convention, for this still allowed self-governing dominions to decide for themselves whether or not to adhere to it, which Canada did not do until 1928.[94] Reduced to its simplest form, the effect of all this was that American reprints of British books could be sold in Canada, and that British publishers could not even protect themselves by authorizing Canadian reprints of their own because that could undermine their rights elsewhere in the Empire. The really significant fact for British publishers was the effective loss of the Canadian market to the Americans. The Chase Act, by providing a means by which British copyrights could be secured and rewarded in the United States, eased the situation a little, but even so, from the middle of the nineteenth century onwards, Canada was no longer a part of the cultural empire of the British publishing industry.

European, American and colonial copyright problems proliferated throughout the nineteenth century. The various attempts made to address them were pragmatic rather than idealistic. Within Europe, treaties and conventions provided a relatively simple mechanism for reciprocal protection, a practice which reached its zenith with the signature of the Berne Convention in 1886. No such agreements were possible with the United States, and British authors and publishers were forced to take what advantage they could of the very limited protection afforded to them by domestic legislation. In the rapidly expanding British Empire, the most advanced country, Canada, provided difficulties of its own; although the concept of 'imperial copyright' was established by the 1842 Act, the 1847 Foreign Reprints Act provided a means of undermining that very concept almost as soon as it was recognized.

By the end of the nineteenth century, international copyright was generally accepted in legal, literary and publishing circles. Provisions might vary, but there was a broad recognition that an author or other copyright owner was entitled to some form of protection of rights in any country in the world. Despite the reluctance of the protectionist United States, and even of some of Britain's own more recalcitrant overseas territories, the principle itself was barely open to challenge. Even in practice, protection was widespread and effective. One consequence, however, was that British copyright law could no longer be considered in a purely national context. In the United Kingdom after 1886, any revision of the law had international implications which legislators would have to take into account. Moreover, the great copyright debates of the nineteenth century, both domestic and international, had made authors everywhere more aware of the economic power which grew out of their artistic talents. It was in this ethos that the 1842 Act operated in the United Kingdom, and in which it gradually came to be seen to be somewhat less ideal than its proponents had hoped.

7 Challenge and Change 1842–1988

In the turmoil of his first American tour, Dickens wrote to his friend and future biographer, John Forster: 'The effect of all this copyright agitation has at least been to awaken a great interest on both sides of the subject . . .'[1] That interest, however, soon subsided, and for long periods even the search for an Anglo-American copyright agreement lay dormant or was pursued through quiet diplomacy or covert bribes. The international question, at least in relation to the United States, did, from time to time, arouse some public debate, although more often because of its patriotic dimensions than because of the literary or legal issues which were at stake. Domestic copyright was of almost no concern whatsoever, except to a very few; those few were a minority even among authors and publishers. To them, it was a crucial issue, and there have indeed been four brief periods since 1842 when their concerns became more general and more public. In general, developments in domestic law have been driven as much by international necessity, in making British law consistent with international conventions to which the United Kingdom wished to adhere, and by rapid and continuous technological change, as they have by the wishes and views of authors and publishers.

The Copyright Act of 1842 had fulfilled at least one of the ambitions of its progenitors. The most important provision for authors was that the period of copyright had been significantly lengthened. At worst, there was lifetime protection for the author, with a 7-year *post mortem* term, and 42-year protection for posthumous works. The compromise which had enabled Mahon to succeed where Talfourd had failed was not ideal, but it provided a reasonable level of protection for authors and their families. In many other respects, however, the Act was unsatisfactory. When copyright was investigated by a Royal Commission in the late 1870s,[2] the Commissioners observed of the Act that 'The first observation . . . is that its form, as distinguished from its substance, seems to us bad'.[3] They went on to use such words as 'incomplete', 'obscure' and 'ill-expressed', referring largely to the wording of the Act, but also, from time to time, to its contents as well.

The truth was that the 1842 Act was, like its predecessor of 1710, designed to solve a specific problem. As a result, it created other problems in its wake, because its authors had failed to identify or to address some other important issues. In 1710, Parliament had legislated for the booksellers; in 1842 it legislated for the authors. In particular, it had legislated for the authors of books. The Act had little to say, although it implied much, about the authors and editors of periodicals, and nothing at all about such matters as performance rights, rights in music and lyrics, and rights in works of visual art. Other laws dealt with some of this, but there were gross inconsistencies between them, and there were some formats and media, and some creative or imitative activities, which were not covered at all, or whose coverage was ambiguous and imperfect. The 1842 Act was a rather backward-looking piece of legislation, which protected the classic form of the late eighteenth and early nineteenth centuries – the printed book – while almost entirely ignoring the proliferation of reproducible and marketable formats and manifestations which already existed even as early as the 1840s.

The diversification of media is an essential part of the history of copyright in the nineteenth and twentieth centuries. It has its roots in technological change, in itself an alien concept in the book trade in the year 1800. At the beginning of the nineteenth century, book production had barely changed in the 350 years since the invention of printing. Printing itself was the only medium of reproduction which could be used for text; its ability to reproduce pictures accurately and effectively was very limited. It was a hand-craft process; typesetting, printing and binding were all done by hand. All the ancillary arts and processes were in the same state; these included the various graphic processes, which involved engraving or cutting in wood or in a metal plate, and even the manufacture of the basic materials of the craft itself, paper, type and ink. Within less than half a century, almost all of this changed.

The details of the changes are not important for the present purpose, but the consequences and the chronology are. The invention (or perhaps more accurately, the re-invention) of stereotyping came first; this process, which allows an exact copy to be made of a page of type, was used commercially from about 1800 onwards, and reduced both the time and the cost of reprinting. It was no longer necessary either to reset the type, or to keep large quantities of type made up (or 'standing' in the printers' terminology) in order to reprint a text. The plates (or moulds from which the plates were made) could be stored easily, used many times, and, when they were worn, easily reproduced for continued use. Stereotyping was the process which made cheap reprinting possible on a previously unimagined scale.[4]

The second great development was the invention of the papermaking machine. The inventor was Louis Robert, a Frenchman, but its practical development took place in England with the capital of the Fourdrinier brothers, who were wholesale stationers in London. The Fourdrinier machines, whose principle still remains essentially unchanged, displaced hand papermaking for commercial purposes very rapidly, after their first introduction in 1807. Much machine-made paper was of a lower quality than its handcrafted predecessor, but the sheer quantity that could be produced inevitably brought down the price.[5] This was a major contribution to the cheapening of printed matter.

The third innovation was in printing itself. Iron displaced wood as the material from which printing presses were made from 1800 onwards, which made the press more efficient, and increased the speed of production. The revolutionary change, however, was in the application of steam power to printing from 1814 onwards. Although the steam presses were at first used almost entirely for newspapers, by the 1840s nearly all books were being printed by steam-driven presses. Printing was easier, faster and cheaper as a result.[6] The mechanization of typesetting was less easily achieved, and the problems which it presented were not solved until almost the end of the century, when, in the late 1880s and early 1890s, two similar systems, Linotype and Monotype, were introduced.[7]

Graphic processes underwent equally important, and even more radical, change. The traditional hand processes survived until the end of the nineteenth century and into the twentieth, but there was one important nineteenth-century addition to the range. This was lithography, which allowed for far more detailed and accurate drawings and diagrams, and was particularly useful for printing maps and music as well as representational illustrations.[8] From the 1840s onwards, however, all the hand processes were under continuous and growing challenge from the wholly new process of photography. Indeed, with photography, we move away from technical innovations in printing towards more general developments in communication media, although techniques were indeed developed for reproducing photographs as part of the printing process.[9]

New media, and new means of reproduction, transmission and communication, have revolutionized the world of books and information since the middle of the nineteenth century. Recorded sound was first heard in 1877, moving photographic pictures were first made in 1887, and the two were linked as 'talkies' in 1926. Before that, signals had been transmitted by cable (1844) and by wireless telegraphy (1896), and commercial broadcasting for entertainment and other purposes had begun in Britain in 1922. Television followed in 1936. After World War Two, the pace of innovation was, if anything, even faster. The use of small-format photographic film, with high-quality lenses, made microform reproduction easy and widespread by the late 1940s. Photocopying, in a primitive form, existed by the 1870s, and the plain-paper dry copying processes were also under development by 1940. Sound recording on magnetic tape had been invented in the 1920s, but tape recorders were not commercially available until the mid-1950s. All the time, equipment was becoming more sophisticated, and, in real terms, cheaper. During the good economic times of the 1950s, the ownership of televisions, tape-recorders and record-players soared in Britain, while libraries equipped themselves with microfilm and microcard readers. By the mid-1960s, the photocopier was ubiquitous in libraries and offices alike.

All of this made reproduction cheap and easy. Photocopiers allowed anyone to make a copy of anything on a piece of paper, text or diagram, manuscript or printed. Tape recording made it possible to copy the sound from radio broadcasts or from gramophone records. It was hard to sustain traditional ideas about the inviolability and integrity of reproducible works in such conditions. Later developments exacerbated the situation. Video recording made all television programmes (which included many cinema films) vulnerable to virtually uncontrollable copying. New communications systems, especially satellite television broadcasting, made it virtually impossible to control transmission and reception outside a single jurisdiction. Above all, computers transformed the information world.

The first computers were built as code-breaking devices during World War Two. They began to be used for complex mathematical calculations in the late 1940s, and spread slowly but pervasively in the scientific world during the 1950s. By the mid-1960s, computers were in use for handling textual data, but they were expensive and difficult to use, and were largely confined to universities. Gradually, they spread into business and industry, as the multiplicity of uses with which we are now familiar were developed from the late 1960s onwards. The development of the microprocessor – the 'silicon chip' – in the 1970s brought a second computer revolution before the first was complete. Computers joined photocopiers in every office, and televisions in many homes, as the visible symbol of the information society. The vast industry which has developed around the computer is creating products which are perhaps more easily reproducible than anything else ever invented. The software which drives a computer, and the stored data which it contains, can be reproduced without error and, almost instantaneously, in a form which is virtually indistinguishable from the original. Even more than photocopying, this presents a challenge to the very idea of copyright, and one which is still not fully answered.

Against this background, the cosy world of books which produced the 1842 Copyright Act has changed almost beyond recognition. Indeed, even in 1842, it was changing. That law was devised at the very time when steam printing, stereotyping and machine-made paper had brought the price of books, in real terms, to unprecedentedly low levels. Other innovations in transport and communications, and in commercial systems such as wholesaling and banking, tended towards the same end. Moreover, as books became cheaper, the market for them increased. Rising literacy rates, the increase of leisure time, and the development of both commercial and public libraries all created new markets for the book trade. The trade itself was transformed. It was increasingly dominated by a small number of publishers and an even smaller number of wholesalers, with a vast and diffuse network of bookshops and circulating libraries through which the public obtained their books. The chain of supply was long, and many people along it were looking to make a profit out of their transactions.

Books no longer stood alone in the trade. Newspapers had, of course, been familiar since the late seventeenth century, and magazines since the early eighteenth, but cheap printing allowed both to proliferate in the nineteenth century. The reduction, and eventual abolition, of taxation on newspapers brought them within reach of virtually the entire population, and by the end of the century, the popular press was well-established and highly profitable. For authors, the newspapers and magazines were a major new source of income in the nineteenth and twentieth centuries, rivalling and perhaps often superseding the writing of books.[10]

Journalism, at whatever level, was not, however, the only new source of income. All the new media of the late nineteenth and twentieth centuries provided new outlets for creative work. Music had to be composed before it could be recorded, and scripts written before talkies could be made. Radio and television both showed an apparently inexhaustible appetite for writing of all kinds, whether original material, or adaptations of existing books. Old simplicities vanished. A novel written in 1891, by an author who did not die until 1940, could have been published originally in a magazine, in both Britain and the United States, reprinted as a book in both countries, in special editions for Canada and for other parts of the British Empire, and subsequently as a cheap edition for the domestic market. It could also have been dramatized for the stage, read in whole or in part on the radio, adapted either from the novel itself or from the stage version for dramatization on radio or television, and used as the basis for a cinema film. The history of the transformation of Shaw's *Pygmalion* from play to film to musical to film of the musical shows that this is not far-fetched. At every stage in the process, new income was generated as new outlets were created by new technology and by social change.

The Copyright Act of 1842 was still in force when much of this innovation began. Indeed, throughout the nineteenth and twentieth centuries, the law has failed to keep up with the pace of change, even when it has tried to do so. Instead, practices have developed within the law, supported by it if they were tested, which have become commercial relationships between the various producers and distributors of created works. The law of copyright has underpinned some of these developments, and sometimes provided a context for them, but, more often, it has had to be changed to accommodate practice rather than being an active driver of change.

The changing relationship between the writers, publishers and sellers of books was built around the increased importance of money in determining how they worked together. During the eighteenth century, as authors had begun to assert some of the powers accidentally conferred upon them in 1710, they had been able to forge new kinds of agreements with publishers.[11] In essence, these involved the publisher buying the copyright from the author, on conditions which were agreed between them which might include payments to the author based on length, sales, revision for new editions, and so on. In the early nineteenth century, the outright sale of the copyright to the publisher was still normal, and was alleged to be popular with authors. A few publishers even made subsequent *ex gratia* payments if a book was particularly successful. For most writers, however, outright sale represented the only form of income from their work, and they were thus paid once only for each book.[12] This could lead to great complications, for an author lost both financial and artistic control of his or her works, and a later collected edition would often involve complicated transactions with a number of parties.[13]

Gradually, outright sale came to be replaced by other methods, most of which were more favourable to the author. The earliest were the profit-sharing agreements under which the author and publisher shared the profits when the expenses of the edition had been covered. The usual division of the spoils was 50:50, and the system consequently was known as 'half-profits'. From the 1830s to the 1860s, this was probably the most common form of payment for most authors. It certainly was for novelists, the producers of the dominant literary form of the period.[14] The system was, however, fraught with difficulties. It depended on the existence of mutual trust between author and publisher, and especially on the author's willingness to accept the publisher's accounting procedures and results. Too often, such trust was lacking, and it was, indeed, occasionally misplaced.[15]

In the second half of the century, a second kind of agreement began to be reached, which was, eventually, to displace all the others almost entirely. This was the royalty agreement, under which the author was paid an agreed percentage of the publisher's income from the book. The percentage was usually of the order of 10 to 12½ per cent. It was normally paid on the trade price, and continued however many editions were published so long as the book remained in copyright. Some publishers began to pay on a royalty basis in the 1860s, and it was probably normal by the 1880s.[16] The author thus gained a continuing interest in the book, and some control over it.

The 1842 Act made no attempt to define copyright, but, by partly associating the term of copyright protection with the author's life, at least implicitly recognized that it was essentially an author's right. The evolving new forms of agreement between authors and publishers also implicitly acknowledged the author's role as the creator of the property. The point which had caused so much trouble to the eighteenth-century lawyers was thus settled pragmatically in the nineteenth century.[17] The assertiveness of authors was not only financial; they also began to claim the right to control their property in an artistic or literary sense, by controlling the forms and versions in which it was disseminated. It was these claims which lay at the root of the difficulties which were to arise about translations, dramatizations and abridgements, and even about the publication of cheap editions of the whole of the original text.[18]

Eventually, the authors began to come together to defend their interests, and indeed to promote them. In 1883–84, twelve writers formed the Society of Authors and quickly persuaded many others to join them. The prime mover in the Society was Walter Besant, a novelist and journalist; the first group of members included Matthew Arnold, Wilkie Collins and Charlotte Yonge, all recruited as Vice-Presidents, and, in Besant's greatest coup, the recently ennobled Tennyson as President.[19] The Society's main interests were in the relations between publishers and authors, and with copyright law reform, both domestic and international, but especially with the still festering issue of Anglo-American copyright.[20] The foundation of the Society of Authors was one of the ways in which the authors professionalized themselves. Some, especially among the younger generation, were beginning to use agents to represent their interests in dealings with their publishers, much as they might have used a solicitor. The first of the great agents, A. P. Watt, was active by the mid-1870s, and, despite the suspicions and hostility of some of the more traditional publishers, literary agents soon became a familiar part of the London book world.[21] The work of the Society of Authors and the activities of literary agents both made authors more aware of their interests, their status and their rights. The generation of Arnold Bennett and H. G. Wells were very clear that, however much they might love literature and wish to serve the republic of letters, they also expected to earn a reasonable living as a reward for their talents and achievements.

It was not only the authors who became more professional and more commercial at the end of the nineteenth century. Throughout the century, there had been intermittent attempts among both the booksellers and the publishers to form societies and associations of various kinds.[22] These organizations had failed, but in the 1890s new organizations were founded on both sides of the trade which were to prove to be permanent.[23] The immediate cause of the foundation of both the Associated Booksellers of Great Britain and Ireland (later to become the Booksellers' Association) in 1895, and of the Publishers' Association in 1896, was the need for representative bodies in the discussions which led to the formulation of the Net Book Agreement in 1900.[24] Indeed, once that Agreement was concluded, both bodies policed the trade to ensure its enforcement. The Publishers' Association also assumed a larger role in representing the interests of its members in a wide range of matters, including copyright. The Net Book Agreement itself was important to the authors in a quite unintentional way; by allowing publishers to determine the minimum retail (or 'net') price at which a book could be sold in the United Kingdom, it provided a touchstone against which royalty percentages could easily be measured without the ambiguity inherent in considering trade prices.

The technological and commercial changes in the book trade were all ultimately dependent on the market for books. This expanded throughout the century, as education and literacy spread down the social scale. To provide for the needs of a diverse and multi-layered market, the trade developed its own norms and practices, especially in the publication of novels. Scott established the convention of three-volume publication, and the 'three-decker' became the standard format of the mid-nineteenth-century novel.[25] The typical three-decker was sold at the considerable price of 31*s*. 6*d*. (one-and-a-half guineas), far beyond the reach of many readers, and expensive even for the middle classes in search of light entertainment. In fact, the three-deckers were almost entirely the preserve of the circulating libraries, which, from humble origins in the late seventeenth century and through a period of fashionable popularity in the eighteenth, became one of the great institutions of mid-Victorian Britain. The two great national libraries, Mudie's and Smith's, came to dominate the market. They demanded three-deckers (because they charged by the volume for loans), and the publishers provided them.[26] When, in 1894–95, Mudie's changed their policy and refused to accept three-deckers, the form vanished overnight, and was never revived.

The libraries provided a safe market for the expensive first editions of novels, but, for the bookshops, the mainstay of the trade was the cheap reprint in one volume, typically priced at 6*s*. 0*d*. Some of these were in series, others were not; whatever the case, it was the cheap editions, containing the full authorized text, in which the Victorian novelists, both greater and lesser, reached the mass market. Cheap reprints became the flagship of the public conscience of the publishing industry, with its claims to serve all classes of society at prices which they could afford.[27] They also, of course, provided additional income, and, for authors, additional royalties. Even the demise of the three-deckers did not kill the reprints. Indeed, in the early twentieth century, they proliferated, with both copyright and public domain texts being issued in such series as Nelson's Sixpenny Classics, Everyman's Library and World's Classics, a pattern of publishing which reached its climax in the work of Allen Lane in the 1930s when he founded Penguin Books.[28]

It is against this complex history of social, economic and cultural change that the development of copyright since 1842 has to be considered. Perhaps the most important difference from earlier periods was the greater prominence of the authors. This was partly a direct consequence of the 1842 Act, but authors, individually and collectively, were also more willing and able to use the law, and to demand that it be changed for their benefit. At the same time, the publishing industry and the book trade had become a vast network of interlocking interests, with massive capital investments and ever-growing costs. Finally, throughout the period, the book, and even the printed word itself, was under continuous challenge from an ever-increasing number of technological marvels, each one more accomplished than its predecessor and some displacing the art of reading itself as the prime means of human communication through time and space.

The 1842 Act was ill-designed to cope with these changes, for that had not been its purpose; yet it had to do so. Ideas about such basic concepts as 'copying' and 'plagiarism' were themselves becoming more complicated, and the practical application of the law to the socially unacceptable was less easy as a consequence.[29] The move to change or augment the Act, however, was not driven principally by perceptions of its conceptual inadequacy. On a purely practical level, authors and publishers alike were concerned with international copyright as much as with domestic law. Especially after 1886, they wanted the United Kingdom to play a full and active part in the growing arena of international copyright protection. More than anything else, especially in the first half of the twentieth century, it was the demands of the international conventions which provided the driving force for reform.

Domestically, the forces at work were somewhat different. Authors and publishers alike were interested in a clear and enforceable law, which required better definitions of rights and penalties. As time went on, however, their interest shifted towards the growing number of subsidiary rights, and the need to protect the integrity of literary properties against the adapters, abridgers and translators, and later the recordists and cinematographers. Apparently clear distinctions between the written and the spoken word, and between publication and performance, were blurred in the face of technological innovation. To confront this was a law largely written at the instigation of a few old men who wanted to protect their families' claims to the income from their writings, together with a multiplicity of statutes, going back to Hogarth's Act of 1735, which sought to offer some form of protection to other products of the human brain. In this morass, there was not even an adequate definition of copyright itself.

The need for consolidation and codification of the law was apparent even in the 1840s, but it was not until 1857 that a Bill was brought forward which would have had this effect. The Copyright Acts Consolidation Bill of that year would have repealed and replaced Hogarth's Act, the 1842 Act, the Dramatic Performances Act of 1833, and a host of other legislation, to give a 42-year term for everything, and a wide range of protection of rights. After a formal First Reading in the Commons, it was withdrawn by its sponsors.[30] The problem remained, however, and the need for a solution was becoming ever more urgent. A similar Bill was introduced in 1864; this went to a Select Committee after its Second Reading.[31] The Select Committee held five meetings in the spring and early summer of 1864, and recognized the confused and conflicting law in the field, but concluded that they were 'not prepared to recommend any amendment or consolidation of the Law of Copyright . . .'[32] *The Times* rightly took this to indicate that they found the matter too difficult, and it was unimpressed by their proposal to refer it to another Select Committee in the following Session.[33] In fact, eleven years were to elapse before Parliament returned to the question of domestic copyright, and the immediate upshot even then was no more than some minor modifications to performing rights.[34]

The Performing Rights Act of 1875, however, provided the occasion for a general debate on domestic copyright in the House of Commons, apparently for the first time since 1842. In the course of that debate, Edward Jenkins, a recently elected Liberal member, declared himself disappointed with the narrow scope of the proposal, and indicated that he hoped that a future Bill would come closer to addressing the key issues of copyright law.[35] In the following Session, he returned to the matter, and took an active part in trying to force a change. Jenkins, the Talfourd *manqué* of copyright law reform in the late 1870s, was an interesting man.[36] He was born in Canada, and educated there at McGill University before coming to London to be called to the Bar of Lincoln's Inn in

1864. He was a Liberal in politics, but an early example of the imperialist faction in the Liberal Party, strongly favouring measures which tended towards the unity of the British Empire, especially imperial preferences. This put him in a very different camp from his notional leader, Gladstone, but also in a position to attract some cross-party support. To Jenkins, copyright was primarily an imperial issue. He wanted to consolidate domestic and imperial law so as to have a uniform copyright regime throughout the British Empire, including the self-governing dominion of which he was a native.

In the spring of 1875, Jenkins was active in promoting the copyright issue. He was at a meeting held (significantly) at the Canadian Agency in London on 1 March 1875 at which a number of authors and others formed an organization which was to be known as the Association for the Protection of the Rights of Authors. The main business of the meeting was actually to hear an address on the present state of copyright law, especially in relation to the colonies.[37] The group, however, also discussed Jenkins's proposal for a Select Committee on copyright, and, in that way, took a more general interest in reform.[38] At first little happened, but during Prime Minister's Questions on 10 May, Jenkins asked Disraeli whether the government would appoint a Select Committee on copyright. Disraeli replied, somewhat anodynely, that he had received a delegation on the matter that morning, and regarded their representations as being of 'a grave character and deserving the consideration of the government'. The matter of the Select Committee was not yet, however, decided.[39]

The question was not unexpected, and nor was the reply. Jenkins knew all about the delegation, because he had been a member of it, as had Charles Reade, the novelist, Charles Dickens the younger, Charles August Sala, Blanchard Jerrold and other writers and writers' heirs and assigns. In fact, the delegation was from the Association for the Protection of the Rights of Authors, in whose formation all of these men had played a part in the previous year.[40] Jenkins raised three issues with Disraeli, all of which concerned the members of the delegation. These were: first, the need for an inquiry into British domestic copyright law; secondly, the particular issue of the dramatization of novels without the consent of the author of the novel; and finally, the state of imperial law on copyright. W. May Thomas, a lawyer who had been helping the Association, elaborated on all three points, particularly on the need to clarify the law on some specific issues, including the copyright in newspaper articles (which was in dispute between authors and proprietors), the effect on the ownership of U.K. rights if a book by a British subject were first published abroad, and the question of stage adaptations. Disraeli was rather overwhelmed by the detail, but he was not unsympathetic; he was reported as saying:

> . . . I will give the most active attention to what is before me, and I will endeavour to take such a course as I think will remove some of the burdens, annoyances and vexations that now exist . . .

Perhaps the memory of that early self-proclaimed parliamentary triumph inspired him,[41] for he did indeed agree that a committee of inquiry was the best way forward.

In his parliamentary question that afternoon, Jenkins did not go into detail on the issue; indeed parliamentary custom would have precluded this. The only specific matter he raised was in relation to the 'new' Canadian copyright Act, which was indeed causing a good deal of worry to authors and publishers in Britain. This Act,[42] if it had come into full force, would have granted to Canadian publishers the right to pay a fixed royalty to the owners of out-of-print British copyright books and then to reprint them freely. Although there were some safeguards against the export of these books, and against the import into Canada of unauthorized reprints, this was a very large step towards the recognition of a Canadian copyright which was distinct from that in the United Kingdom, while also giving wide-ranging rights to Canadian reprinters.[43] For Jenkins, a Canadian and an imperialist, the real issue was the need to maintain uniformity of legislation through the Empire.

In the event, a Royal Commission was established, after some delay, and Earl Stanhope was designated as its Chairman. There could have been no man more appropriate for the job, for Stanhope was in fact Lord Mahon, the author of the 1842 Act. He never served in this office, however, for he died within weeks of his appointment, and his successor, Lord James Manners, the Postmaster-General, was not appointed until March 1876.[44] Only then did the Commission begin its work.

The Royal Commission of 1875 was the first of four great inquiries into copyright law between the 1870s and the 1970s, and in many ways it was both the most thorough and the least conclusive.[45] It sat for almost three years, heard dozens of witnesses, and deliberated for hundreds of hours. It produced a report which is the most thorough analysis which has ever been made of the late-nineteenth-century law of copyright in Britain, but it had almost no practical effect.[46] The members of the Commission were representative of the literary and legal world, as well as of the political interests involved. They included Jenkins, of course, but also Anthony Trollope, Sir Louis Mallet, now serving at the India Office, but formerly at the Board of Trade (which was the parent Department of the Commission), Farrer Herschell, Liberal M.P., barrister and future Lord Chancellor, J. A. Froude, the historian, and Fitzjames Stephen, a lawyer and future judge who belonged to one of the great intellectual clans of late Victorian England.[47] Their combined intellects, however, were unable to reconcile the differences between competing interest groups, and unable, in the end, to propose a course of action which was generally acceptable.

The Commissioners were unequivocal in their view of the law: 'The first observation . . . is that its form, as distinguished from its substance, seems to us bad . . .'[48] The 1842 Act, in particular, was badly arranged, 'incomplete', 'obscure' and 'ill-expressed'; the whole body of copyright law was riddled with inconsistencies, and was in urgent need of codification.[49] To that extent, no one acquainted with the law would have disagreed with their conclusions. The concerns of the Commissioners were, like their brief, wide-ranging; the Terms of Reference left them with unlimited scope, for they were charged 'to make Inquiry with regard to the Laws and Regulations relating to Home, Colonial and International Copyright . . .',[50] and they did indeed look at all three of these, and also at the problems of copyright or similar protection for forms other than the printed word. In the course of their work, a whole series of issues arose, both general and specific. At the most basic level, they were forced to consider what copyright actually was, and indeed its purpose. They found themselves embroiled in issues of free trade and protectionism. They had to adjudicate on the apparent conflict between private rights in works and the public benefits which resulted from the availability of cheap books. At a more specific level, they confronted, among many other matters, the length of the term of copyright, what were not yet called subsidiary rights, imperial and colonial issues, and the rights, status, income and contractual position of authors. All of this was compounded by the views of composers, musicians, actors, artists and architects, as well as authors, publishers, newspaper editors, economists, lawyers and politicians. The Commissioners were, for the two years during which they sat, very busy men. Perhaps it is no surprise that, at the end of it all, they could not agree.

The Commissioners heard evidence from a great variety of witnesses and it was their preoccupations which largely determined both the agenda and the conclusions of the Commission. On the largest question of all, the nature of copyright, witnesses and Commissioners alike were reluctant to commit themselves. John Blackwood, the head of the distinguished Edinburgh publishing house, flatly refused to enter into what he called 'an abstract question about property'. He seems to have regarded copyright as a unique and almost self-defining form of property, denied that it was even comparable to patent law, and clinched his argument with the statement that 'No other man [*sic*] could invent an "Adam Bede"'.[51] Neither of the other major publishers who testified, John Murray and William Longman, entered into the question at all, and, of the other witnesses, only the scientist T. H. Huxley really came to grips with it. Even he concluded, in a pragmatic way, that he regarded his books as being pieces of property which had 'the same right to be protected as any other kind of property'.[52]

In their report, the Commissioners made no serious attempt to define copyright, even though they themselves rightly noted the confusion in the law, and argued that it arose, in large part, from the very lack of definition. Indeed, whenever it tried to deal with the more abstract issues, the Commission found itself confronted by conflicting views, and divided among itself. In the most significant of the several minority reports, Mallet dissented in principle from the assumptions which underpinned the majority view. He asserted that he regarded ideas as a public good, not as a piece of private property. He took a minimalist view of the role of the law in protecting that public good. To Mallet, the only legitimate role of a law of copyright was to give an incentive to authors. His theoretical position seems to have been that these incentives could still be achieved if monopoly copyrights were abolished and all works went into public domain; authors would then be paid a compulsory royalty by whomever chose to publish their works.[53] Mallet's ideas commanded little or no support among his fellow Commissioners, although his implicit contrast between public benefits and private monopolies was one of the underlying themes of their discussions.

Perhaps the most influential of all the witnesses on these general issues was T. H. Farrer, Permanent Secretary of the Board of Trade since 1865, and destined to remain so until his retirement from the

Civil Service in 1886. He was a vastly experienced public official who had been at the Board since 1842, and was an unassailable supporter of free trade. Like many Victorian free traders, he had a generalized dislike of the extension of the power, or, as he saw it, the interference, of the state in any area of commercial or economic life.[54] Farrer was called several times, not least to explain to the Commissioners the present state of the law. Gradually, however, the tone of his evidence changed. At first he was the expert interpreter, although even on the first occasion on which he met the Commission he was expressing strong views on such matters as the extension of the term of copyright, which he opposed.[55]

On his third appearance, however, he came into the open. While not opposed to the idea of a law of copyright, he wanted one which would be of benefit to individual authors, not to the abstraction of 'literature', and certainly not to publishers. In his view, the interests of authors and the public alike were best served when the largest possible number of books was sold at the lowest possible price. On these grounds he supported the royalty system, subsequently also espoused by Mallet, as being most likely to encourage authors to write more books.[56] When, in his final appearance, Farrer was asked to summarize his views and his recommendations he did, at last, make an explicit statement of his position: 'I assume that copyright, as the right to prevent other persons from making copies, is conferred upon authors for the purpose of securing remuneration to them, and thus encouraging them to write for the public.'[57] There were few, if any, members of the Commission who would have disagreed with that, and few of the witnesses would have done so openly; the problem was how to achieve the protection of such rights without interfering with the free flow of trade driven by the demands of the market.

As opposing views began to emerge on how best to give incentives to authors, a parallel argument developed about the price of books. It was agreed that it was in everyone's interests to maximize the sales of books, and there was a strong view that this was best achieved by selling them at low prices. Here the publishers inevitably took a different view from that of some of the other witnesses. This part of the debate began on the very first day on which the Commission heard evidence, when Sir Charles Trevelyan, Macaulay's nephew who had had a distinguished career in the Indian Civil Service, argued that cheap books were a necessity in the colonies, where there were few circulating libraries. To him, the issue was not so urgent in Britain itself.[58] Although his particular view was swamped in subsequent arguments about the price of books in the domestic market, the theme continued to be heard. Blackwood dealt with it at some length. He took the view that book prices were determined by the willingness of people to pay; the circulating libraries were willing to pay for three-deckers, so 'We naturally publish in the form that we think best for the authors and for ourselves'. He added that he wished that people bought books instead of borrowing them, although it was not clear whether he thought that this would be the cause or the result of reducing prices. In any case, Trollope demolished his arguments, and finally forced him to admit that circulating libraries 'have arisen . . . because they have served the wishes and ways of the people'.[59] Farrer again took a different view in due course; in discussing the problem of American and Canadian copyright, he sympathized with the views of both countries that there was no reason why they should be forced to import expensive British books when they could publish cheap reprints of their own.[60] Book prices also became part of the complex tangle of arguments about free trade and protection.

The great issues of the nature of copyright, its philosophical justification and its economic consequences were not, however, the principal preoccupations of the Commission. They spent far more of their time, and of their Report, dealing with the mundane practical problems which the 1842 Act had either generated or ignored.

Inevitably, the length of the term of copyright loomed large among the interests of Commissioners and witnesses alike. Among the publishers, both Longman and Blackwood wanted an extension. Longman, who had 'found that the existing Copyright Act works extremely well', was unspecific, but Blackwood suggested the author's lifetime and 50 years after his death, or 30 if 50 were not acceptable.[61] Both argued that this would be beneficial to authors, but John Murray, the third of the great publishers to testify, was less certain. He did not openly object to the idea of a longer term, but he was clearly reluctant to advocate it when pressed. In truth, he doubted what benefits it would really bring to anyone since, in his view, few copyrights were of any real value for more than a few years after first publication.[62] Murray, however, was in a minority, for, on this issue at least, authors and publishers were generally agreed. The composer Arthur Sullivan, an eloquent witness, supported the idea of the author's lifetime and 50 years thereafter, as did Huxley, although both saw this as being the lesser of two evils. Sullivan said that he:

> . . . could never quite understand why that high moral tone should be taken about the right of the community to brain work, so that the benefit of it to a man's family should cease after a certain time.[63]

Huxley argued for perpetual and absolute rights for the author and the author's heirs, could not understand why he should be 'debarred from making any bargain I please', and regarded a long *post mortem* term as being a poor substitute for an author's natural rights in equity.[64]

There was, however, another side to the argument. Farrer was unhappy about the idea of extending the term at all. It was not a topic on which he spoke at length, but in the end he recommended, perhaps in a rather reluctant tone, a minimal period of protection for the monopoly. He suggested an initial 28 years, followed by a further 14 if the author were still alive, or a single term of 14 years, or the author's lifetime and 7 years thereafter. His real, if implicit, preference was for the shortest possible single term; both his first and third options were attempts at politically acceptable compromises.[65] Other witnesses were less extreme, but there was a view which favoured shorter terms, expressed, among others, by one of the Commissioners, F. R. Daldy, who argued for a single 28-year term.[66] One very authoritative voice argued for limitations and against *post mortem* copyright. This was Sharon Turner, a lawyer and one of the leading authorities on copyright law, whose father had been involved in the debates in 1813 and 1814.[67] As Secretary of the Copyright Association, a group of lawyers and publishers, he argued against any extension of the present 42-year term in any form. Trollope challenged him on this, as did other members of the Commission, but he would not change his mind.[68]

The debate about the term of copyright was important, if only because it introduced, for the first time in public, the possibility of a long period of protection after the death of the author. Despite the extreme positions represented by Farrer on the one hand and Huxley on the other, the real battle in the centre was being fought between the existing system and automatic *post mortem* rights. The latter was an idea imported from Germany, as was pointed out by one witness who advocated it.[69] The Commission ultimately accepted the thrust of the argument, and, with some dissentient voices, accepted the principle involved.[70]

The argument about the length of the term of copyright, like the discussions of book prices and of the very nature of copyright, raised many issues in relation to authors. The 1842 Act had been intended to help them, but they seemed less satisfied with it than the publishers were. Huxley and Sullivan were not alone in making greater claims for their rights than authors had felt able to do before. In the earlier stages of the Commission's work, both Longman and Murry explained how they dealt with their authors. Both normally used half-profits agreements, and Longman added that 'successful authors are not in the habit of selling their copyrights'.[71] Matthew Arnold confirmed the last point, saying that he always retained his copyrights, and would sell them only 'under the pressure of a most extreme necessity'.[72]

For the most part, it seems to have been accepted that half-profits agreements were the normal terms on which authors dealt with their publishers, as, for the most part, it probably was.[73] Towards the end of the Commission's work, however, which was when they heard the evidence of the authors, some new ideas began to emerge. One of the key witnesses here was the philosopher Herbert Spencer. He told the Commission that he generally published his books at his own expense, and that only now, after an active writing life of some twenty-five years, was he beginning to show a profit. He advocated a system of royalties, under which the author would reserve all the rights in his books, and allow publishers to issue them on a percentage basis, but without giving them sole rights.[74] The idea had been raised earlier, but not in so stark a form, and when Farrer followed Spencer in front of the Commission, he admitted that he was influenced by him.[75]

This little episode was not the Commission's only brush with royalties. Indeed, the issue, in various forms, seems to have been bubbling under the surface of many of the discussions of authors' rights and terms.[76] The matter is somewhat confused by the fact that the word was used to describe two different systems of payment. On the one hand, there were the royalties envisaged by Spencer and others as part of a licensing scheme, perhaps combined with perpetual authors' rights, or the *de facto* abolition of copyright as a special form of property and, on the other, there was some discussion of the system of payment by percentage of publisher's income in the sense in which the word is now generally used. The latter was rejected by George Routledge, another publisher witness, as 'an unfortunate thing for an author', although Trollope strongly disagreed with him.[77] The rights of authors were raised in a number of contexts during the sittings of the Commission, and not only in financial terms. One issue, raised by Turner at an early stage, was that of the right to control the adaptation or dramatization of a work, while John Murray and others were concerned about the problem of unauthorized (but currently legal) abridgements of copyright works.[78] The overt concern here was in protecting the integrity of the property of the copyright owner, and, in general, it was indeed expressed in commercial terms. There was, apparently, no explicit statement that the author's artistic or literary integrity was in any way impugned by adaptation of his work without his consent or cooperation, although this was, in due course, to be a matter of great concern.

The questions of subsidiary rights naturally merged into issues of the protection of performing rights in both plays and music. Both John Boosey and Thomas Chappell, two of the leading music publishers in London, advocated a stronger law to protect their particular interests. Boosey was specially concerned with the problems of protecting the scores and libretti of operas, a matter which had already caused him great difficulty.[79] The basic problem, as Boosey saw it, was that the rights in the music, the rights in the lyrics and the rights to perform either or both were different and irreconcilable.[80] Chappell's views were similar, although he was also concerned with other issues, including the unauthorized adaptation of copyright songs, the difficulty of enforcing performing rights, and the practical problems of collecting fees and royalties.[81] On the last issue, John Palgrave Simpson, Secretary of the Dramatic Authors Society, founded in 1832 to support and subsequently enforce performing rights, told the Commission of the very real difficulties which his organization encountered in trying to enforce the existing law.[82] Sullivan went further than any of them, and argued for the right of the composer to control performances of his works, the nearest approach to the explicit advocacy of the moral rights of the author which was heard from any of the witnesses.[83]

The evidence and discussions about royalties, subsidiary rights and performing rights, and the implicit debate about the moral right of the author to control the use as well as the dissemination of his work, reflect the increased complexity of the issues which were beginning to surround copyright by the middle of the nineteenth century. Sharon Turner introduced a further complication, when he pointed out to the Commission that new technical processes of reproduction, such as photography and lithography, also had implications for the law and needed to be considered.[84] A whole succession of witnesses argued the case for new laws to protect designs, works of art, sculptures and architecture.[85] In between, there were lengthy arguments about international and colonial copyright, which had, of course, been the starting-point of the whole investigation,[86] and about such matters as whether the register of copyrights should be kept at Stationers' Hall (as it was under the 1842 Act) or transferred to the British Museum, as was advocated by several witnesses.[87] The latter inevitably raised the question of legal deposit, on which several witnesses expressed their views.[88]

Confronted by all this evidence on such a range of topics, it is not surprising that the Royal Commission took so long to reach its conclusions, and had difficulty in achieving unanimity. In February 1877, *The Times* reported that they were 'still engaged upon the cheerful occupation of taking evidence' and had not even begun to think about how to write a report.[89] In the event, it was not until 1878 that the Commission was able to report to the President of the Board of Trade, and even then ten of the fifteen Commissioners submitted minority reports on one or more aspects of their recommendations. Nevertheless, they had arrived at some recommendations, even if these did sometimes represent the lowest common denominator of compromise.

On the key issue of the length of the term of copyright, only Mallet dissented from the view that the principle of the author's lifetime plus a fixed *post mortem* term should be adopted, with a recommendation that this should be either 30 years or some agreed international standard.[90] They also recommended the standardization of terms of protection for various formats and media, including performing rights. Abridgements, translations and adaptations should all be protected. There were some minor exceptions; photographs were exempted from the 42-year protection, and the copyright in a work of fine art was agreed to belong to the purchaser not the artist.[91] It was all very logical, if rather crude.

In turning to the issue of registration, the Commission enunciated an important general principle, which did not really arise out of the evidence laid before it. Under the 1842 Act, registration at Stationers' Hall was required as proof of ownership of the copyright, a codification of existing practices. This was, in its turn, based upon the long-standing principle of the English law that, as the Commission expressed it, 'copyright attaches upon production and publication, and that registration is only a legal preliminary to the enforcement of the right against a wrongdoer'.[92] To the Commissioners, this was unsatisfactory, and they recommended compulsory registration (at the British Museum) as the means of establishing the ownership of rights.[93]

This recommendation raised a number of issues with which the Commission had not dealt, and with which it did not attempt to deal in its Report. In particular, it seemed to equate the acquisition of copyright with the fact of publication, and thus raised the question of the rights in unpublished works. It also began to suggest a distinction, to become more explicit in twentieth-century jurisprudence, between copyright as a means of forbidding certain acts of copying, imitation, adaptation, and so on, and copyright law as a means of permitting some of these things under certain circumstances and in return for certain considerations.[94] None of this was pursued in the Royal Commission's Report, and leaves a very visible gap in the logic of its recommendations.

Finally, the Report dealt with legal deposit and with colonial and international issues.[95]

The Royal Commission was the most thorough investigation of copyright in the second half of the nineteenth century, and yet it was ultimately unsatisfactory. The Commissioners seem to have been almost overwhelmed by the size and complexity of the subject which they had been called upon to analyse. They tried to be pragmatic. They sought simplicity in a field which was too complicated for simple solutions to be found. The consolidated and consistent law which they sought, especially for the terms of protection, was an attractive solution, but one which conflicted with too many vested interests of publishers, authors, artists, composers, performers and theatrical managers. They did not really come to grips with the central intellectual issue, carefully avoiding any attempt to define the nature or theoretical justification of the rights with which they were concerned. When they did so, in looking at the very practical matter of registration, they raised more questions than they could answer or even properly articulate. The Commissioners, like almost all of the witnesses, were practical men, civil servants, lawyers and successful authors, who wanted a law which was itself practical and which would, without infringing the almost sacred canons of free trade, afford some protection and encouragement to authors and other creative artists. In the end, they did not succeed, because, in their search for a practical solution, they failed, or were perhaps unable, to formulate a conceptual approach which might have guided their pragmatism towards the uniformity and consistency which they so genuinely desired and so painstakingly sought.

The Report was published in the summer of 1878, and in the next Session an attempt was made to transform its recommendations into law. Jenkins himself, frustrated by the failure of the government to bring forward a Bill, introduced his own in December, but withdrew it in February when Manners, as President of the Board of Trade, promised that there would be a government Bill.[96] No Bill appeared until July 1879, and even then it was a provisional document.[97] In introducing it to the House, Manners announced that it followed the recommendations of the Commission, including the proposal to extend the term of copyright to the author's lifetime plus 30 years, rejecting only the proposals about the restriction of legal deposit to the British Museum, and the removal of registration to the Museum from Stationers' Hall. The sting in the tail, however, was that the Bill was placed before the House 'not with the object of becoming law this session', but only for consultative purposes, so that it could be circulated during the recess, and discussed in detail with the colonial governments.[98] There, effectively, the matter came to an end. The Bill reappeared in 1881, but progressed no further than its formal First Reading.[99] There was some public debate,[100] but none in Parliament. Copyright law was not a priority for the government, and there was no reason why it should be so. There was little real public interest, and, as had been clear from the proceedings of the Royal Commission, the publishers, who might have formed the most powerful lobby, were broadly satisfied with the 1842 Act. The authors had not yet formed their own lobbying group, and when they did so, their first concern was with international rather than domestic issues.

When the issue arose again, towards the end of the century, the situation was very different. The United Kingdom's accession to the Berne Convention in 1886, and the passage of the American Chase Act in 1891, seemed to solve the international issues which had dominated the copyright debate ever since 1842.[101] In the meantime, both the authors and the publishers had formed their own professional bodies, and were beginning to act collectively in their various interests. The law was no better in 1895 than it had been in 1875, just twenty years older. The difference was that, this time, it seemed that there were enough interest groups to ensure that some sort of change might be possible.

Copyright was not a political issue in a party sense by the end of the century. It could never entirely escape from the revived debate about free trade and protectionism, but it was essentially non-partisan. Although any legislation would almost certainly require government support, it was unlikely to arise from a government initiative. It was because of this that such bodies as the Society of Authors and the Publishers' Association found for themselves a public role in the reform of copyright law. In 1895, the issue of Canadian copyright arose yet again because a Canadian Act of 1889 had included a manufacturing clause similar to that which was to appear in the American Chase Act of 1891.[102] The effect of the new Canadian law was that no work would be copyright in Canada unless an edition was manufactured in that country within one month of its original publication; if no such edition was published, the work would be in public domain. The Act had received the Royal Assent, but it still required a proclamation from the Governor-General before it could be put into effect. It was this possibility of deferment which allowed the flurry of activity in London in the first half of the 1890s.

The Society of Authors was particularly active in lobbying both in the Colonial Office and in Canada itself; it successfully prevented the implementation of the law. Another body, the Copyright Association, chaired by Frederick Daldy, who had been a member of the Royal Commission, also busied itself in the same cause, and began to work closely with the Publishers' Association when the new body was founded in 1896. Both the Society of Authors and the Copyright Association drafted bills, with help from the Publishers' Association, which were introduced into the House of Lords in the Session of 1897. The House established a Select Committee to consider both of them.[103] The Select Committee, unlike the Royal Commission of twenty years earlier, worked quickly; it heard only four witnesses. All were, essentially, representatives, although they were also individually distinguished. Daldy appeared as the chairman of the Copyright Society; C. J. Longman spoke as President of the Publishers' Association; C. J. Thring was the spokesman for the Society of Authors; and Bram Stoker was there as the manager of the Lyceum Theatre and a representative of the theatrical world.[104]

There was little general discussion of the law. In fact, almost all of the evidence centred around three issues: translations, rights in newspaper articles, and dramatizations. The translation issue, as presented by Daldy, was little more than a technicality arising out of the Berne Convention. This protected English works abroad, and even the translations of works whose original was in the public domain, but the 1842 Act did not appear to offer any protection to the English translations of foreign works published in Britain.[105] As for newspapers, Daldy sought to protect them on the same basis as books, so that articles could not simply be copied without permission from one to another. In the case of dramatizations, Daldy argued that there was a need for greater precision to define the extent to which a dramatist could use the plot taken from a novel. Longman, Thring and Stoker did little more than endorse Daldy's views.

Nothing happened, but the Lords returned to the subject in the following session when another Bill came before them. This was a more ambitious affair, of Daldy's drafting, which was an attempt to consolidate the law along the lines recommended in 1878. Consequently, the Select Committee which considered this Bill was more wide-ranging, and the evidence more generalized.[106] Once again, the witnesses were essentially representatives. John Murray was now the chairman of the Publishers' Association's own committee on copyright matters, and he supported, on their behalf, the idea of a consolidated law. They wanted a proper definition of such basic concepts as what he called an 'original literary work', as well as a 30-year *post mortem* term, and clear resolutions of issues relating to the expiry of copyrights in works with joint authorship, the rights in essays first appearing in collectaneous volumes, the right to use quotations in works of criticism and analysis, and rights in music and opera libretti. The range of Murray's remarks is in itself testimony of the complexity of the publishing industry and associated activities by the end of the nineteenth century. It also reflects more systematic thinking about how some of the issues might be resolved.[107]

None of the other witnesses was as wide-ranging as Murray, but they were cumulatively very impressive. C. F. M. Bell, the manager of *The Times*, explained the issues involved in copyright in newspapers, and especially in the news itself, which, he explained, can only be printed, in the first instance, by those who have expended time and money in collecting it. Arguing that this was analogous to the creative work of an author or composer, he proposed a substantial extension of the law to cover news as well as the 'literary' form in which it appeared.[108] Thring, for the Society of Authors, was perhaps a rather disappointing witness. He had no real ideas, and simply wanted a law which would sort out some of the anomalies which had arisen in such matters as works of joint authorship.[109] Others were more imaginative. Henry R. Clayton, who worked for Novello, the music publishers, and was also the current chairman of the London Chamber of Commerce, told the perhaps rather bemused peers about the need for copyright to protect musical versions of plays, songs in revues and the like. Bulmer Howell introduced them to another aspect of the modern world, speaking as legal adviser to the Photographic Copyright Association.[110]

In the end, this initiative also came to nothing. The Select Committee reported that it had been 'unable to complete the inquiry', having opened Pandora's Box. When the issue was raised for a third time, in the Session of 1899, the conclusion was that the House should not proceed with the Bill, and the attempt to consolidate the law should be abandoned in favour of new legislation which would treat artistic and literary copyright separately.[111] There seemed to be insufficient reason to embark on the complexities of copyright law reform, and neither the authors nor the publishers could exert enough influence to provide such a reason. The same remained true in the new century and the new reign. Despite the promise of copyright reform in Edward VII's speech from the throne in opening his first Parliament, nothing was done.[112] The publishers were absorbed in other matters, and the authors alone were not sufficiently influential. In the end, it was an external event which was to force the government to take action, and, at last although perhaps unwittingly, to take a course of action which was to lead to the end of the 1842 Act.

The external event took place in Berlin in 1908, when the member states of the Berne Convention met to discuss possible changes to its provisions.[113] The conference produced a number of very significant amendments, some of them on subjects which had exercised British publishers and authors for thirty or forty years. By far the most important of these was the agreement in principle that the term of protection should be the author's lifetime plus 50 years after his or her death. Although this was not made mandatory (partly in order to accommodate the United Kingdom's outmoded provisions under the 1842 Act), it was nevertheless a vitally important step towards international uniformity. Other changes included provisions relating to choreography, photographs and translations, all of which were in conflict with British law. For the first time, the delegates also addressed the issues arising out of sound recording and commercial cinematography. The proposals on the former were confused, but on the latter clearly extended protection to this new medium. Finally, there were some technical changes, including a requirement that works should acquire copyright automatically without any need for formal registration.

The Berlin amendments to the Berne Convention were a triumph for the French and German view of copyright and its associated rights as essentially deriving from the creator, and being vested in a producer only as a temporary measure to permit reproduction and dissemination. The mere fact that their views could be expressed in these terms showed how far British law had slipped behind international practice. The need to catch up, in order to ratify the Berlin amendments and thus continue to ensure international copyright protection for British authors, was exactly the incentive which had been lacking, and which was now to lead to the reform of the law.

In fact, the government acted very quickly, and in 1909 the President of the Board of Trade, Sydney Buxton, asked Lord Gorrell to chair a departmental committee on the subject. The terms of reference were explicit; the Gorrell Committee was to 'examine . . . the revised International Copyright Convention signed at Berlin . . . and to consider . . . whether the law should be altered so as to enable His Majesty's Government to give effect to the Revised Convention'.[114] The literary and artistic world was well represented on the Committee, which was less dominated by lawyers and politicians than the 1875 Royal Commission had been. From the literary world, the members included Walter Raleigh, the first Professor of English Literature at Oxford, and the popular novelist Anthony Hope. The theatre was represented by Harley Granville-Barker, art by Lawrence Alma-Tadema, music by the publisher William Boosey and the book trade by Frederick Macmillan. Indeed, the Gorrell Committee was probably the most artistically and intellectually distinguished body of its kind which has ever considered the law of copyright in Britain. The evidence which they heard, and their report, ranged far more widely than might have been expected from their very specific brief. The Committee soon discovered, as some of its members well knew, that the British law was wholly inadequate even for domestic purposes, without even taking into account the United Kingdom's international obligations.

Both authors and publishers were among the witnesses, but there was little serious disagreement between them, and little more than differences of emphasis in the arguments which they presented. For the Publishers' Association, John Murray simply recommended that the Berlin amendments be accepted as a whole and immediately. Significantly, however, he added that he thought that the government should take the opportunity to codify and to clarify

British copyright law in general, especially in relation to some of the long-standing ambiguities about colonial copyright, unpublished manuscripts, abridgements and adaptations. Murray, like virtually every other witness, supported a period of copyright for the author's lifetime and 50 years thereafter, the international standard agreed at Berlin.[115]

On behalf of the Society of Authors, E. J. MacGillivray, a barrister and a member of the Society's Copyright Sub-Committee, took almost exactly the same line, arguing that the provisions of the 1842 Act could sometimes be disadvantageous to authors, while the 50-year *post mortem* term and the other Berlin amendments would meet all their needs and wishes.[116] The Society's Statement of Evidence reiterated these points, and in particular emphasized that its members 'attach great importance to ultimate uniformity in copyright legislation'.[117]

This display of unanimity was, no doubt, very welcome to the Committee, which readily accepted the views of both the authors and the publishers. Indeed, it was easy for them to do so, since they were essentially asking the government to do what it wanted to do in any case, that is, to ratify the Berlin agreement.[118] Other issues, however, persisted in raising their heads. Some were echoes of the past. Both MacGillivray and Murray were keen to emphasize that the revised term of copyright would not affect the publication of cheap reprints, and both pointed out that in fact the majority of cheap editions were actually of works which were still in copyright.[119]

George Bernard Shaw, who appeared on behalf of the Dramatic Sub-Committee of the Society of Authors, added his voice to this chorus. Shaw told the Committee than he was 'a writer whose success, in the commercial sense, came rather late . . .', and as a result his early works were no longer protected under the 1842 Act. This was a little disingenuous; the essence of it was true, but since he was actually born in 1860, only those works which he had published before he was eighteen were no longer in copyright. Nevertheless, his point was a real one, and his concern was that, as his works came out of copyright, American publishers would not be interested in the works in public domain because he could no longer give them sole rights. As a result, '. . . the derelict book has been shunned as dangerous; and the one thing that will bring the book to the public is copyright.' He added that 'the great majority of books are dead in eighteen months . . . The fifty years will apply in practice only to books of exceptional vitality.'[120] No doubt these included Shaw's own, but his evidence was of more than personal interest. In effect, Shaw was arguing the protectionist case for copyright against the rapidly vanishing remnants of Victorian free-trade dogma. He was supported by William Meredith, who had inherited the copyrights of his father, the novelist George Meredith. He explained the difficulties of the operation of the Act for an author's heir, who was, of course, precisely the person whom Wordsworth, Talfourd and Mahon had sought to protect. Copyrights expired at different times; the fixed term after death would ensure that all of an author's copyrights expired simultaneously, and thus the whole situation would be greatly simplified.[121]

Shaw's evidence, however, was important from another point of view, for he raised the whole question of subsidiary rights. He wanted protection for both sound recording rights and film rights in plays, and he wanted them reserved to the original author, the dramatist.[122] So far as plays were concerned, this was still a mere cloud on the horizon, for this was the age of the two-reel silent, but for the musical community, there was already a major issue here. Probably to the surprise of the Committee, its hearings were in fact dominated by the question of sound recording. This raised a range of issues which had simply never been considered before. The most basic was that of performers' and composers' rights. It was argued that composers should have the right to control, by a licensing system, the mechanical recording of their works, and that some benefit should accrue to them for this. It was, however, a vastly complicated matter, for performers, engineers, producers and the owners of studios were involved, and some of these were also the owners of patents or licences in particular recording systems. The details are irrelevant to the history of copyright, but the domination of the proceedings of the Gorrell Committee by this subject is not. The new recording media in all their variety from shellac discs to pianola rolls were beginning to determine the direction which the law would take. The issue of the right of the creator of an artistic work could not be ignored if that right was to include some control over the recording of the work, and, logically, that had implications for the rights of the authors of literary works.

Unlike their predecessors in 1878, the members of the Gorrell Committee did not shrink from the enormity of their task, and they approached it with both firmness and subtlety. They started from a simple premise, from which no one could seriously dissent; they wished to resolve 'the confusion which prevails' in the law of copyright and associated rights, and considered that 'It would be a great advantage if the British law were placed on a plain and uniform basis . . .'[123] In essence, they recommended that the whole of the Berlin agreement should be incorporated into British law, but that it should be done in the context of a general codification of the multitude of existing statutes. They addressed some of the most contentious issues of the previous three-quarters of a century in recommending full protection for translations, abridgements and adaptations, and the reservation of the author's right to control them. Finally, they recommended a licensing system for sound recording, with the rights reserved to the composer, the one point on which there was dissent.[124]

Buxton brought a Bill to the House of Commons within weeks of the publication of the Gorrell Report. It gave effect to all of their recommendations, and seemed unlikely to raise any serious opposition. It was given its formal First Reading following a brief introductory speech by Buxton;[125] then disaster overtook it. Parliament was dissolved when the House of Lords rejected Lloyd George's radical budget proposals for increased taxation and an extended social security system. The Liberals lost their majority in the subsequent election, and were thereafter dependent on the Irish and Labour members to sustain them. The new Parliament, when it met, had to deal first with a major constitutional conflict between the Lords and the Commons, and then with the budget. In the midst of all this Edward VII died, and was succeeded by the well-meaning but politically inexperienced George V. Once again, it seemed that copyright law reform might vanish in the political undergrowth.

That it did not can almost certainly be explained by the government's desire to ratify the Berlin amendments. When the same Bill was reintroduced by Buxton, who kept both his seat and his job in 1910, he emphasized the international dimension.[126] The same point was picked up in *The Times*, which reported that the measure was 'primarily' intended to incorporate the Berlin Convention into British law.[127] Buxton emphasized the consensus which lay behind the proposal. There had, he said, been no objections in principle when the previous Bill had been published, and he could see no reason for any now. Reassuring the House that the extension of the term would have no effect on the availability of cheap books, and that the colonies would be consulted on matters which affected them, he hoped for an easy passage.

He was to be disappointed. In the debate which followed, a number of issues were aired which would have been familiar to anyone who had read the debates of almost a hundred years earlier. Sir Gilbert Parker, who moved the amendment to defer the Bill for six months, which would effectively have killed it, described copyright as 'a restriction of a natural right', although whether of authors, publishers or readers is not clear.[128] William Joynson-Hicks, a lawyer who specialized in the field and had been a member of the Gorrell Committee, was also unhappy, especially about the proposed 50-year term. He saw no need for this, and regarded it as a result of packing the Committee with authors, artists and publishers.[129] It was a powerful speech by an authoritative speaker, which was potentially very damaging. In general, however, there was support for the principle of the Bill, and it was, eventually, given its Second Reading without a division.[130]

At the Committee and Report Stages in the Commons, and again during its passage through the Lords, the Bill was subjected to a number of technical amendments, but none affected the basic principles or interfered with the main recommendations of the Gorrell Committee. Indeed, almost as much time was devoted to legal deposit as to the principles of copyright itself.[131] The Bill received the Royal Assent on 16 December 1911, and became the first general copyright law to be passed by the British Parliament for seventy years.[132]

The 1911 Copyright Act was to prove less long-lived than that of 1842, but was much better conceived. It incorporated a principle which was wholly new in British law, but which had long since been accepted in almost all other European countries. Copyright was now firmly linked to the life of the author, and survived him or her by a substantial period of time. Moreover, the author was explicitly in control of the work; the rights of translation, abridgement, dramatization, or any other form of adaptation, were clearly the author's and only the author's. He or she might make contractual arrangements about the use of those rights, but their origin and the ultimate ownership were not in doubt. Indeed, for practical purposes, authors had to reach agreements with publishers and others for the production and distribution of their works, but the fundamental rights which the Society of Authors, and individual writers, had sought for so long were now firmly incorporated in the law.

The new Act also recognized, for the first time, the wide range of rights which could derive from intellectual products such as written works or musical compositions. Although it was not wholly satisfactory, it did address the problem of sound recording and of cinematographic films, and clearly established the principle of the rights of the primary creator over what was created. Ambiguities remained, but they were comparatively insignificant at the time, although the problems were to be compounded by technical developments during the next thirty years. The success of the Gorrell Committee and the framers of the 1911 Act can, however, be judged by the fact that its basic principles still underpin the law of copyright in Britain and that those principles have proved broadly satisfactory to all the parties involved.

The long-sought reform of the law had, eventually, happened only because of the pressures implicitly exerted on Britain by her fellow signatories of the Berne Convention. In the early 1950s, this particular historical circumstance was repeated. In 1948, the Berne countries came together again, this time at Brussels, and again proposed a series of amendments to the Convention.[133] Few of these affected the central issues of copyright in literary works, but there were many which had important implications for subsidiary rights and for rights in non-printed media. The primacy of the author was reasserted, although the conference rejected a French proposal that recognition of moral rights should be compulsory. The most important proposals were that the ways in which copyright works could lawfully be used should be more precisely defined; and that the rights in public performances, broadcasts and similar diffusions should be brought within the terms of the Convention. As in 1908, there was a need to examine British law to see how it needed to be changed to allow the United Kingdom to ratify the Brussels Amendments.

In 1951, Harold Wilson, as President of the Board of Trade, appointed a Committee under the chairmanship of H. S. Gregory to examine the issue. It was a technical affair, with none of the literary or artistic glitter of its predecessor. It was, however, very businesslike, and within a year was able to report to Wilson's successor, Peter Thorneycroft, with a series of recommendations for changes to the law.[134] Almost all of its proposals were for technical amendments to the 1911 Act in the terms of the Brussels Amendments. Indeed, the Gregory Committee recognized that the Act was 'an enormous advance', but felt that some clarification was still needed.[135] The main reason for this was made explicit in the first paragraph: 'Our Report is inevitably discursive . . . by reason of our need to consider modern technical developments . . .'[136] These developments were in two key areas. One was broadcasting, of which the entire history in the United Kingdom had taken place since 1911, and the other was the emergence of new technologies for copying of printed and written material.

Matters relating to sound recordings, films, broadcasting and 'sporting spectacles and performances of artistes' occupied the greater part of the Committee's time, the longest section of its Report, and nearly a third of its recommendations.[137] The details do not concern us, but all are based on the same general principle that the owner of the copyright has the right to control, and be paid for, the use of the work in any format and any medium. The difficulties arose in considering the copyright position of broadcasting organizations, ultimately resolved by vesting in them the rights in programmes which they originated, even if they had to pay other copyright owners for the materials which they used. Some of this was certainly of interest to authors and publishers. During the 1920s, radio had become a small but significant source of income to some authors, while the cinema had provided a larger income to a much smaller number.[138] Television was still relatively insignificant in Britain in the early 1950s, but it too was beginning to buy more material.[139]

For the publishers, however, the copying of copyright printed matter was of far greater urgency. The Gregory Committee could not avoid this issue even had it wished to do so. In the past, piracy had involved the considerable capital costs of reprinting the work which was being reproduced. Copying for personal use could be done only by hand, and was not a viable means of reproducing a work for sale. By the early 1950s, however, as Gregory noted, 'technical developments such as contact photography and microphotography have . . . [created] means whereby . . . hand-copying can be avoided'.[140] The use of small-format film for document copying had begun in the 1930s, and had reached commercial viability with the foundation of University Microforms Inc. by Eugene Power. Although it was largely used for copying rare research materials, and books long in public domain, it did have some potential as a comparatively cheap means of copying copyright materials. The so-called microfilms (actually ordinary 35-mm monochrome roll films) thus created were, however, dependent upon expensive equipment for both production and reading, and, at the production stage, needed both skilled operators and extensive laboratory facilities.

Photocopying, which was first developed in the late 1930s, had none of these disadvantages. It was cheap, quick and simple. It was this, Gregory's 'contact photography', which was the real threat.

The Brussels Amendments had recognized that certain sorts of copying could not be prevented, but had to be controlled. Gregory found here real conflicts of interests. Publishers objected to a law which would allow large-scale copying of copyright works for any purpose; scholars wanted to be able to make copies for their own use; librarians needed a clear law which would give them unequivocal guidelines. Gregory considered the agreements already reached with some publishers by the Royal Society, which had the general effect of allowing scientists to make copies of articles in learned journals for the purposes of 'private study'. The Committee recommended an extension of this principle, under some general rules about 'Fair Dealing'. Fair dealing, unfamiliar enough to be in quotation marks throughout the Gregory Report, was an important conceptual innovation. Taking the long-established understanding that passages could be quoted for review or criticism, the Gregory Committee suggested that the law should allow reproduction by mechanical or photographic means of extracts up to a certain length for private study, and that these extracts could be made either by the person who required the material or by a librarian acting on that person's behalf. It was an ingenious compromise, which the publishers eventually accepted.[141]

Finally, the Gregory Committee addressed the question of moral rights, the first time that any official body in the United Kingdom had done so in a systematic way. At Brussels, the French had proposed that they should be incorporated into the Convention, but only a very modified version of the proposal was generally acceptable.[142] The British were particularly dubious, and Gregory and his colleagues shared their doubts. The Report refers to moral rights, again in quotation marks, as '*droit moral*', not needing therefore explicitly to condemn it as an inherently continental notion. It was, they wrote, 'a term unknown to our jurisprudence but . . . a convenient phrase to describe certain questions which arise out of copyright protection'.[143] As the lawyers among them must have known, it was far more than a 'convenient phrase'; it was the core of copyright in almost all European countries whose law had developed from the Roman and Napoleonic traditions. It declared that all the rights in the work belonged to its creator from the moment of creation and that, thereafter, his or her control was absolute. The effect was to prevent the use of material for purposes of which the creator did not approve; thus, for example, a piece of music, even if the copyright and performing rights had been sold to a publisher, could not be used in a film or a television advertisement (if such had existed in Britain in 1951–52) without the permission of the composer.

The Gregory Committee would have none of this. There was, they thought, some limited protection along these lines under the Fine Art Copyright Act of 1862,[144] and perhaps at common law, but considered that this was a matter for contractual arrangements between the author or creator and the publisher or disseminator rather than for the law. 'In a field so vague and ill-defined it seems to us to be impossible – even if it were considered desirable – to frame legislative proposals to meet all possible problems.'[145] The Gregory Report was in general, as this suggests, conservative and minimalist in its approach.

This was reflected in the Bill which was, eventually, brought to Parliament in June 1956. In introducing it, Thorneycroft essentially presented it as the embodiment of the Gregory Committee's recommendations, as indeed it was. The measure he proposed was, he said, 'large and complex', although not a subject of party controversy. Nor was it. It was supported from all sides of the House, and passed all its stages without difficulty. There was little serious discussion, and almost none which showed any understanding of the issues which were beginning to emerge. The fair dealing proposals were accepted without any discussion at all, and nothing was said about moral rights. In general, there was little interest in the matter and little appreciation of it. The Bill became law at the end of the Session.[146]

The 1956 Act was as conservative as the 1911 Act had been radical, perhaps suggesting that the political philosophy of the party in power is not wholly irrelevant even to technical legislation such as that on copyright. The fair dealing rules were a step in the right direction, and broadcasts were given some protection, but there was little advance for authors, artists or composers in the provisions of the Act. Moreover, it was inflexible legislation. The Gregory Committee's apparent determination to avoid enunciating general principles, exemplified by their attitude to moral rights, left the United Kingdom with a very specific law which was applicable to the technological, economic and political situation of 1956.

It was almost twenty years before this began to be remedied. In 1973, the Department of Trade (as the Board of Trade had now become) established a committee under Mr Justice Whitford 'to consider and report whether any, and if so what, changes are desirable in the law relating to copyright as provided in particular by the Copyright Act 1956 and the Design Copyright Act

1968 . . .'[147] The Whitford Report was four years in the making, and the most thorough investigation of British copyright law and practice for over half a century. The Committee was confronted with an awesome task. Not only was the 1956 Act inflexible, it was passed at a time when flexibility was about to be needed more than ever before. In looking at an Act which had virtually ignored television, Whitford and his colleagues had to consider satellite broadcasting and domestic video recording, quite apart from all the ramifications of computing. Above all, they sought to clarify the law, and to produce proposals for a law which could cope with continuing change.

The greater part of the Whitford Report is concerned with matters other than copyright in printed matter, although, once again, many of these had implications for the creators, owners and publishers of printed material. In general, however, the basic provisions of the 1911 Act were left intact, as they had been in 1956, with a 50-year *post mortem* term to protect the interests of authors and their heirs. Two of the Whitford recommendations were, however, of interest to publishers and authors. For the former, Whitford's proposed amendment to the fair dealing rules of 1956 were of particular significance. In essence, the Committee recommended that photocopiers, by now a common feature of every office, library and school, should be licensed, and that fees, analogous to those paid to the owners of performing rights, should be paid to the owners of the material copied.[148]

Secondly, Whitford addressed the issue of moral rights, without resorting either to French or to quotation marks. Noting that the United Kingdom offered no protection of these rights which were incorporated in the then current version of the Berne Convention, the Whitford Committee recommended that the law should be amended appropriately. Specifically, there were three proposals: that the author had the right to claim 'paternity' of the work, that the author can control the use of the work, allowing for 'reasonable modifications' (which must be minor), and that it is illegal to claim 'paternity' of a work created by another person.[149]

Eleven years were to pass before the recommendations of the Whitford Committee found their way on to the statute book. The subject was, as Thorneycroft had said in 1956, 'large and complex', but the delays were not entirely without value. When a Bill was brought to the House of Commons in the spring of 1988, it was the result of a good deal of considered debate among lawyers, civil servants, publishers, authors, librarians, broadcasters, designers, industrialists and many others who would be affected by it. The 1988 Bill was no mere amendment to the Act of 1956, but an almost wholesale replacement of it, founded on quite different principles. Introducing it to the House of Commons, Kenneth Clarke drew an implicit contrast with the Act it was designed to replace: 'The Bill sets out to restructure the law on a more logical and consistent basis . . . which takes account of the advances made in the last 30 years . . .', adding that 'we have tried to anticipate future developments . . .'[150] Clarke was right. The Bill, despite the immense complexity of its technical provisions, was indeed based on a principle, and the principle was that of the moral rights of the creator, which, as he rightly pointed out to the House, was now to be incorporated into English law for the first time. This was to be done in the context of a technological climate in which there were media which were 'almost infinitely capable of reproduction'.[151]

The Bill was generally welcomed, but in 1988, unlike 1956, there was a great deal of informed and important debate both in the House and in Committee. The range of subjects was as wide as the provisions of the Bill itself, from the recording of folk songs to the design of replacement parts for cars.[152] There was, however, almost no discussion of any matters of direct concern to publishers and authors. The new fair dealing rules were accepted, and there was never any serious challenge to making the moral right of the creator the basis of the law. Copyright, the creature of the book trade, had outgrown its progenitor.

The 1988 Copyright, Designs and Patents Act is the great consolidated law which some have been seeking for over a century. It is, as yet, young, for precedent would suggest that it will have to serve for at least a generation. The lawyers themselves are still feeling their way around it, and even the standard work shows some doubts and hesitations on its meanings.[153] These will, no doubt, be clarified by the courts and by Parliament in due course. What is clear, however, is that the law of the United Kingdom now adequately protects the authors and the publishers of written works, and of all the products of the human brain. Copyright law has emerged out of a series of compromises between economic and cultural factors, between creators and disseminators, between producers and consumers. It will continue to evolve, as technology and social circumstances change. The almost infinite capacity of modern media for reproduction is, however, already calling into question some of the most fundamental issues of all. The creations of 'authors' can now be distributed around the world without ever taking any non-digitized form. Electronic journals, on-line databases and CD-ROMs present the latest, and perhaps the greatest, challenge to the law and practice of copyright.

Appendix
Statutes

The statutes cited in the text and references are listed here, together with the short title by which they are commonly known. It is not a comprehensive list of British legislation on copyright and other intellectual property.

1624	21 James I c. 3	Monopolies
1662	13 & 14 Charles II c. 33	Printing
1664	16 Charles II c. 8	Printing
1665	16 & 17 Charles II c. 4	Printing
1685	1 James II c. 17	Printing
1693	4 William & Mary c. 24	Printing
1710	8 Anne c. 19	Copyright (Encouragement of Learning)
1734	7 George II c. 24	'Buckley's Act'
1735	8 George II c. 13	Engravings ('Hogarth's Act')
1739	12 George II c. 36	Import of Books
1747	20 George II c. 47	Import of Books
1767	7 George III c. 38	Engravings
1775	15 George III c. 53	Perpetual Copyrights
1777	17 George III c. 57	Engravings
1798	38 George III c. 71	Busts and models
1801	41 George III c. 107	Copyright (Ireland)
1814	54 George III c. 156	Copyright
1833	3 & 4 William IV c. 15	Dramatic Property
1836	6 & 7 William IV c. 59	Engravings (Ireland)
1836	6 & 7 William IV c. 110	Legal deposit
1838	1 & 2 Victoria c. 59	International Copyright
1842	5 & 6 Victoria c. 45	Copyright
1845	7 & 8 Victoria c. 12	International Copyright
1847	10 & 11 Victoria c. 95	Foreign Reprints
1853	15 & 16 Victoria c. 12	International Copyright
1862	25 & 26 Victoria c. 68	Fine Art Copyright
1875	38 Victoria c. 12	Performing Rights
1876	38 & 39 Victoria c. 53	Copyright (Canada)
1911	1 & 2 George V c. 46	Copyright
1956	4 & 5 Elizabeth II 74	Copyright
1988		Copyright, Designs and Patents

A Note on Sources

Primary sources

The primary sources used for this book are cited in the appropriate references. In addition to manuscript material, the following are the main printed sources:

1 the *Journals* of both Houses of Parliament, cited by volume and page numbers, as LJ (House of Lords) and CJ (House of Commons) respectively;

2 the official records of debates, known as *Parliamentary Debates* (or, colloquially, 'Hansard'), cited by series, volume and column numbers as PD;

3 the Sessional Papers of the House of Commons, the official published version of papers tabled in the House or elsewhere by its orders, cited by year, volume number and page reference as PP; for a full explanation of the citations, see Peter Cockton. *Subject Catalogue of the House of Commons Parliamentary Papers 1801–1900*. 5 vols., Cambridge: Chadwyck-Healey, 1988;

4 statutes, cited in the official form by regnal year and chapter up to 11 Elizabeth II, and thereafter in the modern form; see also the Appendix;

5 the published records of legal proceedings, the Law Reports, cited from the official versions, which, up to 1865, are cited by the name of the reporter, preceded by the volume number and followed by the page reference. Most of these will also be found in the series *English Reports* (reprinted in 180 volumes, 1900–32);

6 calendars of documents in the Public Record Office, cited by key titles, monarch, volume and page; the following key titles are used:

APC Acts of the Privy Council
CPR Calendar of Patent Rolls
CSPD Calendar of State Papers (Domestic series)

7 certain unpublished records of the Stationers' Company, especially the minute books of the Court of Assistants (the 'Court Books'); with the exception of the Court Books before 1640 (B and part of C), cited from published editions (see item 8 below), these have been cited from the originals using folio or page references as appropriate; the records are still owned by the Company, and are kept at Stationers' Hall, London, but are also available on microfilm, published by Chadwyck-Healey, for which see Robin Myers. *The Stationers' Company Archive. An account of the records 1554–1984*. Winchester: St Paul's Bibliographies, 1990;

8 published editions of manuscript documents, especially of the records of the Stationers' Company; the principal series cited are:

Edward Arber. *Transcript of the Register of the Company of Stationers of London 1554–1640*. 5 vols., Birmingham: the author, 1875–94, cited by volume and page number as Arber, *Transcript*;

G. E. Briscoe Eyre. *A Transcript of the Registers of the Worshipful Company of Stationers from 1640–1708*. 3 vols., London: the author, 1913–14, cited by volume and page number as Eyre, *Transcript*;

W. W. Greg and E. Boswell. *Records of the Court of the Stationers' Company 1576 to 1602*. London: The Bibliographical Society, 1930, cited by page number as Greg and Boswell, *Records*;

William A. Jackson. *Records of the Court of the Stationers' Company 1602 to 1640*. London: The Bibliographical Society, 1957 cited by page number as Jackson, *Records*.

In addition, many individual contemporary publications are cited, by author [if known], title, and place and date of publication. These include, for the period up to 1800, many documents which, after that date, would have appeared in the Sessional Papers. For particularly rare or obscure documents, or documents with ambiguous or commonly used titles, a library location is given for the copies used. The same practice is followed where a bibliographical point is being made which involves the distinction between editions or issues of the same book.

Secondary sources

A wide range of secondary sources has been used, and is cited in the references. The full reference is given at the first citation in each chapter, and thereafter references are by author, short title and [volume and] page number. The full citation is repeated on the first usage in a subsequent chapter.

Abbreviations

In addition to those noted above, the following abbreviations are used in the references:

BL British Library
Bodl Bodleian Library, Oxford

DNB Dictionary of National Biography
PRO Public Record Office
SC Stationers' Company
STC2 *A Short-title Catalogue of Books Printed in England, Scotland & Ireland and of English Books Printed Abroad 1475–1640*. Second edition, revised and enlarged by W. A. Jackson, F. S. Ferguson and Katherine F. Pantzer. 3 vols., London: The Bibliographical Society, 1976–91.

References

Introduction

1 This school of thought is particularly associated with the French critic, Roland Barthes. His essay, 'The death of the author', is most easily accessible in his *Image, Music, Text*, translated by Stephen Heath, Glasgow: Fontana/Collins, 1977, pp. 142–8.
2 For a different approach, which is primarily a contribution to the history of authorship, see David Saunders. *Authorship and Copyright*. London: Routledge, 1992. Another recent study, Mark Rose. *Authors and Owners. The invention of copyright*. Cambridge, MA: Harvard University Press, 1993, was published after this book was completed. Again, the focus is on authors.
3 See Elizabeth Armstrong. *Before Copyright. The French book-privilege system 1498–1526*. Cambridge: Cambridge University Press, 1990; and Jane C. Ginsbury, A tale of two copyrights: literary property in revolutionary France and America. *Tulane Law Review*, 64, (1990), pp. 991–1031.
4 For an overview, see Lucien Febvre and Henri-Jean Martin. *The Coming of the Book. The impact of printing 1450–1800* (Translated by David Gerard; ed. Geoffrey Nowell-Smith and David Wootton). London: NLB, 1976, pp. 159–66. On the gradual loss of anonymity, see E. Ph. Goldschmidt. *Medieval Texts and Their First Appearance in Print*. London: The Bibliographical Society, 1943, p. 116. For a closely argued particular case, see Joseph Loewenstein, The script in the marketplace. *Representations*, 12 (1985), pp. 101–14.
5 For a general history, see John Feather. *A History of British Publishing*. London: Croom Helm, 1988.
6 Donald W. Nichol, On the use of 'copy' and 'copyright': a Scriblerian coinage? *The Library*, 6th ser., 12 (1990), pp. 110–20.
7 For the general history of authorship in this period, the two books by A. S. Collins are still invaluable: *Authorship in the Days of Johnson. Being a study of the relation between author, patron, publisher and public 1726–1780*. London: Robert Holden, 1927; and *The Profession of Letters. A study of the relation of author to patron, publisher and public 1780–1832*. London: Routledge and Kegan Paul, 1928.

Chapter 1

1 Elizabeth Armstrong, English purchases of printed books from the continent 1465 to 1526. *English Historical Review*, 94 (1979), pp. 268–90;

H. R. Plomer, The importation of books into England in the fifteenth and sixteenth centuries. *The Library*, 4th ser., 4 (1923–24), pp. 146–50.
2 C. Paul Christianson, Evidence for the study of London's late medieval manuscript-book trade. In: Jeremy Griffiths and Derek Pearsall, eds. *Book Production and Publishing in Britain 1375–1475*. Cambridge: Cambridge University Press, 1989, pp. 87–108.
3 Konrad Haebler. *The Study of Incunabula*. New York: The Grolier Club, 1933, p. 192; Leonardas Vytautas Gerulaitis. *Printing and Publishing in Fifteenth-century Venice*. Chicago, IL: American Library Association, 1976, pp. 201–21, 233–5.
4 Lucien Febvre and Henri-Jean Martin. *The Coming of the Book. The impact of printing 1450–1800* (Translated by David Gerard; ed. Geoffrey Nowell-Smith and David Wootton). London: NLB, 1976, p. 241. On France, see Elizabeth Armstrong. *Before Copyright. The French book-privilege system 1498–1526*. Cambridge: Cambridge University Press, 1990.
5 Printed by Sir Walter Greg. *A Companion to Arber*. Oxford: Clarendon Press, 1967, p. 165.
6 John Feather. *A History of British Publishing*. London: Croom Helm, 1988, p. 17.
7 Ibid.
8 The history of the privileges is obscure in detail, as is ownership of individual rights at particular periods. But the general principles are clear enough. There is a list of them, dating from the 1580s, in BL MS. Landsdowne 48, ff. 180–1, 189–94; see Frederick Seaton Siebert, *Freedom of the Press in England 1476–1776*. Urbana, IL: University of Illinois Press, 1965, pp. 38–9. Probably the most comprehensive list of patentees is now that in *STC2*, vol. 3, p. 195, supplemented by the lists in Appendices A–C, ibid., pp. 197–8.
9 CPR Elizabeth I, vol. 2, p. 518.
10 CPR Elizabeth I, vol. 6, p. 93.
11 CPR Elizabeth I, vol. 7, p. 540.
12 CSPD Elizabeth I (1591–94), p. 179.
13 Leo Kirschbaum, Author's copyright in England before 1640. *Papers of the Bibliographical Society of America*, 40 (1946), pp. 43–80.
14 CPR Elizabeth I, vol. 6, p. 266.
15 Greg, *Companion*, p. 127.
16 Cyprian Blagden. *The Stationers' Company. A history 1403–1959*. London: Allen and Unwin, 1960, is a general history. For the early years, see Graham Pollard, The Company of Stationers before 1557. *The Library*, 4th ser., 18 (1937–38), pp. 1–38. The Company's royal charter, the legal basis of its existence, is printed in Edward Arber. *Transcript of the Registers of the Company of Stationers of London 1554–1640*. 5 vols., Birmingham: The Author, 1875–94, vol. 1, pp. xxvii–xxxii; for this, see Graham Pollard, The early constitution of the Stationers' Company. *The Library*, 4th ser., 18 (1937–38), pp. 235–60.
17 I am much influenced by a very important recent paper by Sheila Lambert, State control of the press in theory and practice: the role of the Stationers' Company before 1640. In Robin Myers and Michael Harris, eds.

Censorship & Control of Print in England and France 1600–1910. Winchester: St Paul's Bibliographies, 1992, pp. 1–32. Although, as her title suggests, Lambert is principally concerned with censorship, there is a close relationship between that and copyright in the sixteenth and seventeenth centuries, as we shall see. Lambert argues that the role of the Company in the control of the press was far less important than book trade historians have generally suggested; I would certainly now want to modify some of the statements which I made in 'From rights in copies to copyright: the recognition of authors' rights in English law and practice in the sixteenth and seventeenth centuries'. *Cardozo Arts & Entertainment Law Journal*, 10 (1992), pp. 455–73, the paper on which this chapter is, in part, based.
18 The relevant clause of the Injunctions is printed in Alfred W. Pollard. *Shakespeare's Fight with the Pirates and the Problems of the Transmission of His Text*. Cambridge: Cambridge University Press, 1920, pp. 13–14. The context, however, can be seen only by reading the whole document, printed in P. L. Hughes and J. F. Larkin, eds. *Tudor Royal Proclamations*. 3 vols., New Haven, CT: Yale University Press, 1969, no. 460.
19 Lambert, State control of the press, p. 11.
20 Arber, *Transcript*, vol. 1, pp. 74–5.
21 Ibid., pp. 94–7.
22 Ibid., p. 45.
23 Ibid., p. 70.
24 T. F. Reddaway, The livery companies of Tudor London. *History*, 51 (1966), pp. 287–99.
25 Blagden, *Stationers' Company*, pp. 42–5.
26 Quoted in W. W. Greg. *Some Aspects and Problems of London Publishing between 1550 and 1650*. Oxford: Clarendon Press, 1956, p. 4.
27 I have modified, in the light of Lambert's arguments (see note 17 above), my statement in From rights in copies, p. 460.
28 Arber, *Transcript*, vol. 1, p. 239. Entries were not precisely dated until 1576; before that date they can only be ascribed to a particular year.
29 Ibid., pp. 274, 315.
30 Ibid., p. 93.
31 Ibid., p. 259.
32 Ibid., p. 329.
33 W. W. Greg and E. Boswell, eds. *Records of the Court of the Stationers' Company 1576 to 1602, from Register B*. London: The Bibliographical Society, 1930, p. 9.
34 William A. Jackson, ed. *Records of the Court of the Stationers' Company 1602 to 1640*. London: The Bibliographical Society, 1957, pp. 217, 292. See also Arber, *Transcript*, vol. 4, p. 377.
35 See, among many examples, Arber, *Transcript*, vol. 2, p. 336 (2 September 1578).
36 Ibid., vol. 5, pp. 529–30.
37 Ibid., vol. 2, p. 366. 'The Hall' is Stationers' Hall, situated just to the east of St Paul's Cathedral, which was the Company's home in which it transacted its business. The Master and Wardens seem to have sat, with the

Clerk, in the Hall itself in order to register copies and to undertake other transactions. See Blagden, *Stationers' Company*, pp. 53–5.
38 Ibid., vol. 2, p. 390.
39 Ibid., p. 416.
40 Ibid., p. 421.
41 See Michael Treadwell, Printers on the Court of the Stationers' Company in the seventeenth and eighteenth centuries. *Journal of the Printing Historical Society*, 21 (1992), pp. 29–42.
42 Feather, *History*, pp. 35–40.
43 Feather, *History*, p. 36; Siebert, *Freedom of the Press,* pp. 38–9.
44 H. Anders, The Elizabethan '*ABC* with The Catechism'. *The Library*, 4th ser., 16 (1935–36), pp. 32–48.
45 Greg and Boswell, *Records*, p. 7; Eiluned Rees. *The Welsh Book-Trade before 1820*. Aberystwyth: National Library of Wales, 1988, p. xiv.
46 APC, new ser., 10 (1577–78), pp. 169–70, 188–9.
47 Feather, *History*, p. 37.
48 Harry R. Hoppe, John Wolfe, printer and publishers, 1579–1601. *The Library*, 4th ser., 14 (1933–34), pp. 241–88.
49 APC, new ser., 10 (1577–78), pp. 277–8.
50 Greg, *Companion*, p. 114.
51 Siebert, *Freedom of the Press*, p. 73.
52 Lambert, State control of the press, pp. 12–15.
53 C. L. Oastler. *John Day, the Elizabethan Printer*. Oxford: Oxford Bibliographical Society, occ. publ., 10, 1975, pp. 65–9.
54 Greg and Boswell, *Records*, p. 20.
55 Ibid., p. 21.
56 Arber, *Transcript*, vol. 3, pp. 42–4; Greg, *Companion*, p. 50; confirmed in 1616: Arber, *Transcript*, vol. 3, pp. 679–82; Greg, *Companion*, p. 54. See also Sheila Lambert, Journeymen and Master Printers in the early seventeenth century. *Journal of the Printing Historical Society*, 21 (1992), pp. 13–27, at p. 14.
57 Cyprian Blagden, The English Stock of the Stationers' Company: an account of its origins. *The Library*, 5th ser., 10 (1955), pp. 163–85; Cyprian Blagden, The English Stock of the Stationers' Company in the time of the Stuarts. *The Library*, 5th ser., 12 (1957), pp, 167–86.
58 Greg and Boswell, *Records*, p. 59.
59 Jackson, *Records*, p. 31.
60 Arber, *Transcript*, vol. 3, pp. 288–9.
61 Arber, *Transcript*, vol. 3, p. 248.
62 The latter point is difficult to document, but there is no doubt that it was a well-established practice; the note on Dexter's copies, cited above (note 61), refers to the reversion taking place 'according to a former constitution in suche cases'. It is not clear where, if at all, that 'former constitution' was actually written down, but the practice is referred to as the 'Custom of the Company' in 1626 (Jackson, *Records*, p. 188), and the 'antient Custome' in 1638 (ibid., p. 307).
63 See Lambert, Journeymen, p. 15, and the references in her note 4.

64 Greg and Boswell, *Records*, p. 44.
65 W. W. Greg, ed. *Marlowe's Doctor Faustus 1604–1616*. Oxford: Clarendon Press, 1950, pp. 9–10.
66 Arber, *Transcript*, vol. 3, p. 210. I write 'never *successfully* challenged', because there was some sort of problem with these copies. The entry was made 'by Direction from the wardens under their handes: after yt had ben agreed uppon at ij last courtes'. Unfortunately, Register B (i.e. Greg and Boswell, *Records*) has nothing to say on the matter. The two previous meetings of the Court of Assistants had been on 8 May and 28 June, and, apparently, the case was discussed at neither meeting. There are, however, a number of minor errors and confusions in Register B in 1602 (ibid., pp. 86–90) and some minutes may not have been properly written up in the Court Book. It might be speculated that the discussion concerned the transfer of ownership from the estate of their deceased owner, Cawood, to Leake, rather than on the proof of Cawood's ownership, but this cannot be substantiated.
67 Arber, *Transcript*, vol. 3, p. 365.
68 E. K. Chambers. *The Elizabethan Stage*. 4 vols., Oxford: Clarendon Press, 1923, vol. 3, pp. 291–2.
69 Arber, *Transcript*, vol. 3, p. 431.
70 Information from Dr Maureen Bell, based on work done by her and Professor John Barnard.
71 Greg and Boswell, *Records*, p. 12.
72 Arber, *Transcript*, vol. 2, p. 438.
73 Jackson, *Records*, p. 105.
74 See above, pp. 11.
75 Greg, *Companion*, pp. 50, 153. The book is *STC* 23138. This was part of an effort to introduce the cultivation of the silkworm into England.
76 Greg, *Companion*, pp. 51, 154.
77 Ibid., pp. 56, 162.
78 Ibid., pp. 51–2, 157. See also Sarah L. C. Clapp, The beginnings of subscription publication in the seventeenth century. *Modern Philology*, 29 (1931–32), pp. 199–244.
79 R. A. Foakes and R. T. Rickert, eds. *Henslowe's Diary*. Cambridge: Cambridge University Press, 1961.
80 Literary scholars have tended to assume that Shakespeare was unique in a commercial as well as a literary sense; there is no evidence for this. There is, of course, a vast literature on all of this, much of it of little relevance for our purposes. The organization of the theatrical companies does, however, have some bearing on the matter. Chambers, *Elizabethan Stage*, is the standard, massively detailed and virtually unreadable authority. For a useful summary, however, see Andrew Gurr. *The Shakespearian Stage 1574–1642*. Cambridge: Cambridge University Press, 1970, pp. 19–59.
81 Foakes and Rickert, *Henslowe's Diary*, pp. 21–30.
82 Compare the titles in Foakes and Rickert (as cited in note 81) with Chambers, *Elizabethan Stage*, vol. 3, *passim*, and with W. W. Greg. *A*

Bibliography of the English Printed Drama to the Restoration. 4 vols., London: The Bibliographical Society, 1939–59.
83 The period from the formation of the Company to the retirement of Shakespeare.
84 See Chambers, *Elizabethan Stage*, vol. 3, *passim*; and Greg, *Bibliography, passim*.
85 For an exhaustive study, see Peter Alexander. *Shakespeare's Henry VI and Richard III*. Cambridge: Cambridge University Press, 1929.
86 Arber, *Transcript*, vol. 2, p. 646.
87 Ibid., vol. 3, p. 204.
88 W. W. Greg. *The Shakespeare First Folio. Its bibliographical and textual history*. Oxford: Clarendon Press, 1955, p. 68.
89 Jackson, *Records*, p. 110.
90 Their reasons need not concern us; they relate to the preliminary stages of assembling the First Folio. See Greg, *Shakespeare First Folio*, pp. 28–75.
91 The discussion began with A. W. Pollard. *Shakespeare's Fight with the Pirates and the Problems of the Transmission of his Text*. Cambridge: Cambridge University Press, 1920, pp. 42–4, and was most judiciously ended by Greg, *Aspects and Problems*, pp. 112–22, where he gives a measured account of these so-called 'blocking' entries in the Register and related issues.
92 Chambers, *Elizabethan Stage*, vol. 3, p. 325.
93 This continued throughout the seventeenth century; see Harold Love. *Scribal Publication in Seventeenth-century England*. Oxford: Clarendon Press, 1993.
94 Percy Simpson. *Studies in Elizabethan Drama*. Oxford: Clarendon Press, 1955, pp. 186–92.
95 For James I's patents, see Arber, *Transcript*, vol. 5, p. lvii; Siebert, *Freedom of the Press*, pp. 128–33.
96 Greg, *Aspects and Problems*, p. 75; but see also Allan Pritchard, George Wither's quarrel with the Stationers: an anonymous reply to *The Schollers Purgatory*. *Studies in Bibliography*, 16 (1963), pp. 27–42; and Norman E. Carlson, Wither and the Stationers. *Studies in Bibliography*, 19 (1966), pp. 210–15.
97 J. E. Neale. *Elizabeth I and Her Parliaments 1584–1601*. London: Jonathan Cape, 1957, pp. 376–93; and Conrad Russell. *Parliaments and English Politics 1621–1629*. Oxford: Clarendon Press, paperback ed., 1982, pp. 190–1.
98 21 James I c. 3.
99 Ibid., para. 10.
100 See below, pp. 37–40.
101 Greg, *Companion*, p. 220.
102 W. W. Greg. *Licensers for the Press &c to 1640*. Oxford: Oxford Bibliographical Society (new ser. 10), 1958, p. 63.
103 The decree is printed in Arber, *Transcript*, vol. 4, pp. 528–36. See also Blagden, *Stationers' Company*, pp. 117–25; and Lambert, State control of the press, p. 22.

Chapter 2

1 See John Philipson, The King's Printer in Newcastle upon Tyne in 1639. *The Library*, 6th ser., 11 (1989), pp. 1–9. For subsequent travels, see William K. Sessions. *The King's Printer at Newcastle-upon-Tyne in 1639, at Bristol in 1643–1645 and at Exeter in 1645–1646*. York: Ebor Press, 1982.
2 See W. M. Clyde, Parliament and the press, 1643–7. *The Library*, 4th ser., 13 (1932–33), pp. 399–424; W. M. Clyde, Parliament and the press, II. *The Library*, 4th ser., 14 (1933–34), pp. 39–58; Frederick Seaton Siebert. *Freedom of the Press in England 1476–1776*. Urbana, IL: University of Illinois Press, 1965, pp. 179–233.
3 Sheila Lambert, The beginning of printing for the House of Commons, 1640–42. *The Library*, 6th ser., 3 (1981), pp. 43–64.
4 This had been a problem for much of the seventeenth century, but was certainly deteriorating in the 1630s; for a recent account, see David McKitterick. *A History of Cambridge University Press. Volume 1. Printing and the book trade in Cambridge 1534–1698*. Cambridge: Cambridge University Press, 1993, pp. 195–6.
5 Cyprian Blagden, The Stationers' Company in the Civil War period. *The Library,* 5th ser., 13 (1958), pp. 1–17.
6 Lambert, The beginning of printing, p. 43.
7 John Milton. *Complete Prose Works. Volume II. 1643–1648*. New Haven, CT: Yale University Press, 1959, p. 570.
8 CJ, vol. 2, pp. 71, 79, 84.
9 LJ, vol. 4, p. 174. See also Lambert, The beginning of printing, pp. 44, 47.
10 SC, Court Book C, f. 178. In using Court Books C and D, I am indebted to R. P. Johnston, The Court Books of the Stationers' Company 1641–1679: a complete index and selected entries. Victoria University of Wellington M.A. dissertation, 1983.
11 CJ, vol. 2, p. 402.
12 Franklin B. Williams, Jr., The Laudian imprimatur. *The Library*, 5th ser., 15 (1960), pp. 96–104; Jackson, *Records*, p. 234.
13 C. H. Firth and R. S. Rait, eds. *Acts and Ordinances of the Interregnum 1642–1660*. 3 vols., London: H.M.S.O., 1911, vol. 1, pp. 184–7.
14 On this practice, see N. Frederick Nash, English licences to print and grants of copyright in the 1640s. *The Library*, 6th ser., 4 (1982), pp. 174–84.
15 G. E. Briscoe Eyre. *A Transcript of the Registers of the Worshipful Company of Stationers from 1640–1708*. 3 vols., London, 1913–14, vol. 1, p. 66.
16 Ibid., vols. 1 and 2, *passim*.
17 Firth and Rait, *Acts*, vol. 1, pp. 1021–3.
18 Ibid., vol. 2, pp. 245–54.
19 See Joseph Frank. *The Beginnings of the English Newspaper 1620–1660*. Cambridge, MA: Harvard University Press, 1961, pp. 199–267.
20 Firth and Rait, *Acts*, vol. 2, p. 251.
21 Ibid., vol. 2, pp. 696–9.
22 SC, Court Book C, p. 279^{v}.

23 SC, Court Book D, pp. 11, 11^{v}. The relevant entry (to Leach) is, apparently, Eyre, *Transcript*, vol. 2, pp. 33–4 (12 March 1656).
24 Eyre, *Transcript*, vol. 2, p. 62.
25 Ibid., vol. 2, p. 78.
26 Ibid., vol. 2, p. 119.
27 CSPD Charles II (1660–61), p. 189.
28 See J. Walker, The censorship of the press during the reign of Charles II. *History*, 25 (1950), pp. 219–38.
29 SC, Court Book D, p. 60^{v}.
30 Ibid., p. 61.
31 CJ, vol. 8, p. 288.
32 See CSPD Charles II (1661–62), pp. 44–5.
33 CJ, vol. 3, p. 312 (25 July 1661).
34 CJ, vol. 8, pp. 313, 314.
35 Ibid., p. 315. For the amendment, see CSPD (Charles II), p. 57, a document dated 3 August 1661.
36 Siebert, *Freedom of the Press*, p. 238.
37 CJ, vol. 8, p. 417 (10 May 1662).
38 13 & 14 Charles II c. 33. CJ, vol. 8, pp. 417 (1st Reading, 2 May), 418 (2nd Reading, 3 May), 434 (Report Stage, 17 May), 435 (Report Stage and ingrossment, 19 May), and 436 (agreement to Lords amendments and Royal Assent, 19 May).
39 Cyprian Blagden. *The Stationers' Company. A history 1403–1959*. London: Allen and Unwin, 1960, p. 148.
40 SC, Court Book D, p. 76^{v}, the minutes of a meeting of the Court on 6 October 1662, records a payment to Mr Secretary Nicholas for two letters which he had sent to Parliament in support of 'the Bill', presumably the Bill which became the 1662 Act.
41 CSPD (Charles II), pp. 372–3, the petition of Richard Hutchinson and others.
42 Cyprian Blagden, The 'Company' of Printers. *Studies in Bibliography*, 13 (1960), pp. 1–15.
43 Eyre, *Transcript*, vol. 2, p. 394.
44 McKitterick, *Cambridge University Press*, vol. 1, pp. 202–4, 347, 352; Harry Carter. *A History of the Oxford University Press. Volume I to the year 1780*. Oxford: Clarendon Press, 1975, pp. 78–80. For the long-running disputes between Oxford and the Stationers in the late seventeenth century, see John Johnson and Strickland Gibson. *Print and Privilege at Oxford to the Year 1700*. Oxford: Clarendon Press, 1946, pp. 109–30.
45 This was the notorious pirate, Henry Hills. For this episode, see Bernard Capp. *Astrology and the Popular Press. English almanacs 1500–1800*. London: Faber and Faber, 1979, p. 40. For the almanac trade in general, see Cyprian Blagden, The distribution of almanacs in the second half of the seventeenth century. *Studies in Bibliography*, 11 (1958), pp. 107–16.
46 *Stationers' Company v. Patentees of Roll's Abridgements* (Michaelmas Term, 18 Charles II) reported at Carter 89–92.
47 *Stationers' Company v. Seymour* (Trinity Term, 29 Charles II) reported at 3 Keble 792.

48 Ibid.
49 Generally, see R. C. Bald, Early copyright litigation and its bibliographical interest. *Papers of the Bibliographical Society of America*, 36 (1942), pp. 81–96.
50 SC, Court Book D, p. 191^{v}.
51 The first use of this form of words which I have seen. See above, p. 5.
52 Ibid., pp. 294–310.
53 Ibid., p. 317.
54 SC, Court Book E, p. 160.
55 Bald, Early copyright litigation, p. 87; Francis Mott Harrison, Nathaniel Ponder: the publisher of *Pilgrim's Progress*. *The Library*, 4th ser., 15 (1934–35), pp. 257–94, at pp. 270–5. See also below, p. 49.
56 *Company of Stationers v. Seymour* (Trinity Term, 29 Charles II) reported at 1 Mod. 256–8.
57 Ibid.
58 See above, p. 11.
59 CSPD Charles II (1661–62), p. 52, for the grant.
60 SC Court Book D, p. 118^{v} (Ogilvy: confirmed in 1667, ibid., p. 130); and ibid., p. 85^{v} (Fuller).
61 Eiluned Rees and Gerald Morgan, Welsh almanacks, 1680–1835: problems of piracy. *The Library*, 6th ser., 1 (1979), pp. 144–63, at p. 144.
62 See Nicholas Temperley, John Playford and the Stationers' Company. *Music and Letters*, 54 (1973), pp. 203–12.
63 John Feather. *A History of British Publishing*. London: Croom Helm, 1988, p. 61.
64 SC, Court Book D, p. 236^{v}.
65 Ibid., p. 271^{v}.
66 Feather, *History,* pp. 56–7, 101, and the references cited there.
67 Terry Belanger, Tonson, Wellington and the Shakespeare copyrights. In: R. W. Hunt, I. G. Philip and R. J. Roberts, eds. *Studies in the Book Trade in Honour of Graham Pollard*. Oxford: Oxford Bibliographical Society (new ser., 18), 1975, pp. 195–209.
68 Timothy Crist, Government control of the press after the expiration of the Printing Act in 1679. *Publishing History*, 5 (1979), pp. 49–77.
69 SC, Court Book D, p. 341^{v}.
70 Ibid., p. 236; and above, pp. 44–5.
71 See above, p. 46, and note 55.
72 Eyre, *Transcript*, vol. 3, p. 49; see also Roger Sharrock. *John Bunyan*. London: Macmillan, 1968, p. 69.
73 On this period, see A. W. Pollard, Some notes on the history of copyright in England 1662–1774. *The Library*, 4th ser., 3 (1922–23), pp. 97–114, at pp. 103–7.
74 CJ, vol. 9, p. 729 (5 June 1685).
75 LJ, vol. 14, p. 71.
76 1 James II c. 17, s. 15.
77 For this period, see Raymond Astbury, The renewal of the Licensing Act in 1693 and its lapse in 1695. *The Library*, 5th ser., 33 (1978), pp. 296–322.

78 Ibid., at pp. 300–3, and especially the contemporary sources cited in notes 19 and 27. It should be noted that Astbury (like many others) relied on Siebert, *Freedom of the Press*, rather more often than is sensible. But this certainly does not invalidate his paper, much of which is based on primary sources.
79 Ibid., at pp. 309–11, and the sources cited in notes 65 and 66.
80 CJ, vol. 11, p. 228.
81 See J. A. Downie. *Robert Harley and the Press*. Cambridge: Cambridge University Press, 1979, pp. 149–50; and Laurence Hanson. *Government and the Press 1695–1763*. Oxford: Clarendon Press, 1936, pp. 8–10. Bills which relate solely to the taxation of printed matter are excluded from my calculation.
82 Astbury, Lapse, pp. 311–15.
83 P. D. G. Thomas. *The House of Commons in the Eighteenth Century*. Oxford: Clarendon Press, 1971, pp. 60–4.
84 Downie, *passim*. For Harley's notes on newspapers, one symptom of this obsession, see J. M. Price, A note on the circulation of the press. *Bulletin of the Institute of Historical Research*, 32 (1958), pp. 215–24; Henry L. Snyder, The circulation of newspapers in the reign of Queen Anne. *The Library*, 5th ser., 23 (1968), pp. 202–35; and Henry L. Snyder, A further note on the circulation of newspapers in the reign of Queen Anne. *The Library*, 5th ser., 31 (1976), pp. 387–9.
85 Peter Fraser. *The Intelligence of the Secretaries of State and their Monopoly of Licensed News 1660–1688*. Cambridge: Cambridge University Press, 1956, pp. 39–56; and P. M. Handover. *A History of the London Gazette 1665–1965*. London: H.M.S.O., 1965, pp. 5–6.
86 John Feather, From censorship to copyright: some aspects of government control of the press in England 1695–1775. In: Kenneth E. Carpenter, ed. *Books and Libraries in History and Society*. New York: Bowker, 1983, pp. 173–98.
87 See below, pp. 54–5.
88 SC, Court Book E, p. 217^{v}.
89 CJ, vol. 11, p. 289.
90 Ibid.
91 Ibid., vol. 11, p. 354.
92 *Reasons humbly offer'd to the Consideration of the Honourable House of Commons shewing the great Necessity of having a Bill for the Regulating of Printing and Printing-Presses*. [London: 1696]. (BL, 1887.b.58.(7.)). This is dated [1698?] in the BL catalogue, but there is no Commons business in that year to which it could refer. The 1696 Bill reached the stage at which petitions would have been tabled, and I therefore ascribe it to that year.
93 CJ, vol. 11, p. 706.
94 Ibid., vol. 14, p. 338.
95 BL, 816.m.12.(37.).
96 CJ, vol. 11, p. 765.
97 Harold Love. *Scribal Publication in Seventeenth-century England*. Oxford: Clarendon Press, 1993, pp. 9–22.

98 I have discussed these cases at length in John Feather, The book trade in politics: the making of the Copyright Act of 1710. *Publishing History*, 8 (1980), pp. 19–44, at pp. 25–9, the paper on which part of this chapter is based.
99 Downie, *Robert Harley,* p. 55.
100 Ibid., pp. 57–79.
101 Published on 7 January 1704; see John Robert Moore. *A Checklist of the Writings of Daniel Defoe*. 2nd ed., Hampden, CT: Archon, 1971, no. 68. It was reprinted by the Luttrell Society in 1948, but references here are to the 1704 edition.
102 Defoe, *An Essay*, pp. 4, 7.
103 Ibid., pp. 11–18.
104 Ibid., p. 18.
105 See, for example, Richmond P. Bond, The pirate and *The Tatler. The Library*, 5th ser., 17 (1963), pp. 257–74. See also Pollard, Some notes, pp. 106–7.
106 On the King's Bench prosecutions, see Donald Thomas. *A Long Time Burning. A history of literary censorship in England*. London: Routledge and Kegan Paul, 1969, pp. 34–62.
107 W. A. Speck. *Tory and Whig. The struggle in the constituencies 1701–1715*. London: Macmillan, 1970, pp. 98–109.
108 CJ, vol. 15, p. 313.
109 For the congers and the trade sales, see Terry Belanger, Publishers and writers in eighteenth-century England. In: Isabel Rivers, ed. *Books and the Readers in Eighteenth-century England*. Leicester: Leicester University Press, 1982, pp. 1–25, at pp. 13–16. For the congers, see also Norma Hodgson and Cyprian Blagden, eds. *The Notebook of Thomas Bennet and Henry Clements (1686–1719) with Some Aspects of Book Trade Practice.* Oxford: Oxford Bibliographical Society (new ser., 6), 1956, pp. 209–14. For the trade sales, see also below, pp. 65–6.
110 SC, Court Book G, p. 138^{v}.
111 CJ, vol. 15, p. 316.
112 See below, pp. 99–100.
113 See above, p. 45, and Carter, *A History*, pp. 157–78.
114 CJ, vol. 16, pp. 260–1.
115 SC, Court Book G, p. 173^{v}.
116 SC, Wardens' Accounts, 7 Jan–6 Mar 1710; they spent 11*s*. 6*d*. 'at the Kings head . . . when we came from Parliam^{t}', and paid 5*s*. 0*d*. for 'Coach hire twice to Westminster'.
117 This is based on a manuscript copy in Bodl. MS Rawl. D. 922, ff. 380–6, for which see below, pp. 61–2.
118 CJ, vol. 16, p. 291.
119 BL, 1887.b.58.(3.).
120 Bodl., John Johnson Collection.
121 See below, pp. 81–94.
122 Bodl., John Johnson Collection.
123 CJ, vol. 16, p. 294.

124 Ibid., p. 339. The manuscript version of the Bill (see note 117) derives from the Report Stage, and has been amended by a Member as he sat through the debate. It is the basis for this and the following paragraphs.
125 The Act is 8 Anne c. 19, conveniently printed in Harry Ransom. *The First Copyright Statute*. Austin, TX: University of Texas Press, 1959, pp. 110–17.
126 SC, Court Book G, pp. 178^{v}, $179–179^{v}$.

Chapter 3

1 This statement is based on two aspects of the procedures adopted in the Commons: (1) the petitions followed the tabling of the Bill, rather than preceding it, as was the case for Private Bills; and (2) it went to a Committee of the Whole House after its Second Reading, a Public Bill procedure. By contrast, the 1707 Bill was Private. This may explain, in parliamentary terms, why it failed. On procedural matters, see P. G. D. Thomas. *The House of Commons in the Eighteenth Century*. Oxford: Clarendon Press, 1971, pp. 51, 57–8.
2 See John Feather. *The Provincial Book Trade in Eighteenth-century England*. Cambridge: Cambridge University Press, 1985, pp. 1–11, 44–68.
3 See John Feather. *A History of British Publishing*. London: Croom Helm, 1988, pp. 68–9; and Norma Hodgson and Cyprian Blagden. *The Notebook of Thomas Bennet and Henry Clements*. Oxford: Oxford Bibliographical Society (new ser., 6), 1953, pp. 78–9.
4 The phrase used by Richard Royston, who was one of them, in his will in 1686; Feather, *History*, p. 69.
5 See Stephen Parks. *John Dunton and the English Book Trade*. New York: Garland, 1976, p. 207.
6 Hodgson and Blagden, *Notebook of Thomas Bennet*, p. 84.
7 See above, pp. 56–7 and Table 2.2, p. 58.
8 See above, pp. 18, 42 and 57.
9 See above, pp. 25–6.
10 See Cyprian Blagden, Booksellers' trade sales 1718–1768. *The Library*, 5th ser., 5 (1950–51), pp. 243–57; Terry Belanger, Booksellers' trade sales, 1718–1768. *The Library*, 5th ser., 30 (1975), pp. 281–302; and Terry Belanger, Publishers and writers in eighteenth-century England. In: Isabel Rivers, ed. *Books and Their Readers in Eighteenth-century England*. Leicester: Leicester University Press, 1982, p. 15.
11 See above, pp. 61–2.
12 See above, pp. 32–3.
13 For a recent analysis, see Peter Lindenbaum, Milton's contract. *Cardozo Arts & Entertainment Law Journal*, 10 (1992), pp. 439–54.
14 Kathleen M. Lynch. *Jacob Tonson, Kit-Cat Publisher*. Knoxville, TN: University of Tennessee Press, 1971, p. 16.
15 In 12 George II c. 36, for which see below pp. 75–6, the clauses on price controls were repealed.
16 See below, p. 100.

17 Belanger, Publishers and writers, pp. 16–17.
18 For *Ponder v. Burrill*, see above, pp. 46 and 49. See also Alfred W. Pollard, Copyright in Josephus. *The Library*, 2nd ser., 8 (1917), pp. 173–6.
19 BL 593.c.20. is a copy of the first edition, and BL T.1053.(4) is the second.
20 Bodl. Vet. A5 e. 5045(2) is a copy of the piracy.
21 The papers are PRO C11/2642/49.
22 The father of the Byng executed for cowardice in 1757. See DNB for both men.
23 Shirley Strum Kenny, Eighteenth-century editions of Steele's *Conscious Lovers*. *Studies in Bibliography*, 21 (1968), pp. 253–61.
24 PRO C11/2558/47.
25 David Foxon. *Pope and the Early Eighteenth-century Book Trade*, rev. and ed. by James McLaverty. Oxford: Clarendon Press, 1991, pp. 47–8.
26 For which see below, pp. 77–9. I can find no similar statements, for example, among pre-1731 agreements listed in James E. Tierney, ed. *The Correspondence of Robert Dodsley 1733–1764*. Cambridge: Cambridge University Press, 1988, pp. 508–29; nor do there seem to be any in the papers discussed in G. E. Bentley, Jr., Copyright documents in the George Robinson archive: William Godwin and others 1713–1820. *Studies in Bibliography*, 35 (1982), pp. 67–110; and there were none among the contracts used in John Feather, John Nourse and his authors. *Studies in Bibliography*, 34 (1981), pp. 205–26.
27 See David Hunter, Copyright protection for engraving and maps in eighteenth-century Britain. *The Library*, 6th ser., 9 (1987), pp. 128–47, at pp. 131–2.
28 CJ, vol. 22, p. 364.
29 The point is made by Hunter, Copyright protection, p. 133.
30 CJ, vol. 22, pp. 364, 380.
31 Hunter, Copyright protection, pp. 133–6.
32 CJ, vol. 22, p. 400.
33 Ibid., pp. 411–12.
34 Ibid., p. 482.
35 There are copies of this Bill in Bodl. MS Carte 114, ff. 391–6, and MS Carte 207, ff. 31–5, 36–9, 40–3, and 44–7. A different edition is at ibid., ff. 54–9. For Carte, see below, pp. 74–5.
36 See M. Pollard. *Dublin's Trade in Books 1550–1800*. Oxford: Clarendon Press, 1989, pp. 66–87, for a measured account of the real extent of the Irish problem. For some aspects of the Dutch problem, see John Feather, English books in the Netherlands in the eighteenth century: reprints or piracies? In: C. Berckvens-Stevenlinck, H. Bots, P. G. Hoftijzer and O. S. Lankhorst, eds. *Le magasin de l'univers. The Dutch Republic as the centre of the European book trade*. The Hague: E. J. Brill, 1992, pp. 143–54.
37 *Reasons Humbly Offered to the Consideration of the Honourable House of Commons, in support of a Bill for making more effectual an Act passed in the eighth year of her late majesty Queen Anne, intitled, An Act for the Encouragement of Learning*. [London: 1735]. Copy in Bodl. John Johnson Collection.

38 See CJ, vol. 22, pp. 411–12; and the manuscript 'Draft Report of the Committee' in BL 357.c.2.(39.).
39 [London: 1735]. Copy (printed) in Bodl. MS Carte 207, ff. 69–72.
40 So far as France was concerned this was true, although somewhat disingenuously expressed since the main purpose of French legislation was to prevent the import of books not allowed to be published in France by the censors, rather than to protect commercial interests. See Giles Barber, French royal decrees concerning the book trade 1700–1789. *Australian Journal of French Studies*, 3 (1966), pp. 312–30.
41 [London: 1735]. Copy (printed) in Bodl. MS Carte 207, f. 31.
42 See above, pp. 58–63.
43 Patents were protected for fourteen years only, under a law of 1623; see C. H. Greenstreet, History of patent systems. In: F. Liebesny, ed. *Mainly on Patents*. London: Butterworth, 1972, p. 7. There are some parallels in the development of patent and copyright laws in the eighteenth century, for which see Sir William Holdsworth. *A History of English Law*. 7th ed., 16 vols., London: Methuen, 1966–72, vol. 11, pp. 426–30.
44 *A Letter from an Author to a Member of Parliament. Occasioned by a late Letter concerning the Bill now depending in the House of Commons, for the Encouragement of Learning &c.* [London:] 17 April 1735. Copy in Bodl. John Johnson Collection.
45 *A Second Letter from an Author to a Member of Parliament, containing some further remarks on a late letter concerning the Bill now depending in the House of Commons, for the Encouragement of Learning, &c.* [London: 23 April 1735]. Copy in Bodl. John Johnson Collection (with contemporary MS date).
46 Fixed-term legislation was not unusual in the eighteenth century, as we shall see with the Import of Books Act (see below, p. 76), and had been used as a device since the Restoration; the Printing Act of 1662 was, of course, an example.
47 CJ, vol. 22, p. 482.
48 LJ, vol. 24, pp. 543–4, 548, 550.
49 See Foxon, *Pope*, pp. 131, 244; J. McLaverty, The first printing and publication of Pope's letters. *The Library*, 6th ser., vol. 2, pp. 264–80; and Pat Rogers, The case of *Pope v. Curll. The Library*, 5th ser., 27 (1972), pp. 326–31.
50 *The Case of the Authors and Proprietors of Books*. [London: 1735]. Copy (printed) in Bodl. MS Carte 207, ff. 67–8.
51 See below, pp. 81–3.
52 For Carte, see DNB. His notes are in Bodl. MS Carte 114, ff. 19–20 ('Reasons for amending an Act of Parliament made in the 10th [*recte* 8th] year of the late Queen entitled an Act for the Encouragement of Learning &c'), 21 ('Reasons for renewing the Privilege of the Term of 21 years in old Copies'), and 22 ('reasons for granting authors Privilege for 21 years rather than for 14'). See also Donald W. Nichol, On the use of 'copy' and 'copyright': a Scriblerian coinage? *The Library*, 6th ser., 12 (1990), pp. 110–20, at p. 113.

53 There are at least two printed editions of the Bill. The first is reproduced from the copy in Guildhall Library in Sheila Lambert, ed. *House of Commons Sessional Papers of the Eighteenth Century*, Wilmington, DE: Scholarly Resources Inc., 1975, vol. 7, pp. 266–81. There are copies of the later edition, which incorporates amendments made in MS in the Guildhall copy in BL B.S.68/16(1), and Bodl. MS Carte 207, ff. 11–18.
54 CJ, vol. 22, p. 741.
55 For the stamp duties, see John Feather, The English book trade and the law 1695–1794. *Publishing History*, 12 (1982), pp. 51–75, at pp. 52–6.
56 *Farther Reasons Humbly Offered to the Consideration of the honourable House of Commons*. [London: 1737]. Copy in Bodl. MS Carte 207, ff. 27–8.
57 *Reasons Humbly Offered to the Consideration of the House of Commons, in support of a Bill for making more effectual an Act passed in the eighth year of the Reign of her late Majesty Queen Anne, intitled, An act of the Encouragement of Learning*. [London: 1737]. Copies in BL 816.m.12.(51.) and Bodl. MS Carte 114, ff. 338, 412.
58 See note 56, above.
59 LJ, vol. 25, p. 81.
60 CJ, vol. 23, pp. 157, 320; LJ, vol. 25, pp. 242, 244, 251, 254, 255–6, 259, 362, 363, 368, 370, 372, 374, 395, 418–19. The Act is 12 George II c. 36; it was renewed in 1747 as 20 George II c. 47, and again in 1754.
61 SC, Court Book I, pp. 271–4.
62 Congreve, for example, had done so; see D. F. McKenzie. *The London Book Trade in the Later Seventeenth Century*. [Cambridge:] privately circulated reproduction from typescript, 1976, pp. 35–54.
63 See Foxon, *Pope*, pp. 63–86.
64 J. McLaverty, The contract for Pope's translation of Homer's *Iliad*: an introduction and transcription. *The Library*, 6th ser., 15 (1993), pp. 206–25.
65 BL. MS Egerton 1959, f. 1.
66 See J. McLaverty, Lawton Gilliver: Pope's bookseller. *Studies in Bibliography*, 32 (1979), pp. 101–24, based on McLaverty's A study of John Wright and Lawton Gilliver, Alexander Pope's printer and bookseller. Oxford University B.Litt. dissertation, 1974, where the available evidence will be found. See also J. McLaverty. *Pope's Printer, John Wright: a preliminary study*. Oxford: Oxford Bibliographical Society (Occasional Publications, 11), 1976, pp. 11–28. Pope was apparently involved in helping at least two other booksellers to establish themselves in the trade: Robert Dodsley, to whom he lent £100 (George Sherburn, ed. *The Correspondence of Alexander Pope*. 5 vols., Oxford: Clarendon Press, 1956, vol. 3, p. 346) and perhaps Henry Woodfall (John Nichols. *Literary Anecdotes of the Eighteenth Century*. 9 vols., London: the author, 1812–15, vol. 1, p. 300).
67 BL MS Egerton 1951, f. 9.
68 James R. Sutherland, The Dunciad of 1729. *Modern Language Review*, 31 (1936), pp. 347–53; D. L. Vander Meulen, The printing of Pope's *Dunciad* 1728. *Studies in Bibliography*, 35 (1982), pp. 271–85; and Foxon, *Pope*, pp. 108–14.

69 His memory failed him on this point, and indeed the history of the assignment and entry of *The Dunciad* is even more complicated than Gilliver recalled. See Foxon, *Pope*, pp. 110–12. The whole situation was very confused, but the key points, so far as the present argument is concerned, seem to be clear enough.
70 PRO C11/2581/36.
71 Harry Ransom. *The First Copyright Statute.* Austin, TX: University of Texas Press, 1959, pp. 111–12.
72 The confusion was largely created by Pope himself; see Sutherland, The Dunciad; and Foxon, *Pope*, loc. cit.
73 PRO C33/351/284.
74 PRO C11/549/39. See Foxon, *Pope*, pp. 249–50; and Howard P. Vincent, Some *Dunciad* litigation. *Philological Quarterly*, 18 (1939), pp. 285–9.
75 PRO C11/837/14. Foxon, *Pope*, p. 250.
76 David Hunter, *Pope v. Bickham*: an infringement of *An Essay on Man* alleged. *The Library*, 6th ser., 9 (1987), pp. 268–73. Foxon, *Pope*, pp. 250–1.
77 See Michael Harris, Journalism as a profession or trade in the eighteenth century. In: Robin Myers and Michael Harris, eds. *Author/Publisher Relations During the Eighteenth and Nineteenth Centuries*. Oxford: Oxford Polytechnic Press, 1983, pp. 37–62.
78 See A. S. Collins. *Authorship in the Days of Johnson. Being a study of the relation between author, patron, publisher and public, 1726–1780*. London: Robert Holden, 1927, pp. 114–212.
79 See Raymond Williams. *Keywords. A vocabulary of culture and society*. Rev. ed., Glasgow: Fontana, 1983, pp. 230–1.
80 See Mark Rose, The author as proprietor: *Donaldson v. Becket* and the genealogy of modern authorship. *Representations*, 23 (1988), pp. 51–85, at pp. 55–6; Mark Rose. *Authors and Owners. The invention of copyright*. Cambridge, MA: Harvard University Press, 1993, pp. 154–8; and Martha Woodmansee, The genius and the copyright: economic and legal conditions of the emergence of the 'author'. *Eighteenth-century Studies*, 17 (1984), pp. 425–48, at pp. 426–31.
81 P. J. Wallis, Book subscription lists. *The Library*, 5th ser., 29 (1974), pp. 255–86.
82 Clayton Atto, The Society for the Encouragement of Learning. *The Library*, 4th ser., 19 (1938–39), pp. 263–88.
83 James Ralph. *The Case of Authors by Profession or Trade Stated*. London: Ralph Griffiths, 1758, pp. 59–60.
84 7 George II c. 24.
85 Ralph, The *Case of Authors*, p. '67' [*recte* 75].
86 Feather, *Provincial Book Trade*, pp. 109–21.
87 David Fleeman, The revenue of a writer. Samuel Johnson's literary earnings. In: R. W. Hunt, I. G. Philip and R. J. Roberts, eds. *Studies in the Book Trade in Honour of Graham Pollard*. Oxford: Oxford Bibliographical Society (new ser., 18), 1975, pp. 211–30.
88 Feather, John Nourse, *passim*.
89 See above, pp. 71–2.

90 Pollard, *Dublin's Trade*, pp. 110–226; and Richard Cargill Cole. *Irish Booksellers and English Writers*. London: Mansell, 1986, pp. 40–61.
91 Warren McDougall, Copyright litigation in the Court of Session, 1738–1749, and the rise of the Scottish book trade. *Edinburgh Bibliographical Society Transactions*, 5 (1988), pp. 2–31, at pp. 9–22.
92 Ibid., pp. 4–6; Feather, *Provincial Book Trade*, p. 7.
93 McDougall, Copyright litigation, pp. 5–8.
94 Their statement was printed as *Unto the Right Honourable the Lords of Council and Session. The petition of Daniel Midwinter, William Innes, Aaron Ward, and others, all of London Booksellers, and William Elliot Writer in Edinburgh their Attorney or Factor, Partners*. [Edinburgh:] 9 December 1747. In fact, the prime mover was probably Andrew Millar, who was consistently active against the Scots reprinters; see McDougall, Copyright litigation, *passim*; and below, pp. 87–9.
95 Henry Home, Lord Kames. *Remarkable Decisions of the Court of Session*. Edinburgh: 1766, pp. 154–61.
96 McDougall, Copyright litigation, pp. 7–8. This and the previous case started as one, but were apparently separated for procedural reasons.
97 *Memorial for the Booksellers of Edinburgh and Glasgow, relating to the process against them by some of the London booksellers; which depended before the Court of Session and is now under appeal*. [Edinburgh:] 1747.
98 Ibid., p. 3.
99 See above, pp. 77–8.
100 *Memorial for the Booksellers of Edinburgh and Glasgow*, pp. 10–11, 14.
101 McDougall, Copyright litigation, p. 8.
102 BL MS Egerton 1959, ff. 20–1, 23–4.
103 For this episode, see Feather, *Provincial Book Trade*, p. 8; Gwyn Walters, The booksellers in 1759 and 1774: the battle for literary property. *The Library*, 5th ser., 29 (1974), pp. 287–311; and Graham Pollard, The 2English market for printed books. *Publishing History*, 4 (1978), pp. 7–48, at pp. 30–1. The letters and other documents are printed in Alexander Donaldson. *Some Thoughts on the State of Literary Property*. London, 1764.
104 Christine Ferdinand, Benjamin Collins, the *Salisbury Journal*, and the provincial book trade. *The Library*, 6th ser., 11 (1989), pp. 116–38.
105 Reported in 1 Black. W. 301–11.
106 See above, pp. 77–9.
107 1 Black. W. 321–45.
108 1 Black. W. 345 note (d).
109 Richard Schlatter. *Private Property. The history of an idea*. London: Allen and Unwin, 1951, pp. 151–8, 164–72. Richard Tuck. *Natural Rights Theories. Their origin and development*. Cambridge: Cambridge University Press, 1979, pp. 83–4.
110 Ibid., pp. 162–3.
111 1 Black. W. 329.
112 Donaldson, *Some Thoughts*; see note 103, above.
113 John MacLaurin, Lord Dreghorn. *Considerations on the Nature and Origin of Literary Property*. Edinburgh, 1767.
114 4 Burr. 2303–417.

115 Ibid., 2303.
116 In addition to the official report, details can be found in Sir James Burrow. *The Question Concerning Literary Property, determined by the Court of King's Bench on 20th April 1769, in the cause between Andrew Millar and Robert Taylor*. London, 1773. A slightly variant version of the judges' speeches can be found in *Speeches or Arguments of the Judges of the Court of King's Bench, viz. Mr Justice Willes, Mr Justice Aston, Sir Joseph Yates, and Lord C. Justice Mansfield; in April 1769 in the Cause of Millar against Taylor, for printing Thomson's Seasons*. Leith, 1771.
117 4 Burr. 2318.
118 Ibid., 2315.
119 Ibid., 2335.
120 Ibid., 2341.
121 Ibid., 2377.
122 Ibid., 2386.
123 Ibid., 2390.
124 Ibid., 2408.
125 For *Becket v. Donaldson*, see *The Cases of the Appellants and Respondents in the Cause of Literary Property, before the House of Lords: wherein the decree of Lord Chancellor Apsley was reversed, 26 Feb. 1774*. London 1774. [The appellant was, of course, Donaldson.] See also Rose, The author as proprietor; and Walters, The booksellers.
126 The judge was Lord Coalston, the Lord Ordinary, in *MacKenzie v. Robertson (1771)*. See David Rae, Lord Eskgrove. *Information for John MacKenzie of Delvine, Writer to the Signet, and others, Trustees appointed by Mrs Anne Smith, widow, of Mrs Thomas Ruddiman, Gate Keeper to the Advocates' Library, Pursuers, against John Robertson, Printer in Edinburgh, Defender.* [Edinburgh:] 1771.
127 Deliberately echoing Yates? See above, p. 85.
128 The judges were the four judges of each of the three common-law courts, King's Bench, Exchequer and Common Pleas. In fact, Mansfield did not vote on any of the issues in this case. The procedure was that after the judges had given their opinions, other peers could speak, and the House then divided. See Rose, The author as proprietor, p. 67.
129 There is, unfortunately, a problem about this crucial vote; I have accepted the account in Rose, The author as proprietor, p. 67, which concludes that the vote was 6 : 5 in favour of the question, not 5 : 6 against it. The misapprehension arises from an error made by the Clerk of the House of Lords.
130 Catherine Macaulay. *A Modest Plea for the Property of Copy Right*. London & Bath, 1774. For other contributions to the debate, see Walters, The booksellers, pp. 309–11.
131 Letter to Strahan, dated 7 March 1774, and cited in J. Alan Pfeffer, Samuel Johnson on copyright. *Journal of English and Germanic Philology*, 47 (1948), pp. 165–72, at p. 170.
132 CJ, vol. 34, p. 513. The petition is printed in *Petitions and Papers Relating to the Bill of the Booksellers Now Before the House of Commons*. London, 1774, pp. 3–4.

133 CJ, vol. 34, pp. 588–90.
134 Ibid.
135 CJ, vol. 34, pp. 665–6; *Petitions and Papers*, pp. 7–8.
136 CJ, vol. 34, p. 698; *Petitions and Papers*, pp. 8–12.
137 CJ, vol. 34, p. 679; *Petitions and Papers*, pp. 4–6.
138 [London, 1774]. Copy in MS Carte 207, ff. 25–6. This used to be wrongly dated [1735?] in the Bodleian catalogue, but there is a reference to the verdict in *Becket v. Donaldson* which means that the manuscript date of '1773/4' written on the document must be substantially correct. It cannot have belonged to Carte (who died in 1754), and was presumably confused with his collection of material on copyright when the Carte MSS were sorted and bound in the nineteenth century.
139 *Observations on the Case of the Booksellers of London and Westminster*. [London, 1774]. Copy in BL 215.i.4.(99.).
140 *An Account of the Expense of Correcting and Improving Sundry Books*. [London, 1774]. Copy in BL 215.i.4.(98.). The critical comments are in *Observations*, for which see note 139, above.
141 SC, Court Book M, pp. 480–1.
142 These issues are variously discussed in Terry Belanger, From bookseller to publisher: changes in the London book trade, 1750–1850. In: Richard G. Landon, ed. *Book Selling and Book Buying: aspects of the British and North American book trade*. Chicago, IL: American Library Association, 1978, pp. 7–16; Feather, *History*, pp. 116–22; Pollard, English market, pp. 34–9; Rose, The author as proprietor, pp. 70–8.
143 This brief account is based on the authoritative study by Cyprian Blagden, Thomas Carnan and the almanack monopoly. *Studies in Bibliography*, 14 (1961), pp. 23–43.
144 LJ, vol. 34, p. 470.
145 The case is reported in 3 Swans. 672–81 App.
146 Robert Maugham. *A Treatise on the Laws of Literary Property*. London, 1828, pp. 128–9.
147 See Robert R. Allen, Dr Johnson on abridgement – a re-examination. *Papers of the Bibliographical Society of America*, 60 (1969), pp. 215–19.
148 In *Gyles v. Wilcox (1740)*, this was the decision in Chancery. Reported at 2 Atk. 143.
149 1 East 363.
150 *Trusler v. Murray*, together with the similar *Wilkins v. Atkins* (reported at 17 Vesey 422), was cited by Maugham, *Treatise*, pp. 132–6, to support this view.

Chapter 4

1 See above, p. 68; and John Feather, The English book trade and the law 1695–1799. *Publishing History*, 12 (1982), pp. 51–75, at p. 57.
2 See J. C. T. Oates, The deposit of books at Cambridge under the Licensing Acts, 1662–79, 1685–95. *Transactions of the Cambridge Bibliographical Society*, 2 (1954–58), pp. 290–304; J. C. T. Oates. *Cambridge University Library. A history from the beginnings to the*

Copyright Act of Queen Anne. Cambridge: Cambridge University Press, 1986, pp. 416–29; R. C. Barrington Partridge. *The History of the Legal Deposit of Books*. London: The Library Association, 1938, pp. 23–31; and I. G. Philip. *The Bodleian Library in the Seventeenth and Eighteenth Centuries*. Oxford: Clarendon Press, 1983, pp. 52–5.
3 See above, pp. 43–4.
4 Philip, *The Bodleian Library*, p. 27; Jackson, *Records*, pp. 48–9.
5 Philip, *The Bodleian Library*, pp. 27–30.
6 Partridge, *History*, pp. 287–8.
7 Oates, *Cambridge University Library*, p. 417.
8 SC, Court Book D, pp. 85, 88.
9 Oates, *Cambridge University Library*, pp. 420–8.
10 Philip, *The Bodleian Library*, p. 55.
11 J. H. Monk. *The Life of Richard Bentley*. 2 vols., London, 1833, vol. 1, p. 99.
12 See above, pp. 56–8.
13 For Charlett, see S. G. Gillam, The Correspondence of Arthur Charlett. Oxford University B.Litt. dissertation, 1957, pp. 1–21.
14 Philip, *The Bodleian Library*, pp. 76–7.
15 Bodl. MS Ballard 38, f. 145.
16 The tradition was recorded by William Reading, Librarian of Sion College in *The History of the Ancient and Present State of Sion-college*. London, 1724, pp. 38–9; see also E. H. Pearce. *Sion College and Its Library*. Cambridge: Cambridge University Press, 1913, pp. 281–2.
17 C. E. Doble, ed. *Remarks and Collections of Thomas Hearne. Vol. 2 (March 20 1707–May 23 1710)*. Oxford: Oxford Historical Society, 7, 1886, p. 1.
18 8 Anne c. 19.
19 Philip, *The Bodleian Library*, pp. 78–9. See also John Chalmers, Bodleian Copyright Deposit Survivors of the First Sixteen Years of the Copyright Act of Queen Anne, 10 April 1710–25 March 1726. Oxford University D.Phil. dissertation, 1974.
20 C. P. Finlayson and S. Murray Simpson, The history of the library 1710–1737. In: Jean R. Guild and Alexander Law, eds. *Edinburgh University Library 1580–1980*. Edinburgh: Edinburgh University Press, 1982, p. 55.
21 John Durkan, The early history of Glasgow University Library 1475–1710. *The Bibliotheck*, 8 (1977), p. 126.
22 Reading, *A History*, p. 38.
23 Philip, *The Bodleian Library*, pp. 102–3.
24 P. Ardagh, St Andrews University Library and the Copyright Acts. *Edinburgh Bibliographical Society Transactions*, 3 (1948–55), pp. 183–209, at pp. 187–8.
25 Audrey Nairn, A 1730 copyright list from Glasgow University archives. *The Bibliotheck*, 2 (1959) pp. 30–2.
26 S. Murray Simpson, An early copyright list in Edinburgh University Library. *The Bibliotheck*, 4 (1963–66), pp. 202–12.

27 41 George III c. 107. The original Bill had proposed that only Trinity should have deposit privileges; it is printed in PP 1801 (112) I. 381–8. King's Inn was added in an amendment in the Lords.
28 They were: in England, the British Museum (which had inherited the deposit privilege of the Royal Library on its foundation in 1754), the Bodleian, Cambridge University and Sion College; in Scotland, the Faculty of Advocates (added to the original list of 1710), and the four universities (the two Aberdeen colleges having now merged); and in Ireland, Trinity and King's Inn. In addition, the printer had to retain a twelfth copy, for possible inspection by the magistrates, under the provisions of the Seditious Societies Act of 1799, for which see Feather, The English book trade, p. 59.
29 Basil Montagu. *Enquiries and Observation Respecting the University Library*. Cambridge, 1805. See J. C. T. Oates, Cambridge University and the reform of the Copyright Act 1805–1813. *The Library*, 5th ser., 27 (1972), pp. 275–92, to which I am heavily indebted for the next part of this chapter. For a view of all the events down to 1818, as seen from Cambridge, which had a key role in them, see David McKitterick. *Cambridge University Library. A history. The eighteenth and nineteenth centuries*. Cambridge: Cambridge University Press, 1986, pp. 395–445.
30 Edward Christian. *Vindication of the Right of the Universities of Great Britain to a Copy of Every New Publication*. Cambridge, 1807; it was reprinted in 1808, and there were further editions in 1814 and 1818 when the issues were again relevant to current debates.
31 Oates, Cambridge University, p. 276.
32 The Bill is in PP 1808 (314) I.783–6.
33 PD, 1st ser., vol. 11, cols. 918–19.
34 The amended Bill is PP 1808 (321) I.799–802. See CJ, vol. 63, pp. 461, 463, and, for the debate, PD, 1st ser., vol. 11, cols. 988–93.
35 R. G. Thorne. *The History of Parliament. The House of Commons 1790–1820*. 5 vols., London: History of Parliament Trust, 1986, vol. 5, pp. 454–7.
36 PP 1818 (280) IX, 257, pp. 83–5; Oates, Cambridge University, pp. 280–1; and James J. Barnes. *Free Trade in Books*. Oxford: Clarendon Press, 1964, pp. 2–3.
37 For Wynne, see Thorne, *History*, vol. 5, pp. 587–95; and for Romilly, ibid., vol. 5, pp. 36–43.
38 *Strictures on the Copyright Bill Now Before Parliament*. London: 1808. The text is dated 23 June, and the Postscript, which deals with the term of copyright, 24 June, which I take as the probable date of publication.
39 Ibid., p. 1.
40 Ibid., p. 5.
41 Ibid., p. 11.
42 16 East 317; Oates, Cambridge University, pp. 281–4.
43 CJ, vol. 68, pp. 79–80; PD, 1st ser., vol. 24, cols. 308–11.
44 CJ, vol. 68, p. 300; PD, 1st ser., vol. 25, cols. 10–12.
45 For Giddy (who changed his name to his wife's maiden name of Gilbert when he inherited her uncle's property in 1814), see Thorne, *History*, vol. 4,

pp. 18–21; DNB; and A. C. Todd. *Beyond the Blaze. A biography of Davies Gilbert*. Truro: D. Bradford Barton, 1967, pp. 151–68.
46 Thorne, *History*, vol. 5, p. 219.
47 CJ, vol. 68, pp. 300, 301; PD, 1st ser., vol. 25, cols. 12–16.
48 For Parry, see Ian Maxted. *The London Book Trades 1775–1800*. Folkestone: Dawson, 1977, p. 170. For his evidence, see PP 1812–13 (341) IV.1006.
49 The Minutes of Evidence are PP 1812–13 (341) IV.1003–40.
50 For Longmans in this period, see Philip Wallis. *At the Sign of the Ship. Notes on the House of Longman 1724–1974*. London: Longman, 1974, pp. 12–15.
51 PP 1812–13 (341) IV.1007–18.
52 Ibid., p. 1022.
53 Ibid., pp. 1030–1 (Davies), 1033–4 (Taylor).
54 Ibid., pp. 1032–3.
55 There is a copy in Bodl. J. Pros. 438.
56 The original letter is bound in BL 515.1.20.
57 PP 1812–13 (341) IV.1024–5.
58 Letter bound in BL 515.1.20.
59 PP 1812–13 (341) IV.1028.
60 E. J. O'Dwyer. *Thomas Frognall Dibdin*. Pinner: Private Libraries Association, 1960, p. 18.
61 PP 1812–13 (341) IV.1028–9.
62 J. G. Cochrane. *The Case Stated Between the Public Libraries and the Booksellers*. London, 1813.
63 Ibid., p. 19.
64 Ibid., pp. 21–6; and PP 1812–13 (341) IV.1026.
65 Cochrane, *Case Stated*, pp. 28–9.
66 Richard Taylor. *A Short Plea in Behalf of Learning*. [London, 1813].
67 Sharon Turner. *Reasons for a Modification of the Act of Anne Respecting the Delivery of Books, and Copyright*. London, 1813, pp. 37–56.
68 PP 1812–13 (341) IV.1036.
69 Report of the Select Committee on 8 Anne and 15 & 41 George III, in ibid., 999–1002, tabled on 17 June 1813 (CJ, vol. 68, p. 576), and debated on 18 June (PD, 1st ser., vol. 26, pp. 708–10).
70 CJ, vol. 689, pp. 254, 261; PD, 1st ser., vol. 27, cols. 810–11.
71 18 and 19 May 1814; CJ, vol. 69, p. 284; PD, 1st ser., vol. 27, pp. 965–6. The amended Bill from these two days is in PP 1813–14 (184) II.673–80.
72 CJ, vol. 69, pp. 329, 344, 355, 365, 381.
73 James Couper. *Memorial and Representation of the University of Glasgow*. Glasgow, 1813. Couper was Vice-Rector of Glasgow University.
74 Ibid., vol. 69, pp. 419, 435; McKitterick, *Cambridge University Library*, p. 412.
75 CJ, vol. 69, pp. 303, 396.
76 Ibid., p. 455; PD, 1st ser., vol. 28, cols. 684–6.
77 Todd, *Beyond the Blaze*, p. 162.

78 CJ, vol. 69, p. 470; PD, 1st ser., vol. 28, col. 712; Mary Katherine Woodworth. *The Literary Career of Sir Samuel Egerton Brydges*. Oxford: Clarendon Press, 1935, pp. 20–1.
79 CJ, vol. 69, p. 476; PD, 1st ser., vol. 28, cols. 751–5.
80 LJ, vol. 49, pp. 1129–30.
81 CJ, vol. 69, p. 514.
82 Ibid., p. 517.
83 54 George III c. 156.
84 See below, pp. 124–5.
85 Ardagh, St Andrews, pp. 194–5.
86 McKitterick, *Cambridge University Library*, pp. 417–22.
87 The figures are in Appendix I of the *Report from the Select Committee on the Copyright Acts, 5 June 1818*, in PP (402) IX.249–56, for which see below, pp. 115–18. Reports of books entered were tabled in the House of Commons in 1815 (CJ, vol. 70, p. 378) and 1817 (ibid., vol. 72, p. 207).
88 McKitterick, *Cambridge University Library*, pp. 415–16; W. D. Macray. *Annals of the Bodleian Library*. 2nd ed., Oxford: Clarendon Press, 1890, pp. 302–3.
89 CJ, vol. 72, p. 372.
90 PD, 1st ser., vol. 26, , cols. 1063–4.
91 Chester W. New. *The Life of Henry Brougham to 1830*. Oxford: Clarendon Press, 1961, pp. 146–97.
92 PD, 1st ser., vol. 26, col. 1069.
93 New, *Life*, p. 173; Arthur Aspinall. *Lord Brougham and the Whig Party*. Manchester: Manchester University Press, 1939, pp. 225–7.
94 PD, 1st ser., vol. 26, col. 1068.
95 CJ, vol. 73, pp. 125, 183; PP 181 (126), I.243–6.
96 Some of this had been iterated in the summer of 1814 by John Britton. *The Rights of Literature*. London, 1814, pp. 9–13, 24. It was only in 1817–18, however, that these views entered the mainstream of the debate.
97 CJ, vol. 73, pp. 129, 186, 218, 247, 293, 309, 334, 338, 350, 357.
98 Ibid., pp. 217, 219.
99 Ibid., pp. 226, 235.
100 Ibid., pp. 258, 266.
101 The importance of Brydges' role is clear from a letter from James Lackington to Rogers Ruding in BL 515.l.20.
102 *Copyright Bill . . . To the Honourable the Commons . . . The Humble Petition of George Lackington, Richard Hughes, Joseph Harding, George Fordyce Mavor, and Thomas Jones*. [London, 1818]. Copy in Bodl. 2581 c. 5(30).
103 The Minutes of Evidence, on which this account is based, are PP 1818 (280)IX.257–423.
104 H. Kay Jones. *Butterworths. History of a publishing house*. London: Butterworth, 1980, p. 6. See also C. H. Timperley. *Encyclopaedia of Literary and Typographical Anecdote*. Rev. ed., London, 1842, p. 872; DNB; and Thorne, *History*, vol. 3, pp. 348–9.
105 Ibid., vol. 4, pp. 498–512. See also Jane Rendall, The Political Ideas and Activities of Sir James Mackintosh (1765–1832): a study in Whiggism

between 1789 and 1832. London University Ph.D. dissertation, 1972, pp. 216–27.
106 They were William Smith (Thorne, *History*, vol. 5, pp. 206–14); Lord Althorp (ibid., pp. 238–41); Charles Marsh (ibid., vol. 4, pp. 533–4); Lord Morpeth (ibid., pp. 250–1); and John Lambton (ibid., pp. 364–70).
107 Leonard Cooper. *Radical Jack*. London: Cresset, 1959, p. 58; CJ, vol. 73, p. 226.
108 Notably Charles Long (Thorne, *History*, vol. 4, pp. 448–52); Hudson Gurney (ibid., pp. 120–1); and George Dawson (ibid., vol. 5, pp. 578–9).
109 Ibid., vol. 3, pp. 128–33.
110 Ibid., vol. 5, pp. 113–15; vol. 4, pp. 745–9; vol. 5, pp. 348–50; ibid., p. 219; and vol. 4, pp. 837–40.
111 For details, see John Feather, Publishers and politicians: the remaking of the law of copyright in Britain 1775–1842. Part I: Legal deposit and the battle of the library tax. *Publishing History*, 24 (1988), pp. 49–76, upon which parts of this chapter are based, at pp. 64–6.
112 See DNB.
113 For the book, see *The Gentleman's Magazine*, 89:1 (1819), pp. 460–1.
114 PP 1818 (280) IX.303–9.
115 Sir Egerton Brydges. *A Summary Statement of the Great Grievance Imposed on Authors and Publishers*. London, 1818, p. 12.
116 PP 1818 (280) IX.341–8 (Webb), 359–69 (Gaisford) and 381–5 (Baber). For the last, however, see also Edward Miller. *That Noble Cabinet. A history of the British Museum*. London, 1973, pp. 95, 109.
117 Feather, Publishers, 65–6; William Webb. *Observations on the Copyright Bill*. Cambridge, 1818, p. 7; and Villiers' evidence in PP 1818 (280) IX.348–9.
118 Feather, Publishers, p. 66.
119 The Report is PP 1818 (402) IX.249–56.
120 PD, 1st ser., vol. 38, cols. 1256–64.
121 CJ, vol. 74, p. 255.
122 There are minutes of their meetings in Bodl. MS. Eng. misc. c. 143, ff. 275–92.
123 Ardagh, St Andrews, p. 200.
124 See DNB; and Joel H. Wiener. *The War of the Unstamped*. Ithaca, NY: Cornell University Press, 1969, pp. 71–2.
125 PD, 3rd ser., vol. 33, cols. 440–64; CJ, vol. 91, p. 301.
126 Macray, *Annals*, p. 331, says that in May 1836 the Curators of the Bodleian rejected a proposal for financial compensation in lieu of books.
127 CJ, vol. 91, p. 666. The amended Bill is PP 1836 (441) II.389–92.
128 CJ, vol. 91, pp. 795, 798, 801–2; LJ, vol. 68, pp. 847, 862, 866, 873, 877.
129 6 & 7 William IV c. 110.
130 See below, p. 147, for the 1842 Act. Clauses 6 and 7 deal with legal deposit.
131 For which see pp. 185–94 below.
132 See McKitterick, *Cambridge University Library*, pp. 750–2; Sir Edmund Craster. *History of the Bodleian Library 1845–1945*. Oxford: Clarendon Press, 1952, pp. 63–4.

133 Louis Fagan. *The Life of Sir Anthony Panizzi*. 2nd ed., 2 vols., London, 1880, vol. 1, pp. 286–92.
134 Craster, *History*, pp. 62–4.
135 McKitterick, *Cambridge University Library*, pp. 574–82.
136 For which see below, pp. 202–3.
137 For which see below.
138 PD [H.L.], 5th ser., vol. 10, cols. 173–98; *Library Association Record*, 13 (1911), pp. 211–15. See Partridge, *History,* pp. 107–8, 335–40.
139 R. J. L. Kingsford. *The Publishers Association 1896–1946*. Cambridge: Cambridge University Press, 1970, pp. 39–40.
140 Craster, *History*, p. 174; Partridge, *History*, pp. 108–11.
141 Jan T. Jasion. *The International Guide to Legal Deposit*. Aldershot: Ashgate, 1991, pp. 177–8.
142 Ibid., p. 144.
143 Partridge, *History*, p. 138.

Chapter 5

1 See above, pp. 93–4.
2 See above, pp. 77–9.
3 See John Feather. *A History of British Publishing*. London: Croom Helm, 1988, pp. 129–49; and John Feather, Technology and the book in the nineteenth century. *Critical Survey*, 3 (1990), pp. 5–13.
4 For a general study, see A. S. Collins. *The Profession of Letters. A study of the relation of author to patron, publisher and public 1780–1832*. London: Routledge and Kegan Paul, 1928, pp. 128–70. The realities of the life of the hack writer of the period are exposed in Robin Myers, Writing for the booksellers in the early nineteenth century: a case study. In: Robin Myers and Michael Harris, eds. *Author/Publisher Relations During the Eighteenth and Nineteenth Centuries*. Oxford: Oxford Polytechnic Press, 1983, pp. 119–55.
5 For Maugham, see DNB.
6 Robert Maugham. *A Treatise on the Laws of Literary Property*. London, 1828, pp. 2, 27–32.
7 See above, pp. 95–6.
8 Maugham, *Treatise*, pp. 181–2.
9 Ibid., p. 187.
10 See above, p. 112.
11 3 & 4 William IV c. 15. See G. W. M. McFarlane. Copyright: development and exercise of performing right. London University Ph.D. dissertation, 1975, pp. 41–52.
12 Maugham, *Treatise*, p. 220.
13 CJ, vol. 92, p. 386. The Bill is PP 1837 (380) I.573–87.
14 See *A Memoir of Mr Justice Talfourd. By a member of the Oxford Circuit*. London, 1854; Robert S. Newdick. *The First 'Life and Letters' of Charles Lamb*. Columbus, OH: University of Ohio Press (Ohio State Contributions in English, 6), 1935; William S. Ward, An early champion of

Wordsworth: Thomas Noon Talfourd. *Publications of the Modern Language Association of America*, 68 (1973), pp. 992–1000; and Tim Chilcott. *A Publisher and His Circle. The life and work of John Taylor, Keats's publisher*. London: Routledge and Kegan Paul, 1972, pp. 133, 137, 153.
15 In a letter to Leigh Hunt in June 1836, printed in Charles Richard Sanders, ed. *The Collected Letters of Thomas and Jane Welsh Carlyle*. Durham, NC: University of North Carolina Press, 1981, vol. 8, p. 353.
16 Ernest de Selincourt, ed. *The Letters of William and Dorothy Wordsworth. The later years*. Oxford: Clarendon Press, 1939, p. 796.
17 See Susan Eilenberg, Mortal pages: Wordsworth and the reform of copyright. *ELH*, 56 (1989), pp. 351–74; Paul M. Zall, Wordsworth and the Copyright Act of 1842. *Publications of the Modern Language Association of America*, 70 (1955), pp. 132–44; and Russell Noyes, Wordsworth and the Copyright Act of 1842: an addendum. *Publications of the Modern Language Association of America*, 76 (1961), pp. 380–3.
18 Ernest de Selincourt, ed. *The Letters of William and Dorothy Wordsworth. The middle years*. 2 vols., Oxford: Clarendon Press, 1937, vol. 1, p. 242.
19 Ibid., vol. 2, p. 844.
20 de Selincourt, *Letters . . . Later years*, p. 826.
21 Mary Moorman. *William Wordsworth, A biography. The later years 1803–1850*. Oxford: Clarendon Press, 1965, pp. 551–2.
22 de Selincourt, *Letters . . . Later years*, p. 912.
23 PD, 3rd ser., vol. 37, pp. 866–80.
24 *A Speech by Thomas Noon Talfourd . . . in the House of Commons, on Thursday, 11th May, 1837*. London, 1837, p. 6.
25 Ibid., p. iv.
26 T. N. Talfourd. *Three Speeches Delivered in the House of Commons in Favour of a Measure for an Extension of Copyright*. London, 1840, pp. 30–1.
27 CJ, vol. 92, p. 522.
28 See DNB; Ian Maxted. *The London Book Trades 1775–1800*. Folkestone: Dawson, 1977, pp. 222–3; Philip A. H. Brown. *London Publishers and Printers c.1800–1870*. London: The British Library, 1982; and Charles Humphries and William C. Smith. *Music Publishing in the British Isles*. 2nd ed., Oxford: Blackwell, 1970, p. 306.
29 Thomas Tegg. *Remarks on the Speech of Serjeant Talfourd*. London, 1837. The phrase is on p. 6.
30 Ibid., pp. 15–18.
31 Ibid., p. 12.
32 Ibid., p. 19.
33 CJ, vol. 93, p. 200; the Bill is PP 1837–38 (164) I.489–504.
34 PD, 3rd ser., vol. 39, cols. 1091–3.
35 See below, pp. 155–7.
36 W. F. Monypenny. *The Life of Benjamin Disraeli*. 2 vols., London, 1912, vol. 2, pp. 15–16.
37 CJ, vol. 93, p. 313.
38 The petitions are noted in CJ, vol. 93, pp. 430, 442, 451, 460–1, 468, 473, 485, 510, 628.

39 For this Association, see Ellic Howe. *The London Compositor*. London: The Bibliographical Society, 1947, pp. 237–8.
40 W. M'Dowall. *Serjeant Talfourd's Copyright Bill*. London, 1838, pp. 2–3. M'Dowall was Secretary of the Association of Master Printers, and this broadside consists of the minutes of the meeting of 5 April, and the text of the petition itself. It was apparently circulated to members of the Association to persuade them to go to M'Dowall's house to sign the petition. The copy in Bodl. (2581 c.55(33b)) is addressed in manuscript to John Nichols.
41 *Sergeant Talfourd's Copyright Bill and the Printing Business. Bill to be read a second time on the 11th of April, 1838*. This is of the same origin as the previous document (note 40, above); the copy in Bodl. (2581 c.55(a)) is bound with that item, and has clearly always been associated with it.
42 Scott Bennett, John Murray's Family Library and the cheapening of books in early nineteenth-century Britain. *Studies in Bibliography*, 29 (1976), pp. 138–66.
43 See DNB.
44 Robert Mudie. *The Copyright Question and Mr Serjeant Talfourd's Bill*. London, 1838, pp. 4, 23–5, 33.
45 *Areopagitica Secunda: or speech of the shade of John Milton, on Mr Sergeant Talfourd's Copyright Extension Bill*. London, 1838, p. 18.
46 *A Proposed New Law of Copyright . . . in a letter addressed to Mr Sergeant Talfourd . . . By a Friend to Authors*. London, [1838]. The date is from the BL catalogue, where the pamphlet is T.2387(3.). It is confirmed by the other items in this tract volume, which relate to the 1838 Bill. The catalogue ascribes the work to one William Day, giving no authority; I do not know who he was.
47 I am grateful to Chris R. Vanden Bossche, of the University of Notre Dame, for allowing me to see her paper on 'Copyright and the constitution of authorhood', which deals with the effects of what she calls the 'moral and economic interests of copyright'. The paper was delivered to a conference on Interdisciplinary Nineteenth Century Studies, at the Yale Center for British Art, in April 1991.
48 Quoted in Zall, Wordsworth, p. 134.
49 *Observations on the Law of Copyright, in reference to the Bill introduced into the House of Commons by Mr Sergeant Talfourd*. London, 1838. Copy in BL T.2387.(6.).
50 Ibid., p. 23.
51 de Selincourt, *Letters . . . Later years*, pp. 910–13; this is the letter in which he claims credit for bringing the matter to the attention of the House of Commons for which see above, p. 126.
52 Ibid., p. 916.
53 See above, note 48.
54 de Selincourt, *Letters . . . Later years*, pp. 919–20.
55 Ibid., p. 921.
56 Ibid., pp. 123–4.

57 W. J. B. Owen and Jane Worthington Smyser, eds. *The Prose Works of William Wordsworth*. 3 vols., Oxford: Clarendon Press, 1973, vol. 3, pp. 309–12.
58 On 27 April 1838, the printers of Kendal joined the others who had petitioned the House to reject it; CJ, vol. 93, p. 468.
59 de Selincourt, *Letters . . . Later years*, p. 930. Wordsworth was referring to the possibility of Tegg reprinting his works when he was dead, but more immediate fears may well have been in his mind after Tegg's outburst in 1837.
60 PD, 3rd ser, vol. 42, pp. 559–60; the whole debate, and the division lists, is in ibid., 555–96.
61 Norman Gash. *Mr Secretary Peel. The life of Sir Robert Peel to 1830*. London: Longmans, 1961, pp. 562–3.
62 de Selincourt, *Letters . . . Later years*, pp. 932–4.
63 Ibid., pp. 934–6.
64 Ibid., p. 939. What, one might ask, did Wordsworth think that *he* was doing?
65 According to Wordsworth, writing to Talfourd, in de Selincourt, *Letters . . . Later years*, p. 933. The Bill, as then drafted, would, of course, have restored Scott's copyrights to his heirs, which would have emancipated Abbotsford with more than a little to spare.
66 Mary E. Burton, ed. *The Letters of Mary Wordsworth 1800–1855*. Oxford: Clarendon Press, 1958, p. 212.
67 Letter to Henry Crabb Robinson, dated May 1838, printed in Thomas Sadler, ed. *Diary, Reminiscences and Correspondence of Henry Crabb Robinson*. 2 vols., London, 1872, vol. 2, pp. 205–6.
68 CJ, vol. 93, p. 502.
69 Ibid., p. 500.
70 PD, 3rd ser., vol. 42, cols. 1056–75.
71 Joseph O. Baylen and Norbert J. Gossman, eds. *Biographical Dictionary of Modern British Radicals. Volume 2. 1830–1870*. Brighton: Harvester Press, 1984, pp. 528–31.
72 Wiener, *War of the Unstamped*, pp. 267–8.
73 The amended Bill is in PP 1837–38 (164) I.505–22.
74 CJ, vol. 93, pp. 502, 523. The Bill was a private one, which meant that all public bills took precedence over it (as still happens) if time were short. This was a particular problem in the late 1830s, when the House was being overwhelmed by the number of bills seeking authority to build railway lines. Indeed, it began to reform the private bill procedure to cope with precisely this problem, by allowing private bills to go to a Select Committee rather than to a Committee of the Whole House as had been the practice for centuries. Talfourd's 1838 Bill was sent to a Committee of the Whole House, where an opposed Bill was always vulnerable to problems of time. See O. Cyprian Williams. *The Historical Development of Private Bill Procedure*. 2 vols., London: H.M.S.O., 1948, vol. 2, pp. 76–85.
75 M. R. D. Foot, ed. *The Gladstone Diaries. Volume 2. 1833–1839*. Oxford: Clarendon Press, 1968, p. 378.
76 de Selincourt, *Letters . . . Later years*, pp. 949–50.

77 BL MS Addl. 44,356, f. 97[v].
78 CJ, vol. 94, pp. 22, 23; the Bill is PP 1839 (19) I.505–22.
79 de Selincourt, *Letters . . . Later years*, p. 961.
80 Edith J. Morley, ed. *Henry Crabb Robinson on Books and Their Writers*. 3 vols., London, 1938, vol. 2, p. 566.
81 Ibid., vol. 2, p. 568.
82 Charles Cuthbert Southey, ed. *The Life and Correspondence of Robert Southey*. 6 vols., London, 1850, vol. 6, pp. 354–5.
83 See his letter to Wordsworth printed in Kenneth Curry, ed. *New Letters of Robert Southey*. 2 vols., New York: Columbia University Press, 1965, vol. 2, pp. 473–4.
84 BL MS Addl. 44,356, f. 178.
85 CJ, vol. 94, p. 63.
86 The petition is printed, along with those from individual authors, in Talfourd, *Three Speeches*, pp. 111–46.
87 Printed in Owen and Smyser, *Prose Works*, p. 315.
88 Talfourd, *Three Speeches*, pp. 115–17.
89 Mrs Oliphant. *William Blackwood and His Sons*. 2nd ed., Edinburgh, 1897, vol. 2, pp. 207–8.
90 Ibid., pp. 118–20, 123, 131–32.
91 PD, 3rd ser., vol. 45, cols. 920–43.
92 CJ, vol. 94, pp. 79, 183, 215.
93 Louis G. Dickens, The friendship of Dickens and Carlyle. *Dickensian*, 53 (1957), p. 102.
94 Sanders, *Collected Letters*, vol. 11, pp. 34–36.
95 Ibid., p. 36.
96 Published in *The Examiner*, 7 April 1839, and quoted here from Thomas Carlyle. *Critical and Miscellaneous Essays*. 5 vols., London, 1899, vol. 4, p. 207.
97 CJ, vol. 94, p. 237.
98 Foot, *Gladstone Diaries*, vol. 2, p. 592.
99 de Selincourt, *Letters . . . Later years*, pp. 969–70.
100 For the night's events, see CJ, vol. 94, pp. 238–40; and PD, 3rd ser., vol. 47, cols. 699–715.
101 Gladstone, *Diaries*, vol. 2, p. 597.
102 CJ, vol. 94, pp. 257, 262, 284, 290, 309, 318, 365, 371, 386, 414, 420.
103 The Bill, identical to that of 1839, is PP 1840 (61) I.415–32. For the progress of the Bill, and the tabling of the petitions, see CJ, vol. 95, pp. 59–60, 100, 109, 115, 116, 121, 152, 166, 261, 288, 293, 297, 313, 316, 318, 333, 359, 361, 376, 384, 409, 421, 436, 439, 472, 478, 499, 500, 511, 526, 540. For the only debate (which was procedural rather than substantive), see PD, 3rd ser., vol. 51, cols. 1250–8; ibid., vol. 52, cols. 400–23. One postponement was, yet again, for inquoracy, as Gladstone noted: 'No House: alas for copyright' (M. R. D. Foot and H. C. G. Matthew, eds. *The Gladstone Diaries. Volume 3. 1840–1847*. Oxford: Clarendon Press, 1974, p. 40).
104 See above, p. 137. I assume that the book is his *Three Speeches*.
105 CJ, vol. 96, pp. 10, 14; PD, 3rd ser., vol. 56, pp. 134–5, 146–55.

106 The debate is in PD, 3rd ser., vol. 56, cols. 341–60.
107 Ibid., col. 350.
108 Sir George Otto Trevelyan. *The Life and Letters of Lord Macaulay*. Popular ed., London, 1889, p. 434.
109 Vera Wheatley. *The Life and Work of Harriet Martineau*. London: Secker and Warburg, 1957, p. 142; she is, I think, the 'writer of eminence who has since echoed [Talfourd's] complaint', referred to by Trevelyan, *Life and Letters*, p. 434.
110 Trevelyan, *Life and Letters*, p. 434.
111 CJ, vol. 96, p. 26.
112 For the 1833–37 Parliament, see S. F. Woolley, The personnel of the Parliament of 1833. *English Historical Review*, 53 (1938), pp. 240–62. For the changing character of the House in the 1830s and 1840s, and its consequences for the conduct of business, see Josef Redlich. *The Procedures of the House of Commons*. 3 vols., London, 1908, vol. 1, pp. 73–132; and W. O. Aydelotte, The House of Commons in the 1840s. *History*, new ser., 39 (1954), pp. 247–62.
113 BL MS Addl. 38,109, ff. 360^{v}–61.
114 Foot and Matthew, *Gladstone Diaries*, vol. 3, p. 11.
115 See DNB's life of his father, Stanhope, Philip Henry, for an account of him.
116 W. O. Aydelotte, Parties and politics in early Victorian England. *Journal of British Studies*, 5 (1966), pp. 95–114, at p. 103.
117 CJ, vol. 97, p. 83.
118 The Bill is PP 1842 (79) I.501–18.
119 PD, 3rd ser., vol. 60, cols. 1429–30.
120 Ibid., cols. 694–5.
121 Ibid., cols. 1111–17.
122 CJ, vol. 97, p. 154; the amended Bill is PP 1842 (139) I.519–36.
123 Trevelyan, *Life and Letters*, p. 436.
124 *The Collected Letters of Thomas and Jane Welsh Carlyle. Vol 14. January–July 1842*. Durham, NC: Duke University Press, 1984, p. 139.
125 Thomas Pinney, ed. *The Letters of Thomas Babington Macaulay*. Cambridge: Cambridge University Press, 1977, vol. 4, p. 25.
126 PD, 3rd ser., vol. 63, cols. 777–813.
127 LJ, vol. 74, pp. 327–8.
128 CJ, vol. 97, pp. 442–3, 445; LJ, vol. 74, pp. 382, 386.
129 5 & 6 Victoria c. 45.

Chapter 6

1 Madeleine House and Graham Storey, eds. *The Letters of Charles Dickens. Volume 1. 1820–1839*. Oxford: Clarendon Press, 1965, p. 313.
2 Edgar Johnson. *Charles Dickens. His tragedy and triumph*. London: Gollancz, 1953, p. 213; Robert L. Patten. *Charles Dickens and His Publishers*. Oxford: Clarendon Press, 1978, p. 135.

3 See above, pp. 38–9 and 55.
4 See above, pp. 54–5.
5 See above, p. 76.
6 See above, pp. 93–4.
7 See above, pp. 100.
8 Bernhard Fabian, English books and their eighteenth-century German readers. In: Paul J. Korshin, ed. *The Widening Circle. Essays on the circulation of literature in eighteenth-century Europe*. Philadelphia, PA: University of Pennsylvania Press, 1976, pp. 117–96; Bernhard Fabian. *The English Book in Eighteenth-century Germany*. London: The British Library, 1992, pp. 1–36. See also Giles Barber, Galignani and the publication of English books in France from 1800 to 1852. *The Library*, 5th ser., 16 (1961), pp. 267–86, at p. 267; and Giles Barber, J. J. Tourneisen of Basle and the publication of English books on the continent *c.*1800. *The Library*, 5th ser., 15 (1960), pp. 193–200.
9 See the general account by John Tebbel. *A History of Book Publishing in the United States. Volume I. The creation of an industry 1630–1865*. New York: R. R. Bowker, 1972, pp. 203–62; and James J. Barnes. *Authors, Publishers and Politicians. The quest for an Anglo-American copyright agreement 1815–1854*. London: Routledge and Kegan Paul, 1974, p. 49.
10 See Raymond Birn, The profits of ideas: *Privilèges en librairies* in eighteenth-century France. *Eighteenth-century Studies*, 4 (1970–71), pp. 131–68; Martha Woodmansee, The genius and the copyright: economic and legal conditions of the emergence of the 'author'. *Eighteenth-century Studies*, 17 (1984), pp. 425–48, at pp. 437–40.
11 Frederick R. Goff. *The First Decade of the Federal Act for Copyright 1790–1800*. Washington, DC: Library of Congress, 1951.
12 David Saunders. *Authorship and Copyright*. London: Routledge, 1992, pp. 90–5; Jane C. Ginsburg, A tale of two copyrights: literary property in revolutionary France and America. *Tulane Law Review*, 64 (1990), pp. 991–1031.
13 This, and the following paragraphs, is heavily indebted to Barber, Galignani, for which see note 8, above.
14 Barber, Galignani, p. 271.
15 Barnes, *Authors,* pp. 97–9.
16 Ibid.; and James J. Barnes, Galignani and the publication of English books in France: a postscript. *The Library*, 5th ser., 25 (1970), pp. 294–313. The papers in *Bentley v. Baillière* are PRO C31/514/Part I and PRO C13/2702.
17 For Bentley, see Royal A. Gettman. *A Victorian Publisher. A study of the Bentley papers*. Cambridge: Cambridge University Press, 1960. See also John Sutherland, Henry Colburn publisher. *Publishing History*, 19 (1986), pp. 59–84.
18 William B. Todd and Ann Bowden. *Tauchnitz International Editions in English 1841–1955. A bibliographical history*. New York: Bibliographical Society of America, 1988, p. 3.

19 Ibid., p. 4; and Simon Nowell-Smith. *International Copyright Law and the Publisher in the Reign of Queen Victoria*. Oxford: Clarendon Press, 1968, pp. 42–4.
20 Barnes, *Authors*, pp. 53–9; James J. Barnes, Edward Lytton Bulwer and the publishing firm of Harper & Brothers. *American Literature*, 38 (1966–67), pp. 35–48.
21 Barnes, *Authors*, pp. 1–29.
22 Ibid., p. 100.
23 Clarence Golden. *American Literature in Nineteenth-century England*. New York: Columbia University Press, 1944, pp. 14–46.
24 Barnes, *Authors*, p. 96.
25 *Publisher's Circular*, 5 (1842), p. 97.
26 See above, pp. 133–4.
27 See DNB. The Bill is PP 1837–38 (295) I.523, with the amended version at ibid. (509) I.529. The 20 March proceedings are in PD, 3rd ser., vol. 41, cols. 1096–1108.
28 Ibid., col. 1097.
29 Ibid., cols. 1098–9.
30 Nowell-Smith, *International Copyright Law*, p. 41.
31 Barber, Galignani, p. 280.
32 Barnes, *Authors*, pp. 61–6; see below, p. 158.
33 PD, 3rd ser., vol. 41, cols. 1103–4.
34 Ibid., col. 1107.
35 Ibid., cols. 1105–6.
36 Ibid., cols. 1101–2, 1104–5.
37 Ibid., cols. 1102–3.
38 Ibid., cols. 1107–8.
39 1 & 2 Victoria c. 59.
40 PD, 3rd ser., vol. 41, cols. 1100–1.
41 See above, pp. 132–7.
42 This account is heavily indebted to Barnes, *Authors*, pp. 60–74.
43 Arno L. Bader, Frederick Saunders and the early history of the international copyright movement in America. *Library Quarterly*, 8 (1938), pp. 25–39.
44 See Lawrence H. Houtchens, Charles Dickens and international copyright. *American Literature*, 13 (1941–42), pp. 18–28; and Barnes, *Authors*, pp. 75–7.
45 Alexander Welsh. *From Copyright to Copperfield. The identity of Dickens*. Cambridge, MA: Harvard University Press, 1987, pp. 30–9.
46 Madeleine House, Graham Storey and Kathleen Tillotson, eds. *The Letters of Charles Dickens. Volume 3. 1842–1843*. Oxford: Clarendon Press, 1974, p. 221.
47 Ibid., p. 85.
48 Andrew J. Eaton, The American movement for international copyright, 1837–60. *Library Quarterly*, 15 (1945), pp. 95–122, at p. 112.
49 Reprinted in House, Storey and Tillotson, *Letters . . . 1842–1843*, pp. 256–9.
50 Eaton, American movement, pp. 115–19; Barnes, *Authors*, pp. 80–94.

51 7 & 8 Victoria c. 12.
52 Nowell-Smith, *International copyright law*, p. 41.
53 Barber, Galignani, pp. 280–1.
54 DNB.
55 Labouchère described the negotiations in introducing the Bill to enact the Convention in the House of Commons; PD, 3rd ser., vol. 119, cols. 498–500.
56 Sam Ricketson. *The Berne Convention for the Protection of Literary and Artistic Works 1886–1986*. London: Centre for Commercial Law Studies, Queen Mary College, 1987, p. 20.
57 15 & 16 Victoria c. 12. Introduced 13 February 1853 (CJ, vol. 107, p. 45; PD, 3rd ser., vol 119, cols. 498–502); First Reading, 18 February (CJ, vol. 107, p. 59); Second Reading, 15 March (PD, 3rd ser., vol. 119, col. 1035); Report Stage, 26 March (CJ, vol. 107, p. 127); and Royal Assent (ibid., p. 248). The other stages are unreported.
58 PD, 3rd ser., vol. 119, cols. 500–2.
59 Barber, Galignani, pp. 281 and note 2.
60 Todd and Bowden, *Tauchnitz International Editions*, p. 48.
61 For a full account of these bilateral agreements, see Ricketson, *The Berne Convention*, pp. 27–38.
62 See below, pp. 185–94.
63 See below, pp. 169–71.
64 *Bentley v. Foster (1839)*, reported at 10 Sim. 329.
65 4 Ex. 145–58.
66 Ibid., at 156, 157.
67 *Boosey v. Jeffreys (1854)*, in the House of Lords, reported at IV H.L.C. 815–96; this is another of the cases concerning *La somnambula*.
68 See below, pp. 169–71.
69 This account is largely based on that in Ricketson, *The Berne Convention*, pp. 48–80.
70 As reported in *The Times*, 15 January 1886, p. 7.
71 See below, pp. 180.
72 Victor Bonham-Carter. *Authors by Profession. Volume 1. From the introduction of printing until the Copyright Act 1911*. London: Society of Authors, 1978, pp. 128, 230 (note 6); and *The Times*, 20 March 1886, p. 5.
73 CJ, vol. 141, pp. 126, 127, 248, 305, 308; PD, 3rd ser., vol. 304, cols. 81, 1142–4, 1748–50; ibid., vol. 305, cols. 478–88; ibid., vol. 306, cols. 662, 985, 1250–1.
74 Printed in PP 1886 (156) II.529.
75 Ibid., vol. 304, cols. 1142–3.
76 Ricketson, *The Berne Convention*, pp. 78–81.
77 Ibid., pp. 74–5.
78 N. John Hall, ed. *The Letters of Anthony Trollope*. 2 vols., Stanford, CA: Stanford University Press, 1983, vol. 2, p. 193, in a letter to Alexander Blackwood, a British publisher, dated 4 July 1881.
79 Nowell-Smith, *International Copyright Law*, p. 64.
80 *Routledge v. Samson Low (1868),* reported in LR III 100–21. See also below, pp. 170.

81 Nowell-Smith, *International Copyright Law*, pp. 70–1.
82 This, and following paragraphs, is heavily indebted to Barnes, *Authors*, pp. 177–262. See also, Eaton, American movement, pp. 119–22; and Tebbel, *History . . . Volume I*, pp. 560–1.
83 John Tebbel. *A History of Book Publishing in the United States. Volume II. The expansion of an industry 1865–1919*. New York: R. R. Bowker, 1975, pp. 634–6.
84 Ibid., pp. 638–41.
85 Bonham-Carter, *Authors by Profession. Volume 1*, p. 162.
86 Nowell-Smith, *International Copyright Law*, p. 68.
87 Dan H. Laurence, ed. *Bernard Shaw. Collected Letters 1874–1897*. London: Max Reinhardt, 1965, p. 125.
88 Dan H. Laurence, ed. *Bernard Shaw. Collected Letters 1898–1910*. London: Max Reinhardt, 1972, p. 58.
89 John Feather. *A History of British Publishing*. London: Croom Helm, 1988, p. 203.
90 Nowell-Smith, *International Copyright Law*, pp. 24–33.
91 10 & 11 Victoria c. 95. The measure was never debated; for its passage, see CJ, vol. 102, pp. 778, 807, 862, 868, 874, 931, 951. See also Barnes, *Authors*, pp. 146–8.
92 Barnes, *Authors*, pp. 150–1.
93 See above, note 80.
94 Ricketson, *The Berne Convention*, p. 956.

Chapter 7

1 Madeleine House, Graham Storey and Kathleen Tillotson, eds. *The Letters of Charles Dickens. Volume 3. 1842–1843*. Oxford: Clarendon Press, 1974, p. 85.
2 See below, pp. 185–94.
3 *Report of the Commissioners*, in PP (1878) [C.2036] [C.2036.-I] XXIV.169.
4 Michael L. Turner, Andrew Wilson: Lord Stanhope's stereotype printer. *Journal of the Printing Historical Society*, 9 (1975), pp. 22–65.
5 Dard Hunter. *Papermaking. The history and technique of an ancient craft*. 2nd ed., New York: Knopf, 1947, pp. 309–99.
6 James Moran. *Printing Presses. History and development from the fifteenth century to modern times*. Berkeley, CA: University of California Press, 1978, pp. 101–220.
7 James Moran. *The Composition of Reading Matter. A history from case to computer*. London: Wace, 1965.
8 See Anthony Dyson. *Pictures to Print. The nineteenth-century engraving trade*. London: Farrand, 1984; and Michael Twyman. *Lithography 1800–1850*. London: Oxford University Press, 1970.
9 Geoffrey Wakeman. *Victorian Book Illustration. The technical revolution*. Newton Abbot: David and Charles, 1973, pp. 82–145.

10 Generally, see Richard D. Altick. *The English Common Reader. A social history of the mass reading public 1790–1900*. Chicago, IL: University of Chicago Press, 1957, pp. 260–364.
11 See above, pp. 67–9.
12 Royal A. Gettman. *A Victorian Publisher. A study of the Bentley papers*. Cambridge: Cambridge University Press, 1960, pp. 77–84.
13 For one unusually complicated transaction of this kind, in preparation for the 1829–33 edition of Scott's novels, see Jane Millgate. *Scott's Last Edition. A study in publishing history*. Edinburgh: Edinburgh University Press, 1987, pp. 41–52.
14 Ibid., pp. 84–7, 103–8.
15 J. A. Sutherland. *Victorian Novelists and Their Publishers*. London: Athlone Press, 1976, pp. 88–94.
16 Gettman, *Victorian Publisher*, pp. 115–18.
17 See above, pp. 124–5.
18 See Sutherland, *Victorian Novelists*, pp. 94–98.
19 Victor Bonham-Carter. *Authors by Profession*. 2 vols., London: Society of Authors, 1978–84, vol. 1, pp. 120–5.
20 See above, pp. 168–9.
21 James Hepburn. *The Author's Empty Purse and the Rise of the Literary Agent*. London: Oxford University Press, 1968, pp. 45–66.
22 James J. Barnes. *Free Trade in Books. A study of the London book trade since 1800*. Oxford: Clarendon Press, 1964, pp. 1–18, 30–47.
23 John Sutherland. The institutionalisation of the British book trade to the 1890s. In: Robin Myers and Michael Harris, eds. *Development of the English Book Trade 1700–1899*. Oxford: Oxford Polytechnic Press, 1981, pp. 95–105.
24 Ibid., pp. 96–100; Barnes, *Free Trade*, pp. 143–6; R. J. L. Kingsford. *The Publishers' Association 1896–1946*. Cambridge: Cambridge University Press, 1970, pp. 5–17.
25 For this and the following paragraphs, see John Feather. *A History of British Publishing*. London: Croom Helm, 1988, pp. 151–5, and the authorities cited there.
26 For Mudie, see Guinevere L. Greist. *Mudie's Circulating Library and the Victorian Novel*. Newton Abbot: David and Charles, 1970; for this aspect of W. H. Smith's, see Charles Wilson. *First with the News. A history of W. H. Smith 1792–1972*. London: Jonathan Cape, 1985, pp. 357–63.
27 Altick, *English Common Reader*, pp. 298–9.
28 Feather, *History*, pp. 194–5, 206–11.
29 Alexander Welsh, Writing and copying in the age of steam. In: James R. Kincaid and Albert J. Kuhn, eds. *Victorian Literature and Society. Essays presented to Richard D. Altick*. Columbus, OH: Ohio State University Press, 1984, pp. 30–45; and, for a special but fascinating case which raises many important issues, Jim Swan, Touching words: Helen Keller, plagiarism, authorship. *Cardozo Arts & Entertainment Law Journal*, 10 (1992), pp. 321–64.
30 CJ, vol. 112, pp. 330, 351; the Bill is PP 1857 (Session 2) (142) I.409.

31 CJ, vol. 119, pp. 144, 172. The Bill is PP 1864 (59) I.501, and is virtually identical to that abandoned in 1857.
32 *Select Committee on Copyright (No. 2) Bill*, at PP 1864 (441) IX.1.
33 *The Times*, 12 July 1864, p. 11.
34 38 Victoria c. 12.
35 PD, 3rd ser., vol. 222, cols. 235–6.
36 See the account of him in DNB.
37 Bonham-Carter, vol. 1, p. 98; *The Times*, 2 March 1875, p. 10.
38 Ibid., p. 7.
39 PD, 3rd ser., vol. 224, col. 393.
40 This account of the meeting is based on that in *The Times*, 11 May 1875, p. 10, which seems to be derived from an account given to the newspaper by one of those present, possibly Jenkins.
41 See above, p. 129.
42 38 Victoria c. 88, modified by the Imperial Parliament in 38 & 39 Victoria c. 53.
43 See Simon Nowell-Smith. *International Copyright Law and the Publisher in the Reign of Queen Victoria*. Oxford: Clarendon Press, 1968, pp. 88–9, and above, pp. 170–1.
44 PD, 3rd ser., vol. 228, col. 63.
45 The others were in 1909–10, 1951–52 and 1973–77, for which see below, pp. 199–202 and 204–8.
46 The *Report of the Commissioners* is at PP 1878 [C.2036] XXIV.163–252; the *Minutes of the Evidence Taken Before the Royal Commission on Copyright* is at PP 1878 [C.2036.-I] XXIV.253–668. These are cited as *Report* and *Minutes* respectively, with the pagination from the Sessional Papers, not from the Blue Books.
47 For Herschell, Froude and Mallet, see DNB; for Trollope's work on the Commission, see N. John Hall. *Trollope. A biography*. Oxford: Clarendon Press, 1991, p. 421, although the reference is a passing one only, and Hall says nothing else of this side of Trollope's work. Trollope's *Autobiography*, although not published until 1883, was largely written when the Commission was still sitting, and in the revised version which was actually published, Trollope merely says that he does not propose to discuss its recommendations with which he generally agrees. See Anthony Trollope. *An Autobiography*. Ed. Frederick Page. London: Oxford University Press, 1950, p. 312. For Stephen, see Noel Annan. *Leslie Stephen. The godless Victorian*. London: Weidenfeld and Nicolson, 1984, p. 5.
48 *Report*, p. 169.
49 Ibid., pp. 169–70.
50 Ibid., p. 165.
51 *Minutes (1878)*, p. 299.
52 Ibid., p. 562.
53 *Report (1878)*, pp. 208–19.
54 See DNB. Farrer's own views are in his *Free Trade Versus Fair Trade* (London, 1882), one of several publications on free trade issues. After his retirement, he entered politics himself, as a member of the London County Council.

55 *Minutes (1878)*, pp. 404–21.
56 Ibid., pp. 525–32.
57 Ibid., p. 582.
58 Ibid., p. 260.
59 Ibid., p. 300.
60 Ibid., p. 460.
61 Ibid., pp. 276, 298.
62 Ibid., pp. 318–19.
63 Ibid., p. 368.
64 Ibid., pp. 562–3.
65 Ibid., p. 582.
66 Ibid., pp. 304–11.
67 See above, pp. 108–9.
68 *Minutes (1878)*, pp. 337–8.
69 Ibid., p. 326.
70 See below, p. 193.
71 Minutes (1878), p. 278; see also ibid., pp. 276 (Longman), 322 (Blackwood).
72 Ibid., p. 455.
73 See above, p. 179.
74 *Minutes (1878)*, pp. 515–17, 539–46.
75 Ibid., p. 527.
76 The minutes, of course, record only the formal statements and questioning of the witnesses; there is no record of the private discussions of the Commissioners themselves.
77 Minutes (1878), pp. 498–505.
78 Ibid., pp. 296, 318.
79 See above, pp. 162–3.
80 *Minutes (1878)*, pp. 358–63.
81 Ibid., pp. 363–8.
82 Ibid., pp. 378–87.
83 Ibid., p. 368.
84 Ibid., pp. 337–8.
85 Ibid., pp. 421–35, 552–8.
86 See above, pp. 184–5.
87 *Minutes (1878)*, pp. 279, 290, 317, 338, 354–7.
88 See above, pp. 119.
89 *The Times*, 12 February 1877, p. 9.
90 *Report (1878)*, pp. 171–4.
91 Ibid., pp. 177–82.
92 Ibid., pp. 184–5.
93 Ibid., p. 185.
94 See below, pp. 205–6.
95 See above, pp. 119–20 and 162.
96 PD, 3rd ser., vol. 243, cols. 404, 1308.
97 Copyright (No. 2) Bill, in PP 1878–79 (265) II.3.
98 PD, 3rd ser., vol. 248, cols. 1628–9.

99 PP 1881 (121) I.639; CJ, vol. 136, pp. 130, 143; PD, 3rd ser., vol. 259, col. 1145.
100 See, for example, letters in *The Times* on 16 April 1881, p. 8 and 22 April 1881, p. 4.
101 See above, pp. 163–5 and 168–9.
102 The Canadian Act is 52 Victoria c. 29. See Nowell-Smith, *International Copyright Law*, p. 90; and above, p. 170
103 Bonham-Carter, *Authors by Profession*, vol. 1, pp. 163–4; Kingsford, *The Publishers' Association*, p. 10.
104 PP 1897 (385) X.213–51.
105 Ibid., pp. 223–5.
106 PP 1898 (393) IX.231–548.
107 Ibid., pp. 243–65.
108 Ibid., pp. 293–304.
109 Ibid., pp. 394–8.
110 Ibid., pp. 305–20, 455–8.
111 PP 1899 (362) VIII.541–799.
112 Kingsford, *The Publishers' Association*, p. 18.
113 For the Berlin conference and its work, see Sam Ricketson. *The Berne Convention for the Protection of Literary and Artistic Works 1886–1986*. London: Centre for Commercial Law Studies, Queen Mary College, 1987, pp. 87–96.
114 *Report of the Committee on the Law of Copyright*, in PP 1910 [C. 4946] XXI.241–88, at p. 2. Cited as *Report (1910)*, and by the pagination of the Blue Book.
115 *Minutes of Evidence Taken Before the Law of Copyright Committee*, in PP 1910 [C. 5051] XXI.289–559, at pp. 138–43. Cited as *Minutes (1910)*, and by the pagination of the Blue Book.
116 Ibid., pp. 20–31.
117 Ibid., p. 187.
118 Bonham-Carter, *Authors by Profession*, vol. 1, p. 216, misses this point, and grossly overestimates the influence of MacGillivray and the Society. Kingsford, *The Publishers' Association*, p. 38, is, rightly, far more restrained.
119 *Minutes (1910)*, pp. 25, 138–9.
120 Ibid., pp. 31–2.
121 Ibid., pp. 145–6.
122 Ibid., p. 32.
123 *Report (1910)*, p. 7.
124 Ibid., pp. 10–26.
125 PD [H.C.], 5th ser., vol. 6, cols. 1945–50.
126 Ibid., vol. 23, cols. 2587–604.
127 *The Times*, 3 April 1911, p. 10.
128 PD [H.C.], 5th ser., vol. 23, col. 2605.
129 Ibid., cols. 2611–21.
130 Ibid., col. 2603.
131 See above, pp. 120.

132 The remaining debates are in PD [H.C.], 5th ser., vol. 28, cols. 468, 1902–77 (Report Stage); vol. 29, cols. 2133–93 (Report Stage, continued; Third Reading); PD [H.L.], 5th ser., vol. 9, col. 1154 (First Reading); ibid., vol. 10, cols. 39–54 (Second Reading), 133–66, 168–211 (Committee Stage), 451–87 (Report Stage), 573 (Third Reading); PD [H.C.], 5th ser., vol. 32, col. 2447 (Lords amendments); and PD [H.L.], 5th ser., vol. 10, col. 1167 (Royal Assent). The Act is 1 & 2 George V c. 46.
133 Ricketson, *The Berne Convention*, pp. 105–14.
134 *Report of the Copyright Committee*, in PP 1952–53 [C. 8662] IX.573–704, cited as *Report (1952)*, by the pagination of the Blue Book.
135 Ibid., p. 5.
136 Ibid., p. 1.
137 Ibid., pp. 36–80, 118–21.
138 Bonham-Carter, *Authors by Profession*, vol. 2, pp. 205–82.
139 Ibid., p. 283. See also Malcolm Bradbury. *The Social Context of Modern English Literature*. Oxford: Basil Blackwell, 1971, pp. 144–68.
140 *Report (1952)*, p. 17.
141 *Report (1952)*, pp. 17–21, 117.
142 Ricketson, *The Berne Convention*, p. 110.
143 *Report (1952)*, p. 80.
144 25 & 26 Victoria c. 68.
145 *Report (1952)*, pp. 81–2.
146 The debates were poor and badly attended; PD [H.C.], 5th ser., vol. 553, cols. 715–811 (Second Reading, including a particularly inane contribution from Roy Jenkins at cols. 737–46); ibid., vol. 558, cols. 651–784, 843–930 (Report Stage). There were no divisions. The Act is 4 & 5 Elizabeth II 74.
147 *Report of the Committee to Consider the Laws on Copyright and Designs* [C. 6732] (1977), p. 1. Cited as *Report (1977)*.
148 Ibid., pp. 54–74.
149 Ibid., pp. 16–18.
150 PD [H.C.], 6th ser., vol. 132, col. 526.
151 Ibid., col. 535.
152 See the speech by Tony Blair on the Report Stage, in ibid., vol. 138, cols. 37–43.
153 David Lester and Paul Mitchell. *Joynson-Hicks on UK Copyright Law*. London: Sweet and Maxwell, 1989.

Index

Cambridge University Library 7, 57, 97, 100–1, 110, 114, 117